T0330596

The Future of the Nation-State

The tension between culture, politics and economy has become one of the dominant anxieties of modern society. On the one hand people endeavour to maintain and develop their distinct cultural identity; on the other there are many forces for greater international integration, driven by free trade and political cooperation.

How to understand and explain this fundamental issue is illuminated in nine essays by eminent scholars from various countries and disciplines.

Routledge Advances in International
Political Economy

The Future of the Nation-State
Essays on Cultural Pluralism and Political Integration
Edited by Sverker Gustavsson and Leif Lewin
Co-publication with Nerenius & Santérus Publishers, Stockholm,
Sweden

The Future of the Nation State

Essays on Cultural Pluralism and Political Integration

Edited by
Sverker Gustavsson
and
Leif Lewin

Routledge
Taylor & Francis Group
LONDON AND NEW YORK

Nerenius & Santérus Publishers

First published 1996
by Routledge
2 Park Square, Milton Park, Abingdon, Oxon, OX14 4RN

Simultaneously published in Scandinavia
by Nerenius & Santérus Publishers
P.O. Box 6287, S-102 35, Stockholm, Sweden

Simultaneously published in the USA and Canada
by Routledge
270 Madison Ave, New York NY 10016

Reprinted 1999, 2000

Transferred to Digital Printing 2006

Routledge is an imprint of the Taylor & Francis Group

Phototypeset in Berling and Gill Sans by
Annika Almborg, Stockholm, Sweden

British Library Cataloguing in Publication Data
A catalogue record for this book is available from the British Library

Library of Congress Cataloguing in Publication Data
A catalogue record for this book has been requested

ISBN 0-415-14734-4
ISBN 91-88384-75-6 (Scandinavian edition)

Publisher's Note
The publisher has gone to great lengths to ensure the quality
of this reprint but points out that some imperfections
in the original may be apparent

Table of Contents

Part Two: Institutions

by Sverker Gustavsson and Leif Lewin, Uppsala University

Preface

What is meant, in fact, by the "European"? Few questions have inspired scholars to so many profound reflections, acute definitions and witty characterizations. Is it, perhaps, the respect for the rights of the individual? Or is it rather the brutality that issued in empire and colonization? Is it the Puritan work ethic, or the bent towards frivolity, leisure and entertainment? Is it the focus on immediate progress, or idealism in the tradition deriving from Jerusalem, Athens and Rome?

In a time marked by such contrary patterns as West European integration and East European dissolution, it would seem no one dares any longer to try to capture the "European" in a single formula. "Multiplicity" is the answer, maybe, if any answer be ventured at all. By this interpretation, politics appears as a method for imposing order. In the process of nation-building explored by Stein Rokkan, and (we would add today) in the current efforts to create a supranational order, a tension is evident throughout between, on the one hand, the desire of the peoples to express their distinctive national character, and on the other, their need to bridle international antagonisms by means of a system of cooperation that partly deprives the nations of independence and sovereignty.

7

It was, in short, this perspective that guided us when, together with the representatives of other faculties, we arranged a jubilee symposium at Uppsala University on March 22–25, 1995. The occasion was the 400th anniversary of the re-establishment of the university. The Faculty of Social Sciences wished to commemorate this important event in the intellectual history of our country by assembling distinguished international scholars to a symposium on "The Future of the Nation-State." Two questions lay in the back of our minds: Had political ambitions rendered the national units too small, so that the essays submitted would sooner be epitaphs than visions of the future? Or would the distinctive cultures prove still to be so vital as to make it meaningful to speak of nation-states in the future as well?

The multidisciplinary focus reflected more than a desire to let the symposium be an affair for the entire faculty, with active participation on the part of all of our departments. It also lay in the nature of the problem under consideration. Its multifaceted character called for expertise of the most varied types. So it came to be that, during those days in March, our faculty was a meeting place for scholars who seldom had met before, and whose professional orientation often furnished their colleagues with fruitful surprises and cross-fertilization. Not surprisingly, then, combining the submissions to the conference into a single book presents the editors with something of a challenge. The pluralism of the volume now in the hands of the reader bears witness not only to an uncommon scholarly vitality, but also to the grave difficulties facing those politicians who would force the varied peoples of the European Union into a unitary supranational culture.

The book's first section contains four essays falling under the heading of culture. It is thus natural that they address problems of the most varied sort. The first explores views of authority, individualism, masculinity-femininity, and ways of dealing with uncertainty. The following three take up the more limited matters of eating habits, ethnicity and family policy.

Taking advantage of his unique multidisciplinary professional training, *Geert Hofstede* sets out in the first essay to study "the mental programming" of IBM employees in over fifty countries

8

around the world. These people are similar in all respects except nationality. The picture that emerges shows the extraordinary impact of cultural heritage in the different countries. "Two thousand years of history have not wiped out the difference in mentality between peoples once under Rome and those whose ancestors remained barbarians. Four hundred years of neighbourhood have not unified the mental programmes of Dutch speakers on either side of the Belgian-Dutch border. Ninety years of Swedish-Norwegian Union has not wiped out the difference between Swedes and Norwegians. Some people believe that modern communication media will lead to what history has been unable to achieve. I do not believe it. Even if technology influences mental programmes, these influences are very partial and gradual. At least for the next two hundred years or so, mental programmes will noticeably differ between nation-states."

Anne Murcott devotes her attention to that phenomenon which, more than any other, weaves people together through symbol and rite: the meal, as an expression of national identity. Food satisfies not just a biological but also a social need. And globalization has not brought with it an eradication of the specific traditions of each nation in this area, but rather the import of other countries' culinary customs. So does the national paradoxically triumph in an internationalized world, and the great cities of Europe tempt us with French, Vietnamese, Italian, Lebanese, Singaporean, Thai, Mexican, Japanese, Indian, Columbian, and Chinese restaurants.

What is the place of ethnicity in contemporary Europe? Is integration in the West creating a new European citizen, "inside yet outside, a 'stranger'"? This is the question *Aleksandra Ålund* asks in her essay. "Processes of belonging are filled with tensions between dreams and realities," she writes in her concluding reflection. Immigrants — and perhaps still more their children — are "strangers" in George Simmel's sense, "near yet distant." In their search for identity, inherited and assumed, new patterns of conflict in European societies are contained.

Are women "strangers" as well, deviations from the national cultures of our continent? As they constitute half of the population, it would seem that they should not be. Yet on the labor market they are so nonetheless. *Sandra Scarr* contemplates, from an American perspective, the dilemma faced by European women when their men-folk refuse to shoulder an equal responsibility for children-rearing. "Family-friendly" policies promote women's opportunities to combine work and family life, but they also, in Scarr's view, impede the pursuit of a career. Only those women who "can work like men — single women, childless married women, and mothers who are willing to take on nearly un-manageable burdens for some years while children are young — can achieve like men" in terms of power, prestige and self-esteem.

The second part of the book, which contains the contributions of five authors, concentrates on the European nation-state as an institution. What strengthens or undermines the nation-state is not only, in the view of these authors, the interaction between national culture, economy and political behavior. For relations with the other countries of Europe — and of the world as a whole — play an important role here as well.

Richard Pipes discusses, in his contribution to this volume, the unique course of developments in Russia. His central claim is that the clock of history moves at a different rate in the eastern and western parts of this continent. While, in Western Europe, the question of a new balance between territory, function and identity is being posed, the territorial nation-state — as seen in the England of the 1600s, for example — has not yet begun to function in Russia. During the many centuries of Tsarist autocracy, personal loyalty to the Tsar was at a premium, and the same applied vis-a-vis the Communist Party after 1917. For a variety of historical reasons, no broad-based loyalty to independent institutions ever came into being, and no defence for the rights of the individual was ever established. Legal disputes over land were settled by the Tsar's henchmen. Until 1861, moreover, serfdom embraced not an ethnic minority — as in the case of American slavery — but the greater part of the population. What could have become a bourgeois revolution never became one. The constitutional standard of Russia remains at its medieval starting point. Now, when Western Europe is returning to medieval arrangements in a sense, this does not mean Russia can jump over the modern period.

The road beyond modernity can only go through it, Richard Pipes concludes.

The differences among the four essays on West European integration lie less in how the authors pose the question as in how they formulate the answer. Two opposed theses clearly emerge, each claiming to answer the question of the impact of integration. Does the system of cooperation established in the early 1950s work to strengthen the member states? Or does it instead weaken the nation-state as an institution?

The four concluding essays offer three different answers to this question — all equally interesting and worthy of serving as the point of departure for continued discussion. *Alan S. Milward* opens his essay with the assertion that cooperation will likely lead to a continued strengthening of the member states. This view reflects the analysis contained in his books on the earlier history of West European integration. A long-term historical perspective is important here. For despite the massive use of political symbols and conscript armies, few European states succeeded in the course of the 1800s in strengthening their standing in the eyes of their people. In the years between 1815 and 1914, for instance, 150 million people left their native land. Against this background, the years from 1945 to 1968 stand out as the only period of any length during which the states of Western Europe have succeeded in winning and keeping the confidence of the majority of their population. The construction of welfare states on a foundation of universal suffrage presupposed political integration for the securing of peace, employment and stable prices. It was a question, concretely speaking, of managing the markets for coal, steel and agricultural products on a supranational basis. This collaboration aimed at and led to the strengthening (in the sense of the saving) of each one of the participating democracies.

As a researcher of original sources and a programmatic opponent of all forms of speculation, Alan Milward is compelled to allow that the continued integration of the last thirty years may have had the opposite effect. It remains, however, for empirical research so to demonstrate, he ripostes. Theories of the withering-away of the nation-state do not count as evidence. What counts is

11

whether such a weakening can be demonstrated to have occurred in fact — and not just in utopian or dystopian wishful thinking. Is there any evidence, he asks rhetorically and eager for argument, to show that today's West European governments seek consciously to undermine the long-term loyalty of their people?

The next two authors argue on behalf of the contrary thesis — that the process of integration weakens rather than strengthens the participating states. Both authors discern a new way of combining territory, function and identity. This new form undermines representative democracy in the member countries, without introducing any corresponding accountability at the European level. *Beate Kohler-Koch* is the first of these authors. In her view, the West European state was never — even during its presumed heyday before 1914 — organized according to the principle that the prince or popular majority ruled through orders transmitted to a loyal bureaucracy. It appears, moreover, that this principle applies still less within the EU's administration for regional and technology policy, to which she and other German researchers have devoted such close attention.

Beate Kohler-Koch presents the results of studies of how municipal, regional, national, European, corporative and commercial actors cooperate in practical terms — in unspectacular and everyday settings. The "strength of weakness" characterizing these structures, she claims, gives rise to a new mode of governance, a "governance without government." The practical integration effected in these networks, she argues, represents something new in principle. The upshot is the development of a common system of governance in which such concepts as national loyalty and representative democracy lose their practical significance. To a diminishing extent do the actors of everyday politics feel themselves to be part of a hierarchical system of order-giving and accountability. Another notion governs their thinking and, in increasing measure, their actions as well. This other idea stresses the importance of being, in relation to each particular question, "centrally" and thereby "correctly" placed in the working out of partial norms and the distribution of available resources.

Philippe C. Schmitter is also a proponent of the thesis that representative democracy and parliamentarism are diminishing in importance. Instead of arguing on the basis of empirical research on administration, however, he chooses in this essay to reason in an intuitive and theoretical manner. His contribution is more speculative than empirical in character. If, he asks, the nation-states of Western Europe are withering away, then it is important to try to ascertain what new form might appear for the stabilization of territory, function and identity.

His answer proceeds on the premise that territory and function are more fundamental than identity. He directs our attention to four possible combinations along two dimensions: fixed or differentiated territory on the one hand, and fixed or differentiated function on the other. There is much to indicate, he contends, that today's European system of nation-states will not be succeeded by a complete federal state, or a partial confederation, or a consortium for certain fixed, partial functions — but rather by a condominium. Within the framework of such a condominium, both the territories and the functions included within the competence of the EU may vary. Such variations will occur, he presumes, along lines dictated by which political identities are politically possible. In the end, identity and self-assertion assume a form in many ways recalling medieval conditions.

In the final essay, *Johan P. Olsen* takes up a third line. He deems it scientifically unfruitful to proceed on the basis of either of the two hypotheses about the strengthening or weakening impact of integration. The research strategy should instead be, in his opinion, to avoid investing intellectual prestige in any particular view on the "big" question. With a more modest approach, he avers, the prospects for success increase. Researchers on Europe should pose more limited (but not for that sake less important) questions. As an example, he cites the question of what difference it makes for a country to join the European Union or to remain outside.

Both of the theses in question are expressive of an excessive reductionism, Olsen argues. For none of the relevant levels — European, national or regional — exhibit sufficient uniformity. The question should therefore not be posed in such a manner as to force the researcher to portray any of these levels unambiguously as a dependent or independent variable. For Europeanization leads to new combinations on all three levels at the same time. All three levels are characterized by a looser configuration of territory, function and identity than those pushing the one thesis or the other are forced to assume. It will not in the long be possible, according to Olsen, to confirm or refute either hypothesis. Instead of wrestling with undue simplifications, then, we should direct out efforts from the start on producing a more nuanced picture. A scientifically based account of both strengthening and weakening elements will in that case more easily emerge.

As a research program, Johan P. Olsen's third line enjoys all prospects of winning the practical acceptance both of Alan Milward and of Beate Kohler-Koch and Philippe Schmitter. All of the questions and answers discussed by Olsen's three colleagues are contained within the theoretical framework he sketches. The risk, Olsen would say, is that the theoretical basis for their argumentation on behalf of the one thesis or the other remains deficient and polemically conditioned. His colleagues can reply that theses are needed to give life, nerve and direction to scientific development. We see no reason as editors to take a position on this difference in scientific temperament and long-term research strategy. The critical thing in this context is that a broader intellectual public have the opportunity of judging the issue.

We hope that, with these words of introduction, we have succeeded in conveying to the reader a small part of the intellectual excitement marking the contributions to this book. On account of the central standing of the contributors in their respective areas, these essays give expression to strikingly sharp and interesting disagreements. We believe the prospects are excellent that, in a published form as well, these essays will work to inspire and challenge participants in the interchange between disciplines and research milieu.

In addition to the contributors, we would like to thank professor Stig Strömholm, Vice-Chancellor of Uppsala University, who took the initiative for commemorating this jubilee, and who suggested the idea of faculty symposia. We would also like to thank Marcus Wallenberg Foundation for International Cooperation in Science.

Generous grants have made possible both the symposium and the publication of this book. Finally, we wish to express our special thanks to chairpersons, discussants and assistants, to Laila Grandin for her help with the heavy administrative work involved in the symposium, and to Ludvig Beckman for assisting with the editorial work on this volume.

Uppsala, December 1995

Sverker Gustavsson   *Leif Lewin*

Part One | CULTURE

The Nation-State as a Source of Common Mental Programming: Similarities and Differences Across Eastern and Western Europe

by Geert Hofstede, Institute for Research on Intercultural Cooperation, Maastricht, the Netherlands

The concept of mental programming

"Mental programming" is a computer user's metaphor for the pattern of thinking, feeling and acting that every person has acquired in childhood, and carries along through life. Without such mental programmes people's behaviour would be unpredictable, and social life impossible.

A person's mental programming is partly unique, partly shared with others. We can distinguish three levels of uniqueness in mental programmes:

1. The least unique and most basic is the universal level of mental programming which is shared by all, or almost all, mankind. This is the biological "operating system" of the human body, which includes a range of expressive behaviours such as laughing and weeping, and kinds of associative and aggressive behaviours which are also found in higher animals. This level of our programming has been popularized by ethologists (biologists specialized in animal behaviour) such as Desmond Morris (1968), Konrad Lorenz (1970), and Irenaeus Eibl-Eibesfeldt; the latter has called one of his books "Der vorprogrammierte Mensch" (Man the Pre-Programmed, 1976).

2. The collective level of mental programming is shared with some but not with all other people: it is common to people belonging to a certain group or category, but different among people belonging to other groups or categories. The whole area of subjective human culture (as opposed to objective culture which consists of human artifacts; see Triandis, 1972:4) belongs to this level. It includes the language in which we express ourselves, the deference we show to our elders, the physical distance from other people we maintain in order to feel comfortable, the way we carry out basic human activities like eating, making love, or toilet behaviour and the ceremonials surrounding them.

3. The individual level of human programming is the truly unique part. No two people are programmed exactly alike, not even identical twins reared together. This is the level of individual personality, and it provides for a wide range of alternative behaviours within the same collective culture.

The borderlines between the three levels are a matter of debate within the social sciences. To what extent are individual personalities the product of a collective culture ? Which behaviours are human universals, and which are culture-dependent?

Mental programmes can be inherited, that is transferred in our genes, or they can be learned after birth. From the three levels, the universal level must be entirely inherited: it is part of the genetic information common to the human species. Programming at the individual level should be at least partly inherited, that is genetically determined. It is otherwise difficult to explain the differences in capabilities and temperament between successive children of the same parents raised in very similar environments. But at the middle, collective level all mental programmes are learned. They are shared with people who went through the same learning process, but who do not have the same genes. For an example think of the existence of the people of the U.S.A. Mixing all the world's genetic roots, present-day Americans show a collective mental programming very recognizable to the outsider. They illustrate the force of collective learning.

Mental programming manifests itself in several ways. From the many terms used to describe mental programmes, the following four together cover the total concept rather neatly: symbols, heroes, rituals and values. From these, symbols are the most superficial and values the most profound, with heroes and rituals in between.

Symbols are words, gestures, pictures or objects which carry a particular meaning only recognized as such by those who share the mental programme. The words in a language or jargon belong to this category, as do dress, hair-do, Coca-Cola, flags and status symbols. Heroes are persons, alive or dead, real or imaginary, who possess characteristics that are highly prized by those sharing the mental programme, and thus serve as models for behaviour. Rituals are collective activities, technically superfluous to reach desired ends, but considered socially essential: they are therefore carried out for their own sake. Ways of greeting and paying respect to others, social and religious ceremonies are examples of rituals. Symbols, heroes and rituals together constitute the visible part of mental programmes; elsewhere, I have subsumed them under the term "practices" (Hofstede, 1991:7).

Values are the invisible part of mental programming. Values can be defined as "broad tendencies to prefer certain states of affairs over others" (Hofstede, 1980:19). They are feelings with an arrow to it: a plus and a minus side.

The transfer of collective mental programmes through learning goes on during our entire lives. The most fundamental elements, the values, are learned first, when the mind is still relatively unprogrammed. A baby learns to distinguish between dirty and clean (hygienic values) and between evil and good, unnatural and natural, abnormal and normal (ethical and moral values). Somewhat later the child learns to distinguish between ugly and beautiful (aesthetic values), and between paradoxical and logical, irrational and rational (intellectual values). By the age of ten, most children have their basic value system firmly in place, and after that age, changes are difficult to make.

Because they were acquired so early, values as a part of mental programming often remain unconscious to those who hold them. Therefore they can not normally be discussed, nor can they be directly observed by outsiders. They can only be inferred from the way people act under various circumstances.

21

The transfer of collective mental programmes is a social phenomenon which, following Durkheim (1937 [1895]: 107), we should try to explain socially. Societies, organizations, and groups have ways of conserving and passing on mental programmes from generation to generation with an obstinacy which many people tend to underestimate. The elders program the minds of the young according to the way they were once programmed themselves. What else can they do, or who else will teach the young? Theories of race, very popular among past generations, were an erroneous genetic explanation for the continuity of mental programmes across generations.

"Collective mental programming" resembles the concept of habitus proposed by the French sociologist Pierre Bourdieu. Bourdieu (1980: 88–89) describes this concept in words which I translated as follows: "Certain conditions of existence produce a habitus, a system of permanent and transferable dispositions. A habitus ... functions as the basis for practices and images ... which can be collectively orchestrated without an actual conductor". The fact that Bourdieu associates collective behaviour with orchestration by a conductor reflects his French national mental programming, to which I will come back later.

Levels of mental programming

Collective mental programming, as I just described it, takes place within the collectivities people are part of. Everybody belongs to different categories at the same time; therefore, everybody carries different levels of mental programming. The most obvious ones are:

- a family level, determined by the family or family substitute in which a person grew up;
- a gender level, according to whether a person was born as a girl or as a boy;
- a generation level, according to the decade a person was born in;
- a social class level, associated with educational opportunities and with a person's occupation or profession;

- a linguistic level, according to the language or languages in which a person was programmed;
- a religious level, according to the religious tradition in which that person was programmed;
- for those who are employed, an organizational or corporate culture level according to the way a person was socialized by the work environment;
- a nation-state level according to one's country (or countries for people who migrated during their lifetime);
- within nation-states, possibly a regional and/or ethnic level.

In this chapter I will focus on the level associated with the nation-state. This corresponds partly with what once was called "national character", and later "national culture". National characters are intuitively evident, and have been so for hundreds and even thousands of years. However, because of the values element in national mental programmes, statements about national characters were almost without exception extremely biased. They often contained more information about the person making the statement than about the nation the statement was about.

In order to avoid this bias, I will only use comparative information about differences in nation-state-linked mental programmes that treat every nation-state's data as equivalent.

National culture differences

Human societies as historically, organically developed forms of social organization have existed for at least ten thousand years. Nation-states as political units into which the entire world is divided and to one of which any human being is supposed to belong are a much more recent phenomenon in human history. The concept of a common mental programming applies strictly spoken more to societies than to nation-states. Nevertheless many nation-states do form historically developed wholes even if they are composed of different regions and ethnicities, and even if less integrated minorities live within their borders. This is certainly the case for the nation-states of Central and Western Europe.

Nation-states contain institutions that standardize mental programmes: a dominant language (sometimes more than one), common mass media, a national education system, a national army, a national political system, national representation in sports events with a strong symbolic and emotional appeal, a national market for certain skills, products, and services. Today's nation-states do not attain the degree of internal homogeneity of the isolated, usually nonliterate societies traditionally studied by field anthropologists, but they are the source of a considerable amount of common mental programming of their citizens.

The German sociologist Norbert Elias has described this process in words which I have translated as follows: "The societal units which we call nations distinguish themselves clearly from each other by the nature of their affect transactions *(durch die Art ihrer Affekt-Ökonomie)*, that is by the patterns fashioning the individual's affect life under the pressure of institutionalized tradition and of the actual situation" (Elias, 1969:40–41).

The way mental programme patterns in societies, and often in nation-states, are stabilized over generations is illustrated in Figure 1 (developed from Figure 1.4 in Hofstede, 1980:27). In the center of the diagram is a system of societal norms, consisting of the value systems shared by major groups of the population. Their origins are in historical events plus a variety of ecological conditions (in the sense of elements of the objective environment). The societal norms have led to the development and pattern maintenance of institutions in society with a particular structure and way of functioning. These include the family, education systems, politics, and legislation. These institutions, once they have become facts, reinforce the societal norms and some of the ecological conditions that led to them.

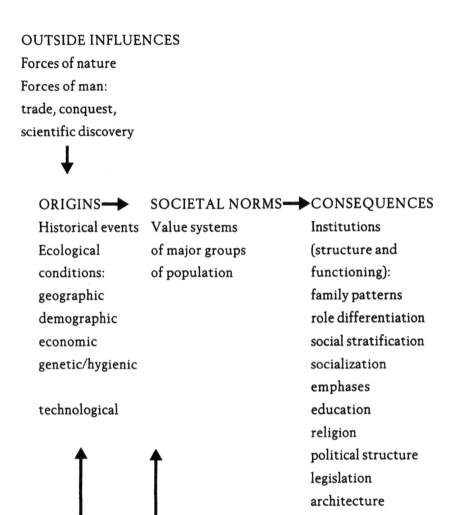

OUTSIDE INFLUENCES
Forces of nature
Forces of man:
trade, conquest,
scientific discovery

ORIGINS→   SOCIETAL NORMS→CONSEQUENCES

Historical events	Value systems	Institutions
Ecological	of major groups	(structure and
conditions:	of population	functioning):
geographic		family patterns
demographic		role differentiation
economic		social stratification
genetic/hygienic		socialization
		emphases
technological		education
		religion
		political structure
		legislation
		architecture
		scientific theories

REINFORCEMENT

Figure 1. The Stabilizing of Culture Patterns

In a relatively closed society, such a system will hardly change at all. Institutions may be changed, but this does not necessarily affect the societal norms; and when these remain unchanged, the persistent influence of majority mental programmes patiently

25

smoothes the new institutions until their structure and functioning is again adapted to the societal norms. Real change comes from the outside, through forces of nature (changes of climate, silting up of harbours) or forces of man (trade, conquest, colonization, scientific discovery). The arrow of outside influences is deliberately directed at the origins, not at the societal norms themselves. I believe that norms change rarely by direct adoption of outside values, but rather through a shift in ecological conditions: technological, economical, and hygienic (Kunkel, 1970:76). Such norm shifts will be gradual unless the outside influences are particularly violent (such as in the case of military conquest or deportation).

A very popular term at the present time is "national identity". National identity is part of a national population's mental programming, but at the conscious level of practices: symbols, heroes, and rituals. There is an increasing tendency for ethnic, linguistic and religious groups to fight for recognition of their own identity, if not for national independence. Ulster, the republics of the former Yugoslavia and parts of the former Soviet Union are evident examples. But the groups fighting are not necessarily very different in terms of their deepest level of mental programmes: values. They may fight on the basis of rather similar values, as I will show to be the case for the Flemish and Walloons in Belgium, and for the Croats and Serbs in the former Yugoslavia.

Dimensions of national cultures

In the first half of the twentieth century, social anthropology has developed the conviction that all societies, traditional or modern, faced and still face the same basic problems; only the answers differ. Attempts at identifying these common basic problems used conceptual reasoning, interpretation of field experiences, and statistical analysis of data about societies. In 1954 two Americans, the sociologist Alex Inkeles and the psychologist Daniel Levinson, published a broad survey of the English language literature on what was then still called "national character". They suggested that the following issues qualify as common basic problems worldwide, with consequences for the functioning of societies, of groups within those societies, and of individuals within those groups:

1. relation to authority

2. conception of self, in particular :
   – the relationship between individual and society, and
   – the individual's concept of masculinity and femininity

3. ways of dealing with conflicts, including the control of aggression and the expression of feelings (Inkeles and Levinson, 1954: 447).

Twenty years later I was given the opportunity to study a large body of survey data about the values of people in over fifty countries around the world. These people worked in the local subsidiaries of one large multinational corporation: IBM. At first sight it may look surprising that employees of a multinational — a very special kind of people — can serve for identifying differences in national value systems. However, a crucial problem in cross-national research is always to sample respondents who are functionally equivalent. The IBM employees represented almost perfectly matched samples: they were similar in all respects except nationality which made the effects of nationality differences in their answers stand out unusually clearly.

A statistical analysis of the answers on questions about the values of similar IBM employees in different countries revealed common problems, but solutions differing from country to country, in the following areas:

1. social inequality, including the relationship to authority;

2. the relationship between the individual and the group;

3. concepts of masculinity and femininity: the social implications of having been born as a boy or a girl;

4. ways of dealing with uncertainty, relating to the control of aggression and the expression of emotions.

These four problem areas could be expressed in four dimensions of national cultures, labelled Power Distance (large versus small), Individualism versus Collectivism, Masculinity versus Femininity,

27

and Uncertainty Avoidance (strong versus weak). Every country studied could be located somewhere between the extremes (poles) of each dimension.

These empirical results covered amazingly well the areas predicted by Inkeles and Levinson twenty years before. I only discovered Inkeles and Levinson's prediction after I had identified the four dimensions in the IBM data. It provided strong support for the theoretical importance of the empirical findings. Problems basic to all human societies should turn up in different studies regardless of the approaches followed.

A dimension associates a number of phenomena in a society that were empirically found to occur in combination; even if at first sight there does not always seem to be a logical necessity for their going together. The logic of societies, however, is not the same as the logic of individuals looking at them.

The IBM research results have been replicated by others on other samples of respondents: on students (Hofstede and Bond, 1984) and on national elites (Hoppe, 1990). They correlate significantly with the results of other cross-national studies of values, like the European Value Systems Study (Stoetzel, 1983; Harding and Phillips, 1986; Ester et al., 1993), and the worldwide values surveys by Schwartz (1994).

More recently a fifth dimension of differences among national cultures was identified, opposing a "Long Term Orientation" in life to a "Short Term Orientation". East Asian nations tend to score Long Term; European countries more Short Term. For this chapter which focuses on differences within Europe, this dimension is less relevant.

Mental programmes in European nation-states: power and uncertainty

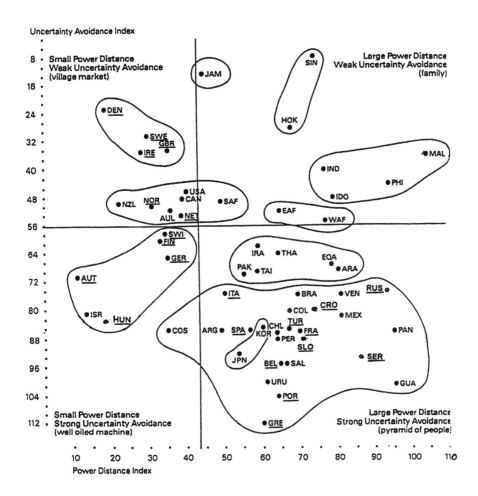

Uncertainty Avoidance Index

Figure 2 The Position of 57 countries or regions on the Power Distance x Uncertainty Avoidance dimensions (for country name abbreviations see Figure 2A)

Figure 2A

ABBREVIATIONS FOR COUNTRY NAMES

ARA	Arab-speaking countries(Egypt, Iraq, Kuwait, Lebanon, Lybia, Saudi-Arabia, United Arab Emirates)	IDO IND IRA IRE ISR ITA	Indonesia India Iran Ireland Israel Italy
ARG	Argentina	JAM	Jamaica
AUL	Australia	JPN	Japan
AUT	Austria	KOR	South Korea
BEL	Belgium	MAL	Malaysia
BRA	Brazil	MEX	Mexico
CAN	Canada	NET	Netherlands
CHL	Chile	NOR	Norway
COL	Colombia	NZL	New Zealand
COS	Costa Rica	PAK	Pakistan
CRO	Croatia	PAN	Panama
DEN	Denmark	PER	Peru
EAF	East Africa (Ethiopia, Kenya, Tanzania, Zambia)	PHI POR RUS	Philippines Portugal Russia
EQA	Equador	SAF	South Africa
FIN	Finland	SAL	Salvador
FRA	France	SER	Serbia
GBR	Great Britain	SIN	Singapore
GER	Germany F.R.	SLO	Slovenia
GRE	Greece	SPA	Spain
GUA	Guatemala	SWE	Sweden
HOK	Hong Kong	SWI	Switzerland
HUN	Hungary	TAI	Taiwan

THA	Thailand	USA	United States
TUR	Turkey	VEN	Venezuela
URU	Uruguay	WAF	West Africa (Ghana,Nigeria, Sierra Leone)

Figure 2 shows the position of the answers by the respondent samples from 57 countries and regions, on the two dimensions of Power Distance and Uncertainty Avoidance. The 22 European countries in the set have been underlined.

Power Distance has been defined as "the extent to which the less powerful members of institutions within a country expect and accept that power is distributed unequally." It represents the degree of social inequality in people's mental programming. All societies are unequal, but some are more unequal than others, and this inequality is reflected in people's mental programmes.

Uncertainty Avoidance has been defined as "the extent to which the members of a culture feel threatened by uncertain or unknown situations." It stands for the need for structure, social conformity, and absolute Truths. People in strongly uncertainty avoiding societies have been programmed to feel that "What is different, is dangerous". People in uncertainty tolerant societies have been programmed to feel that "What is different, is curious". Fundamentalisms thrive in strongly uncertainty avoiding societies; tolerance, mysticism and meditation are characteristic for weakly uncertainty avoiding societies.

The IBM survey data, collected around 1970, did not cover Eastern Europe, except for what was then still Yugoslavia. In 1993 I went back to the old Yugoslavia data, which I could split into data from Croatia, Serbia and Slovenia. More recent replications on samples more or less matched with the IBM employee samples collected data in Hungary (Varga, 1986) and Russia (Bollinger, 1988). Attempts have been made to collect data with the same questionnaire in other Eastern European countries, but the survey populations were poorly matched with the IBM employee population, so that the results are not meaningful.

31

Figure 2 shows that the scores from the 22 European countries covered are found in three quadrants of the diagram.

The top left quadrant contains six North- and West-European countries: Denmark, Sweden and Norway, and Ireland, Britain, and the Netherlands. These combined small Power Distance with weak Uncertainty Avoidance: in their people's mental programmes there is little social inequality and little need for structure.

The bottom left quadrant contains the German speaking countries of Austria, Switzerland and Germany, plus Finland and Hungary. These combine small Power Distance with stronger Uncertainty Avoidance: their people's mental programmes show little social inequality, but more need for structure.

The two quadrants to the left thus host all Germanic countries, plus Finugric Finland and Hungary. In all of these, survey respondents scored low on Power Distance. The closeness of Austria and Hungary is remarkable: the Austro-Hungarian empire is still present in people's minds.

The top right quadrant (large Power Distance but weak Uncertainty Avoidance) contains countries from Africa, Asia, and the Caribbean, not from Europe.

The bottom right quadrant contains all Latin European countries studied: Italy, Spain, France, Belgium, and Portugal, and the South and East European countries Slovenia, Croatia, and Serbia, Turkey, Russia and Greece. In all of these, respondents scored high on both Power Distance and Uncertainty Avoidance.

Power and structure are the key elements in the organizations people build. Other research (described in Hofstede, 1991:140) has suggested that people from different countries tend to hold different mental models on what an organization is. People from the Latin quadrant tend to see an organization as a pyramid of people, functioning on the basis of both power and structure. Remember the quotation from Pierre Bourdieu from France, who associated collective behaviour with orchestration by a conductor. Those from the German-speaking quadrant tend to see an organization as a well-oiled machine, functioning on the basis of its structure, but without the need for a constant exercise of power.

Those from the Anglo-Nordic quadrant tend to see an organization as a market, functioning on the basis of permanent negotiation. Among authors from the Anglo countries it is popular to explain collective behaviour in organizations as a way of minimizing transaction costs; an approach that meets with little understanding in, for example, France.

The roots of these different mental programmes lie evidently in history. The Latin countries of Europe grew out of the remains of the Roman Empire, the Germanic countries did not. The Roman Empire was the first large and effective state to be established in its part of the world. In the same way as early childhood experiences have a major impact on personality, these early societal experiences must have had a lasting impact on polity, affecting not only all institutions that have followed but also the corresponding mental programmes. We still speak of the "Latin mentality". The Roman Empire combined two principles new to Europe: (1) authority centralized in Rome, and (2) a system of codified laws, applicable to every Roman citizen. The centralized authority principle supports a large Power Distance; the codified law principle supports strong Uncertainty Avoidance. From the two principles, the first dominated over the second: the supreme power, the emperor, stood over the law. One historian has described this situation as follows: "By an implied contract the people confer upon the emperor all power and authority over them so that his will has the force of the law" (Smith, 1964:272).

When the Roman Empire disintegrated, the absolute authority of the ruler was maintained by the Germanic invaders of France who mixed with the Romanized population (Pirenne, 1939: 32), but not by the Germanic Anglo-Saxon invaders of Britain who chased the Romanized Celts without mixing with them. In the Germanic tradition the power of the king was subordinate to the assembly of free men. Therefore an absolutist rule could never settle in Britain; when the Norman kings attempted to establish it, they were forced to recognize the rights of the people in the Magna Charta of 1214 (Pirenne, 1939: 257). In Germany up till the nineteenth century a central authority could never last, and the country was composed of small principalities. Federal Germany is still much more decentralized than the countries of Latin Europe.

The Roman and Germanic traditions also divided Europe by their different inheritance laws (Jordan, 1973:69). In the former Roman Empire the practice of divided inheritance was long dominant. This meant that land and other possessions were divided equally among all heirs, leading to all children remaining on ever-smaller farms, and a need for birth control. In Germanic and English common law land was usually inherited by the eldest son only, with the remaining offspring being compensated in other ways, if at all (a familiar picture from several of Grimm's German fairytales). This led in a later stage of history to emigration and urbanization of the younger children. It has been said that the younger sons have made England great (Sauvy, 1966: 26). From 1720 to 1970 the population of Britain grew by a factor 7.9, of Germany by a factor 5.5, but of France only by a factor 2.6 (Jordan, 1973:72). This must have been the result of birth control, because France neither knew neither massive emigration nor higher death rates than other countries (Sauvy, 1966:54). Smaller family sizes support larger Power Distances because parental authority weighs heavier on the children who remain more dependent.

Russia, Greece and Serbia inherited the Byzantine culture, which in turn was an offspring of the Roman culture. We find their scores on the extreme fringe of the Latin quadrant in Figure 2, with extreme Power Distances in Russia and Serbia and extreme Uncertainty Avoidance in Greece. The Byzantine empire seems to have developed and transferred a hypertrophy of Latin mental programming traits.

The Germanic countries in Figure 2 are relatively close on Power Distance but show a wider spread on Uncertainty Avoidance. The countries turned towards the sea avoided uncertainty less than the countries turned towards the land. How, why and when exactly this split took place is a question I have to leave to historians.

Mental programmes in European nation-states: individualism and masculinity

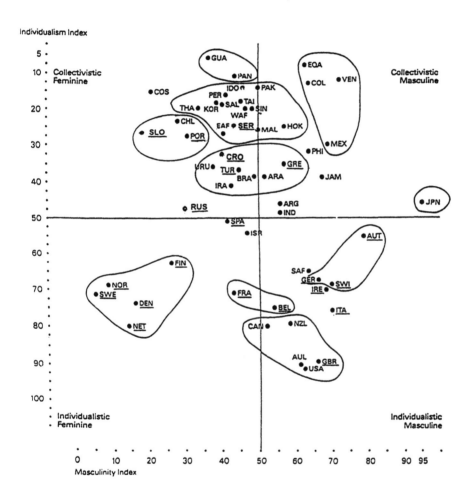

Figure 3. *The Position of 56 countries or regions on the Individualism x Masculinity dimensions (for country name abbreviations see Figure 2A)*

Figure 3 shows the position of the respondent samples from 56 countries and regions, on the two dimensions of Individualism-Collectivism and Masculinity-Femininity. Twenty-one European countries are underlined (for these two dimensions no data are available for Hungary).

Individualism stands for a society in which the ties between individuals are loose: everyone is expected to look after himself or herself and his or her immediate family only; Collectivism stands for a society in which people from birth onwards are intergrated into strong, cohesive ingroups, which throughout people's lifetime continue to protect them in exchange for unquestioning loyalty.

Collectivism is the normal state of mind for agricultural societies; hunting and gathering societies are more individualist. Modern individualism developed in England, Scotland and Holland, and was taken to the U.S.A. by the Pilgrim Fathers. Individualism in countries increases with national wealth (increased individualism is an effect, not a cause of economic growth). Asian nations that have recently become wealthy have also become more individualist, but not as much as Western European countries at the same wealth level.

The scores on Individualism in Figure 3 closely follow the countries' Per Capita Gross National Product. All West-European countries except Portugal scored individualist. The parts of former Yugoslavia, Greece, Turkey and Russia scored collectivist.

Individualist mental programmes are a precondition for a political democracy and for a free market economy. One person, one vote presupposes that those persons have been programmed to hold personal opinions. The invisible hand of the market economy presupposes that persons will attempt to maximize their individual economic advantage. Both do not apply in nations with collectivist mental programmes and institutions. World Bank economists, trained in the U.S.A., prescribed market economies to Third World countries in the past decades, with remarkably little success. They seem to be still following the same approach now to Second World countries, including the parts of the former Soviet Union, with predictably equally little success. Only in the relatively wealthy and therefore more individualist countries of

Central Europe may this approach work out: Hungary, Czechia, maybe Poland and Bulgaria. The economically fast growing countries of Asia have been successful by not following U.S. recipes, but sticking to their own forms of collectivist logic.

The second dimension in Figure 3, Masculinity, stands for a society in which social gender roles are clearly distinct: men are supposed to be assertive, tough, and focused on material success; women are supposed to be more modest, tender, and concerned with the quality of life. Femininity stands for a society in which social gender roles overlap: both men and women are supposed to be modest, tender, and concerned with the quality of life.

On the bottom left, individualist and feminine side of the diagram we find a cluster of Nordic countries: Sweden, Norway, Denmark, Finland, plus the Netherlands; collectivist and feminine scores were obtained for Slovenia. Slightly feminine scores were found for France, Spain and Portugal, Croatia, Serbia, Russia and Turkey.

On the bottom right, individualist and masculine side of the diagram we find the German speaking countries Germany, Switzerland and Austria (moderately individualist but strongly masculine), plus Ireland, Italy and Britain (very individualist and fairly masculine). Belgium and Greece scored slightly masculine.

Masculine mental programmes lead to political choices in favour of a performance society, sympathy for the strong, and reward according to merit. Feminine mental programmes lead to a welfare society, sympathy for the weak, and reward according to need. Among the wealthy nations of Europe, the ones in the bottom half of Figure 3, the percentage of their Gross National Product spent on development cooperation with poor countries is strongly negatively correlated with their masculinity scores in the IBM samples. The correlation is over .80: feminine countries spend much more than masculine ones. The present fashion to reduce development assistance budgets also strikes the masculine countries more than the feminine ones. On the other hand, the percentage of national GNPs spent on armaments is positively correlated with the masculinity scores. Politicians in masculine countries tend to favour economic growth over preservation of the ecosystem; those in feminine countries tend to show the opposite preference.

The origins of Masculinity-Femininity differences are not immediately evident. The feminine nations concentrated in Northwestern Europe (Denmark, Finland, Netherlands, Norway, Sweden) share some of the same history. The elites in these countries consisted to a large extent of traders and seafarers. In trading and sailing, maintaining good interpersonal relationships and caring for the ships and the merchandise are competitive advantages. The Hanseatic League (1200–1500 AD) covered all these countries, plus the free cities of Hamburg, Bremen and Lübeck in Northern Germany and the Baltic states. The Hansa was a free association of trading towns and, for the maintenance of such a system, values associated with Femininity were functional. Women played an active role. An article about the Hansa contains the following description: "Although the wife did not share her husband's legal status, they usually formed a business team. Even in merchant circles, the family was the smallest functional cell of society, where the women and the children had a role to play. This meant that women had a certain degree of emancipation, and their independence and business skills increased. Indeed, some women managed to win the 'battle for the trousers' even while their husbands were still alive" (Samsonowicz, 1970). While the Hansa does not explain the origin of North-European Femininity, it at least benefitted from it and reinforced it.

Mental programmes in Eastern Europe

The Figures 2 and 3 contain no data about the Baltic states, Poland, Czechia, Slovakia, Romania, Bulgaria, Macedonia and Albania, nor about parts of the former Soviet Union other than Russia. However, it should be evident that in terms of mental programming, Eastern Europe is not a homogeneous category. The communist era has been remarkably ineffectual in changing mental programmes; old ways of thinking, feeling and acting resurge. Dostoyevski and Tolstoy are still, I believe, the best guides for those trying to understand the Russian mind.

There is a need for good research into the mental programmes of Eastern European national populations. Good research means that the samples compared should be functionally equivalent. The convenience samples presently surveyed by Western travellers are not good enough.

The joint guesstimate of me and some colleagues is that the Baltic States' mental programming will resemble that of Finland and Sweden, but with lower Individualism. East and West Germany are likely to differ on Individualism, but this difference is bound to disappear, that is, the Easterners will become as individualist as the Westerners. Czechia is likely to resemble East-Germany; Poland and Slovakia should also resemble East-Germany but with larger Power Distance and lower Individualism.

In South-West Europe, Romania is likely to belong to the Byzantine cluster of very large Power Distance, very strong Uncertainty Avoidance, Collectivism, and below average Masculinity. Albania could be similar but more masculine. Bulgaria and Macedonia may be more similar to Turkey, which means moderately high scores for both Power Distance and Uncertainty Avoidance, moderate Collectivism, and average Femininity.

The other parts of the former Soviet Union are all likely to be characterized by large Power Distances and moderate to extreme Collectivism, and to vary on the other two dimensions.

The influence of language and religion

Acting as the devil's advocate, I could use the split between Germanic and Latin Europe in Figure 2 to argue that the differences in scores obtained are due to language rather than to other forms of mental programming. The differences could even be trivial artefacts of the languages used in the surveys, assuming that somehow in Latin languages respondents use different parts of answer scales than in Germanic languages, without there being any substantial difference in the content of what they want to answer.

This argument is refuted by the clustering of Hungary with Austria in Figure 2, and of Finland with Sweden in Figure 3. Countries with Finugric languages, linguistically very different, cluster with neighbouring Germanic countries. A more complete analysis of the role of language is provided by the cases of Belgium and Switzerland, two countries that combine one or more Germanic and one or more Latin languages (Hofstede, 1980:335).

In Belgium about 54 percent of the population speaks Dutch (Flemish), 45 percent French (Walloon), and 1 percent German. In Switzerland, the figures are about 75 percent German, 20 percent French, 4 percent Italian, and 1 percent Raeto-Romanic.

In Belgium and Switzerland the surveys were administered in two national languages each: in French and Dutch in Belgium, and in French and German in Switzerland. Figure 4 shows the dimension scores for each language area separately, as well as the scores of the neighbouring countries with the same languages.

I. Belgium

	NET	BEL-NE	BEL-FR	FRA
Power Distance	38	61	67	68
Individualism	80	78	72	71
Masculinity	14	43	60	43
Unc. Avoidance	53	97	93	86

II. Switzerland

	GER	SWI-GE	SWI-FR	FRA
Power Distance	35	26	70	68
Individualism	67	69	64	71
Masculinity	66	72	58	43
Unc. Avoidance	65	56	70	86

Figure 4. Dimension scores for Belgium and Switzerland by language area, with neighbouring countries

As we see in Figure 4, in Belgium respondents from the two language areas score quite similarly; both resemble the French. The scoring gap between Flemish (Dutch-speaking Belgians) and Dutch is wide. In fact, no two countries in the IBM data base with a common border and a common language produce such different scores. The gap occurs in Power Distance, Uncertainty Avoidance, and Masculinity; only in Individualism do Belgium and the Netherlands come together.

A very different picture is found for Switzerland. German-speaking Swiss score more like Germans, French-speaking Swiss like French, and in this case the scoring gap is between the two language areas, in particular on the dimension of Power Distance. The two parts of Switzerland evidently belong to different culture clusters, the German-speaking part to the Germanic and the French-speaking part to the Latin cluster. The fact that in Figures 2 and 3 Switzerland showed up as part of the Germanic cluster is simply due to the greater numerical strength of German-speaking respondents in the IBM sample.

Curiously, the language split is a hot political issue in Belgium (where, according to the data, the two areas share largely the same culture) and not in Switzerland (where cultures differ). This is undoubtedly due to the different political histories of the two countries.

Belgium was for centuries a distant dependent province of foreign powers (successively of Spain, Austria, France, and the Netherlands) and only gained its independence from the Netherlands in 1831. For the next 100 years French was the only language of government, the upper classes, and of secondary and higher education. Only in the 1950s did the emancipation movement of the Dutch-speaking majority gain momentum, which finally led to the recent restructuring of the country into language regions.

Switzerland was created in 1291 as a voluntary federation of three cantons (small provinces) and grew gradually by the more or less voluntary addition of 19 other cantons, reaching its present size in 1815. Its political structure has always been strictly federal, leaving a large amount of internal independence to the cantons. In one case where a canton was bilingual (Berne) this led in the 1960s to political conflicts not unlike those in Belgium, but these were resolved by splitting the canton (creating the new canton Jura).

The comparison between the Belgian and the Swiss case shows that the institutions rather than the languages account for the respondents' mental programming. In a Latin-dominated governance structure that lasted for more than a century but had roots as old as the Roman Empire, all Belgians maintained the Latin mentality, even those who speak Dutch. It is possible, of course, that now that the country is regionalized the cultures of the language areas will slowly grow apart.

The split between Germanic and Latin countries in Figure 2 could also be explained as as split by religion: protestant versus Roman Catholic. According to the Belgian historian Henri Pirenne (1939:397), the Roman Catholic church is in many respects a continuation of the Roman Empire; therefore the influences of old Rome and new Rome are difficult to separate. However, Ireland, predominantly Roman Catholic but never part of the Empire, scored like Britain and not like, for example, Italy. Which suggests that the crucial factor is the Empire and not the Church.

Religious affiliation anywhere in the world is less tightly associated with mental programming than is often assumed. If we trace the religious history of countries, what religion a population has embraced, and which version of that religion, seems to have been a result of previously existing mental programmes as much as a cause of new programmes. All of the great religions of the world at some time in their history underwent profound schisms: between Roman Catholics, Eastern Orthodox, and various Protestant groups in Christianity; between Sunni and Shia in Islam; between liberals and various fundamentalist groups in jewry; between Hinayana and Mahayana in Buddhism. Differences in mental programming between groups of believers have always played a major role in these schisms.

The future of the nation-state

Nation-states are products of history. What I have tried to show is that this history is not only reflected in artefacts and institutions: it is also present in the minds of people, both on the conscious level of practices and on the unconscious level of values. In the case of the Roman Empire, its traces on the mental maps of the citizens of European countries can be clearly identified after two thousand years. The historical roots of other differences in mental programmes between European nation-states are less easy to identify, but their existence cannot be doubted.

Nation-linked mental programming goes beyond a feeling of national identity. As stated earlier, national identity is conscious and resides in common symbols, heroes and rituals. National mental programmes however contain a large unconscious component of common values. In the cases of Belgium and Switzerland I have shown that conflicting identities may rest on similar mental programmes, and that a joint national identity may bridge different mental programmes.

National identities are a hot topic in Europe these days, much more than national mental programmes. In my native Netherlands I can hardly open a newspaper without striking an article about our national identity. Opinions vary; there are those who think the national identity will be lost and raise the alarm trumpet, those who think it will be lost and this is okay, those who think we never had much of a national identity anyway, and those who believe our national identity is alive and well. Mr. Heineken, a well-known brewer from the Netherlands, has published a map showing how he wants to reshuffle all of Europe into regions, doing away with nation- states altogether. I don't know whether he meant to be serious. On his map I found that in the case of Europe's most meaningful recent re-shuffling, the renewed independence of Estonia, Latvia and Lithuania, Mr Heineken's map left them with Russia.

The fact that ethnic, linguistic and/or religious groups fight for independence in the name of their identity is not a new phenomenon. In Scandinavia, Norway gained its independence from Sweden in 1905, and the Åland-islands got regional autonomy inside Finland after an international crisis in 1921. Such conflicts of differentiation will be with us forever, I guess; they are more likely to become violent in nations combining strong Uncertainty Avoidance with Collectivism (like Croatia and Serbia). Collectivism opposes "us" to "them"; strong Uncertainty Avoidance adds that "what is different, is dangerous" — and therefore we better strike them before they strike us.

At the same time as regional differentiation there is, of course, international integration. Fifteen European nation-states, Sweden among them now, have voluntarily engaged themselves in the European Union, implying a transfer of certain powers to this supra-national body. In fact some believe that this integration is a good thing for regional differentiation, as the Union is more likely to support regional autonomies than were the nation-states before joining.

A very popular question is, whether this international integration:

(1) threatens the nation-states' national identity, and

(2) will wipe out their national mental programmes.

Two thousand years of history have not wiped out the difference in mentality between peoples once under Rome and those whose ancestors remained barbarians. Four hundred years of neighbourhood have not unified the mental programmes of Dutch speakers on either side of the Belgian-Dutch border. Ninety years of Swedish-Norwegian Union has not wiped out the difference between Swedes and Norwegians. Some people believe that modern communication media will lead to what history has been unable to achieve. I do not believe it. Even if technology influences mental programmes (Figure 1), these influences are very partial and gradual. At least for the next two hundred years or so, mental programmes will noticeably differ between nation-states.

However, if national mental programmes continue to differ, national identities will also not seriously be threatened. Some symbols may be lost and replaced by European symbols; fewer heroes may become international heroes; even fewer rituals will change into European rituals. The underlying values will continue to show strong nation-state components.

Differences in national mental programmes are a greater problem for the European Union than the Union is for the differences in mental programmes. It is a very challenging task for the Union to effectively coordinate nations whose citizens think, feel and act as differently as they do. It will be a long time before there is a United States of Europe in the way there is a United States of America. With or without the Union, Europe will remain a "Europe des patries".

Notes

1. Bollinger's 1988 survey of Russians found a Masculinity score of -1. This may have been influenced by peculiarities of the sample. Later research on Individualism and Masculinity among students in 8 countries including Russia arrived at a score of 30 (Hofstede et al., 1994). In the diagram the latter figure was used.

References

Bollinger, D. (1988), unpublished survey report, Paris: CEGOS-Coopération.

Bourdieu, P. (1980), *Le sens pratique*, Paris: Éditions de Minuit.

Durkheim, E. (1937 [1895]), *Les Règles de la Méthode Sociologique*, Paris: Presses Universitaires de France.

Eibl-Eibesfeldt, I. (1976), *Der vorprogrammierte Mensch: Das Ererbte als bestimmender Faktor im menschlichen Verhalten*, München: Deutscher Taschenbuch Verlag.

Elias, N. (1980 [1969]), *Über den Prozeß der Zivilisation: Soziogenetische und psychogenetische Untersuchungen, Erster Band*, Frankfurt am Main: Suhrkamp.

Ester, P., Halman, L. and de Moor, R. (1993), *The Individualizing Society: Value Change in Europe and North America*, Tilburg Neth.: Tilburg University Press.

Harding, S. and Phillips, D. with Fogarty, M. (1986), *Contrasting Values in Western Europe*, London: Macmillan.

Hofstede, G. (1980), *Culture's Consequences: International Differences in Work-Related Values*, Beverly Hills CA: Sage Publications.

Hofstede, G. (1991), *Cultures and Organizations: Software of the Mind*, London: McGraw-Hill.

Hofstede, G. and Bond, M.H. (1984), "Hofstede's culture dimensions: an independent validation using Rokeach's Value Survey", *Journal of Cross-Cultural Psychology*, 15(4): 417–433.

Hofstede, G., Kolman, L., Nicolescu, O. and Pajumaa, I. (1994), *Characteristics of the Ideal Job among Students in Eight Countries*, Paper presented at the XIIth Congress of Cross-Cultural Psychology, Pamplona, Spain, July.

Hoppe, M.H. (1990), *A Comparative Study of Country Elites: International Differences in Work-related Values and Learning and their Implications for Management Training and Development*, unpublished Ph.D. Dissertation, University of North Carolina at Chapel Hill.

Inkeles, A., & Levinson, D.J. (1969 [1954]), "National character: The study of modal personality and sociocultural systems", in G. Lindzey and E. Aronson (eds.), *The Handbook of Social Psychology*, Vol.4, pp. 418–506, Reading MA: AddisonWesley.

Jordan, T.G. (1973), *The European Culture Area: A Systematic Geography*, New York: Harper & Row.

Kunkel, J.H. (1970), *Society and Economic Growth: A BehavioralPerspective of Social Change*, New York: Oxford University Press.

Lorenz, K. (1970), *On Aggression*, New York: Bantam Books.

Morris, D. (1968), *The Naked Ape: A Zoologist's Study of the Human Animal*, New York: McGraw-Hill.

Pirenne, H. (1939), *A History of Europe from the Invasions to the XVI Century*, London: George Allen & Unwin.

Samsonowicz, H. (1970), "Die Bedeutung des Grosshandels für die Entwicklung der polnischen Kultur bis zum Beginn des 16. Jahrhunderts", *Studia Historiae Economica*, 5: 92-120.

Sauvy, A. (1966), *Théorie générale de la population, Volume II: La vie des populations*, Paris: Presses Universitaires de France.

Schwartz, S. (1994), "Beyond Individualism/Collectivism: New cultural dimensions of values", in U. Kim et al. (eds.), *Individualism and Collectivism: Theory, Method, and Applications*, pp. 85–119. Thousand Oaks CA: Sage.

Smith, J.C. (1964), "The theoretical constructs of Western contractual law", in F.S.C. Northrop and H.H. Livingston (eds.), *Cross-cultural Understanding: Epistemology in Anthropology*, pp. 254–283. New York: Harper and Row.

Stoetzel, J. (1983), *Les valeurs du temps présent*, Paris: Presses Universitaires de France.

Triandis, H.C. (ed.), (1972), *The Analysis of Subjective Culture*, New York: John Wiley.

Varga, K. (1986), *Az emberi és szervezeti eröforrás fejlesztése*, Budapest: Akadémiai Kiadó.

by Anne Murcott,
South Bank University,
London

Food as an Expression of Identity

Pistol: Le Roy? a Cornish name. Art thou of Cornish crew?

King Henry: No, I am a Welshman.

Pistol: Know'st thou Fluellen?

King Henry: Yes.

Pistol: Tell him I'll knock his leek about his pate upon
Saint Davy's Day.

Henry V
Act IV Scene I

I was a schoolgirl in Paris then. Every Sunday I was invited together with my brother and a cousin to eat *ful medames* with some relatives. This meal became a ritual. Considered in Egypt to be a poor man's dish, in Paris the little brown beans became invested with all the glories and warmth of Cairo, our home town, and the embodiment of all that for which we were homesick

Claudia Roden
A Book On Middle Eastern Food

Introduction

Associations between food and national identity are not hard to find.[1] We only have to look at the uncomplimentary names that one nation uses to ridicule another. The word Eskimo, for instance, is a derivation of *eskimantsik,* the derisive word meaning "eaters of raw meat", that neighbouring Indians used to refer to the Inuit (Farb & Armelagos 1980:97). North Americans make metaphorical reference to the supposed eating habits of the French, the Germans, and the Italians in speaking of "Frogs", "Krauts" and "Macaronis" and the French, in turn, call English people "rosbif". To this might be added the less widely known reports that Dhor, i.e. eaters-of-beef, is the name given to a subdivision of the Katkari caste of Bombay. And in the Congo, the Western Lange, who eat dogmeat, are known by the other Lange peoples as Baschilambua, i.e. dog-people. It has even been claimed that stereotypes of national character are couched in terms of typical national diets.

> The French subtlety of thought and manners is said to be related to the subtlety of their cuisine, the reserve of the British to their unimaginative diet, German stolidness to the quantities of heavy food they consume, and the unreliability of Italians to the large amounts of wine they drink. (Farb & Armelagos 1980:3–4)

Associations such as these are familiar enough. But why do we use diet to describe national identity? Why do we refer to eating habits to flatter or belittle other nations? Can we say why a humble dish comes to remind an exile so powerfully of home? What is it about food that lends itself to such expression? Thinking about how we might begin to answer these questions is the task I have set myself in this paper. To do so has meant venturing beyond the literatures on food to see what discussions of nationality have to offer in the attempt to bring food and national identity into focus with one another.

Drawing on these separate literatures is reflected in what follows which I have divided into sections. The first is concerned with analyses of food as meaning more than merely "something to eat". It is long accepted amongst social anthropologists and sociologists that food has an expressive, symbolic value. We say things with food at the same time as providing our bodies with essential nourishment. How this may be adequately studied, though, has yet to be settled. The first section of the paper starts by reviewing some of the arguments and then moves on to attempt to draw out the strengths and limitations of the position proposed by Sidney Mintz, professor of anthropology at Johns Hopkins University, among others. In his study of sugar and its symbolic meanings, Mintz insists that both a long historical view and a global perspective is essential.

The second section of the paper temporarily sets discussion of food aside to focus on national identity. It only needs a quick glance at the illustrations with which I began to see that national identity is taken for granted, referred to but not examined, assumed rather than inspected. Turning to the literatures that do examine it, suggests provocative parallels between the position scholars are currently adopting to the study of nationhood and that proposed by Mintz for the study of the expressive aspect of human food use.[2]

From these literatures I single out the work of Benedict Anderson on the history of nation as an idea made real. The supposed stolidity of German food and character, the British reserve attributable to their lack of culinary inspiration, only make sense at certain time and place when the foodways attributable to the peoples of those nations have developed a distinctive image. Equally, the identities concerned only make sense once the nations to which people belong become nameable as such, made possible by the emergence of the very notion of nation. As we shall see, it may not be stretching a point too far to say that what Mintz does for the history of the symbolic value of sugar, Anderson does for the histopect different versions of food as an expression of national identity and to sury of nationality. The paper's final section returns to the main theme to insmmarise the beginnings of answers about why one is adopted to represent the other.

In the process of what follows, I hope it will become apparent that treating food[3] as an expression of national identity is not taken as a given, but is to be dealt with as a matter for enquiry. That it may prove to be an especially potent instance of the expression of

51

identity, national as much as other versions, is a view coincidentally shared by Delamont (1995). She even elects to give her textbook introducing the social anthropology of Western Europe the title *Appetites and Identities*

> because it celebrates the variety of tastes (in food, drink, family life, language and religion) and the variety of identities that can be found in western Europe. (Delamont 1995:1)

Stressing that the identities in question are not neatly bounded by nation states, she notes that

> "(F)ood from our families, our childhood, our homeland, our first foreign holiday, is irrevocably fixed for us as special. Our beliefs about food are usually unexamined and buried deep within ourselves." [4] (Delamont 199:24)

Food as an expression of...

In part, my purpose in this section consists of illustrating the well established analytic position that treats food as an expression of "something" social: social harmony or social display, necessity or luxury, or, of course, identity. As Caplan has observed:

> Food ... can evoke taste, memory, feelings and emotions; for an anthropologist it is also about social relations, identity and selfhood. (Caplan 1992:3)

My main concern in this section, however, is to highlight debates about how the study of food as expression may be best approached. Although there are debates, there is nonetheless a set of underlying assumptions that form a common point of departure, with which we need to begin.

These assumptions run along the following lines. While all living things have to eat, it is only human beings (as far as we can tell) who ponder on what it means to eat. Indeed, we tend to distinguish the human species from all others in terms of the capacity for speech, memory and abstract thought. Eating and reflecting on what and how we eat are facts of life human beings have in common. But where they vary, and vary markedly, is in what they eat and how they think about it.

Certainly, human beings are omnivores and as such are relatively unusual in the animal kingdom. But that does not mean all people everywhere eat any and anything. Indeed, they do not eat everything available to them that is not poisonous and potentially nutritious. They are selective. Since the selections they make are only partly explicable in biological terms, they must, then, be made on a some cultural basis.

The phenomenon captured in the English expression "one man's meat is another man's poison" extends beyond individual idiosyncrasies to whole social groups. We learn the cultural conventions of the group to which we belong and only within that, to the extent that material and ideological circumstances allow, give expression to individually perceived food preferences. For taste, literally and metaphorically, is culturally shaped and socially controlled.[5] Eating may be essential to life and have an inescapably biological nature, but simultaneously food has a socio-cultural character that is learned.

Static approaches and their limitations

Based on such shared assumptions, it has become standard to investigate the learned character of food and eating by treating it as an expression of something social, a matter of non-verbal communication [6] (although, of course, this is not the only way sociologists and social anthropologists are interested in food). Between them, investigators have developed a tell-tale little lexicon. Phrases such as "(f)ood is a ... means of social communication" crop up in passing (eg Harriss-White 1994:1); a whole chapter can be devoted to discussions of the "Meal as Metaphor" (Farb and Armelagos 1980). Many of us seem to find ourselves unable to dispense with terms such as symbol, message, language or code [7] (e.g. Richards 1964 [1932], Monod-Becquelin 1977, Charles and Kerr 1988, Gusfield 1987, Murcott 1986, Whitehead 1994).

A number of my generation with an interest in sociological

aspects of human food use found the work of the structuralists, such as Lévi-Strauss (e.g. 1966, 1969) on cooking or the cultural [8] approaches of social anthropologists such as Mary Douglas (e.g. 1972, 1984, Douglas and Nicod 1974) on meals especially inspiring (e.g. James 1982, Atkinson 1978, 1980 and Murcott 1982). In my own work (Murcott 1982, 1983a, 1983b) for instance, my attention was drawn to concentrating on what my informants defined as a "proper meal" and the importance they attached to it in family life. Finding they used a term "cooked dinner" which was new to me to describe a British meal of meat, potatoes, green vegetables and gravy with which I was only too familiar, I set out to uncover the "rules" for its composition, preparation and presentation which underlay informants' accounts. I showed that roasting and boiling were prescribed, and frying and stewing proscribed; that offal or fish did not "count" as meat, nor did preserved meats such as bacon; and that the gravy as the accompanying sauce was not only regarded as a key to defining the "properness" of the meal its preparation was based on by-products — meat juices, vegetable water — and served to unite the separate elements when served on the plate. These "rules" turned out to be seamlessly of a piece with the valuation of a "cooked dinner" as a regular home-coming meal, with a more elaborate version to mark family "togetherness" on a Sunday. Who was to prepare it (the wife) for whom (the husband/partner and children) was characterised as expressive of a woman's marital (and parental) obligation. This obligation had its counterpart in that of the husband as wage-earner and provider of the means for acquiring the household's food. In the ideal, then the cooked dinner was held to signify the household unit itself along with its members" well-being and their relation to one another.

On the other hand, for his discussions of the significance of health-foods, Atkinson picked out Lévi-Strauss' suggestions that the part played by preparing food, eating and drinking in mythology and ritual is one way of expressing the fact that people are "civilised" rather than wild, savage or animal. While in her analysis of the meaning of children's sweets, James found his ideas provocative, notably his suggestion that food is "good to think with" as much, if not more so than good to eat. Both relied on

Douglas' proposal that a meal can be "deciphered" by examining the combination of foods in different dishes, the ordering of dishes in a meal and the daily, weekly and annual succession of meals to restate the assertion that food and the manner in which it is eaten conveys messages about those who produce and consume it. And both developed imaginative applications and ingenious extensions of Lévi-Strauss' and Douglas' analyses.[9]

I refer to this selection of applications simply to illustrate the influence of the work of Lévi-Strauss and Douglas — authors whom I also select to illustrate a broad school of thought associated with the analysis of food and its social expressions (and in the process fail to do their contributions justice). For present purposes, I am not concerned with locating them in the development of sociological or anthropological theorising about food (for brief introduction see Mennell, Murcott and van Otterloo 1992). Nor am I concerned with some of the intricate criticisms that expose many of their shortcomings (see, for instance, Goody 1982). My purpose here is to draw attention to a limitation in the influence they can have if we rely only on what they have to offer.

In the different ways associated with their theoretical intentions and the scholarly positions they adopt, both Lévi-Strauss and Douglas by-pass historical change as a phenomenon to be analysed. Of course, neither is ignorant of shifts over long periods of time. But any such shifts are only referred to or treated as just "there" in the background. In effect, change is ironed out of the subject matter that is the focus of analytic attention. Though owing allegiance to Lévi-Strauss and Douglas, both James and Atkinson, to their credit, take care to indicate they are well aware, respectively, of the history of sweets in Britain or the fact that the use of so-called health foods is not new.

I, on the other hand, made no mention of the history of the "cooked dinner". I was, however, regularly struck by the tendency for members of sociology seminars where I presented the work to describe the cooked dinner as "traditional" — a designation to which I return briefly below. But such a description also by-passes the analysis of history and of how one meal or another earns the designation. Investigation may confirm that a meal of "meat and

55

two veg" is not much more than a century old showing that it slowly developed a place in conventional British eating: as food supplies became more secure; as distribution systems across the country extended with the development of the railways; as average incomes gradually rose; as domestic appliances for cooking and storing food became more reliable and affordable for increasing numbers of households; as a style of domestic cuisine became enshrined in the training and education of girls with the establishment of schools of home economics — and more. But recognition of histories is not the same as regarding them as integral to the matter to be analysed.

The kind of history I have in mind is one that does not only document the fact that changes have taken place but which also attempts to study the process — the forces, causes and consequences — of change itself. And the reason I have it in mind while discussing the investigation of food as expressive, is that this type of history offers a means, and a powerful one at that, of reducing the danger of arbitrariness. To study eating as expressive of something social by relying on a lexicon of terms and phrases that treat food as language, code, or symbol is the first, not the final analytic step.

Quite often, the term or phrase seems to be introduced simply as an *assertion* of some relationship between food and the something that is social (and c.f. Goody 1982:30–31). The usage is stronger than just alluding, for instance, to "foods (being) linked with social status" (Baldwin 1977:70). But it still seems more akin to a statement of intent or of general focus than a developed mode of analysis — and to that extent, risks being arbitrary. Perhaps even more obviously arbitrary, is the specification of whatever the "something" social which food is said to symbolise. Once it is agreed that the realm symbolised is described in some general way as "social relations", "cultural systems" or "social structures", then any specification beyond that looks suspiciously like little more than an act of social scientific faith and/or based on whatever else the analyst happens to be interested in at the time.

In order to illustrate the point, I shall briefly consider a few examples that also, conveniently return to one of the themes of the whole paper, namely food as an expression of identity. The proposal that food is a medium of communication also provides for its analysis in terms of identity. Mintz — whose work is discussed more fully later — captures the idea when he observes:

> What we like, what we eat, how we eat it, and how we feel about it are phenomenologically interrelated matters: together they speak eloquently to the question of how we perceive ourselves in relation to others. (Mintz 1985:4)

Farb and Armelagos (1980:4–5) remark that the mere fact of sitting down to eat together can convey important statements about a society. They remind us that the civil-rights movements in the southern United States during the 1950s began as a dispute about the right of blacks not just to eat at lunch counters, but to sit down there alongside whites. Blacks, they comment, insisted on that right because it is customary in North America that equality is proclaimed in sitting together to eat.

The next illustration comes from the other side of the Atlantic. Pierre Bourdieu gives us an explanation for working class Frenchmen's distaste for fish.

> ... in the working classes, fish tends to be regarded as an unsuitable food for men, not only because it is light food, insufficiently "filling", ... but also because, like fruit (except bananas) it is one of the "fiddly" things which a man's hands cannot cope with and which make him childlike ... but above all, it is because fish has to be eaten in a way which totally contradicts the masculine way of eating, that is, with restraint, in small mouthfuls, chewed gently ... (because of the bones). The whole masculine identity — what is called virility — is involved in these two ways of eating: nibbling or picking, as befits a woman, or with wholehearted male gulps and mouthfuls ([1979] 1986:190–1)

Now, many of us will find these examples wholly plausible. We readily recognise Bourdieu's explanation of why eating fish affronts French working class masculine identity; we can see only too well how barring blacks from eating alongside whites symbolised an inferior, ethnic identity. Food may well express or mean "something". Observing that it does is a first analytic step. But how does it come to express it and what does it mean?

Dynamic approaches and their strengths

A second analytic step is offered by Sidney Mintz. A good deal of his work is about sugar, its production, consumption, *and* its meanings (Mintz 1979, Mintz 1982, Mintz 1985). In the late twentieth century sugar broadly means a general, and generally available, sweetener; to the nineteenth century working classes it was a necessity; in the seventeenth century it meant luxury, available to the nobility and the wealthy, but in mediaeval Europe it was a medicine and figured among the supposed remedies for the Black Death. What sugar symbolised changed dramatically. Certainly, Mintz agrees, meaning and the symbolic have to be deciphered. But, for example, decoding the amazing displays of sugar confections of the seventeenth century wealthy as conveying a message of wealth cannot be sufficient. Apart from verging on the circular, it wholly ignores the very great contrasts in sugar's meanings of earlier and later periods.

For Mintz, use precedes the symbolic; meaning arises out of use in social relationships. The meanings encoded in sugar, he argues, changed as a result of increased usage. Thus the social forces that led to increased use must also be analysed. So he details the nature, organisation and growth of sugar production that made increased demand possible which over the centuries, in turn, further stimulated supply. What is required is not simply to decipher messages conveyed by food, but to ask how the meanings became possible in the first place and to decode the process of codification.

> "Meaning" ... is not simply to be "read" or "deciphered" but arises from the cultural applications to which sugar lent itself, the uses to which it was put. Meaning, in short, is the consequence of activity. This does not mean that culture is only (or is reducible to only) behavior. But not to ask how meaning is put into behavior, to read the product without the production, is to ignore history once again. (Mintz 1985:14)

Mintz is particularly persuasive.[10] And his warnings not to forget history are reinforced by Jack Goody, Professor of Social Anthropology at Cambridge who has explicitly aligned his own attitude to the study of food with that of Mintz. In his remarkable and broad ranging comparative study of cuisines (1982), Goody offers a telling example. He too is critical of analyses (including, in part those of Douglas and Lévi-Strauss) which overemphasise continuity and holism at the expense of change and difference. It is naive, he remarks, to think that revolution, for instance, either alters all or changes nothing.[11] Change in a cuisine, he observes, also comes about as the result of the "introduction of ingredients and techniques from *outside*" (Goody 1982:36, emphasis added). He goes on:

> It is difficult to conceive of Italian food without pasta and tomato paste. But the use of pasta may have arrived from China via Germany only in the fifteenth century ... Stouff's study of 14th and 15th centuries concludes by denying that there was an original Provencal cuisine in the late Middle Ages ... The outstanding feature of "traditional" Provencal cooking of the nineteenth and twentieth centuries, olive oil, was used only for eggs, fish and frying beans. Otherwise it was the fat of salted pork, used particularly to flavour the soup of peas, beans and above all cabbage. This was the basic food, he claims, of the ordinary folk of Provence, just as it was in the rest of Europe at that time ... "Traditional Provencal cooking", like many other folk-ways, only emerged in recent times, a salutary thought for those attached either to the holistic or to the timeless view of culture" (Goody 1982:36).

I quote Goody's discussion of this example at length, for it illustrates extremely well some of the elements to which we must attend in thinking about food as symbolic of some national identity. It is not simply that Goody pays attention to scholarly historical evidence to show just how recent an olive-oil based image of Provencal [12] cooking probably is. It is also that he is obliged to refer to "outside" in presenting his illustration, reminding us of the importance of the idea of place. Furthermore, in the use of the adjective "traditional", which Goody himself places in quotation marks, he implies that inherent in the olive-oil image of Provencal cuisine (however historically inaccurate) is a sense of time projected backwards to some unspecifiable era that is popularly believed to hold for a definable, named, geographical territory.

Here, then are three elements we need to bear in mind when turning to concentrate on national identity. Reflecting on anything "national" by definition, involves some specification of place. It also, I shall want to emphasise, involves specification of time. As Mintz insists, we must not ignore the study of history. But, as Goody's illustration reminds us, historical analysis needs to be separated from ethno-history, folk concepts that also happen to enshrine notions of time.

...national identity

Let me begin discussing national identity with further reference to Mintz' work. In a very recent paper, he summarises his analytic position by observing that

> ... the cultural materials people employ in creating systems or symbols — foods are a suitable example of such materials — are not givens, but are the precipitate of economic, social and political processes (Mintz 1994:114, emphasis added).

Once again, he is talking about sugar, the case which happened to interest him. Yet his observations do not just apply to the human use of material phenomena but also to abstract phenomena manufactured by human beings which are deployed in the process of attributing meaning and creating symbols. Like the material, abstract phenomena too may not be givens but are also to be understood as the precipitate — the products and outcomes — of economic, social and political processes. In like fashion, nationality as the symbolic object of expression in food and eating, is not be treated as a given, but instead must be understood as a precipitate of the kind to which Mintz refers: it has a history.

The evolution of nation-states, the upsurge of nationalist sentiments and the development of social movements and struggles for independent nationhood all have a history. Much of the scholarly literature is, of course, devoted to accounting for those histories, entailing debates devoted to fundamental questions such as: how modern is the modern nation; what are the forces that brought it into being; what is the place of the modern state, of industrialisation, capitalism, or the intensification of internal communications in the development of the nation (Giddens 1985, Hutchinson 1994). At the risk of doing violence to this extensive body of scholarship, I want to single out just one contribution, presented by Benedict Anderson in his book *Imagined Communities* (Anderson 1991).

His very point of departure is that the phenomena to which terms like "national" refer, are to be understood as manufactured. Nationality, he says:

> or as one might prefer to put it in view of that word's multiple significations, nation-ness, as well as nationalism, are cultural artefacts of a particular kind (Anderson 1991:4)

and nation is to be defined as an "imagined political community" (Anderson 1991:6). It comes into being as a creative act of the imagination as distinct from a process of gradual realisation of its prior existence. It is an idea that is invented. Any community larger than a band of people who all know one another directly, claims Anderson, is imagined. What distinguishes nations from other communities is the style in which it is imagined. And it is to the history of the style of imagining that is encompassed by the idea of nation, to which his extended analysis is devoted. A rough approximation of his argument runs as follows.

Nation is a particular kind of artefact because, once invented, it is, as he puts it, "modular", portable over time and across social terrains. Along with other commentators [13], Anderson inclines to date the early crystallisation of nation towards the end of the eighteenth century. Its earlier origins, he argues, lie in the complex of possibilities created by the secularisation of European societies, the slow but sure decline of dynastic, monarchical rule as a political form and with them alterations in notions and apprehensions of time. The associated and gradual spread of the vernacular, the slow increase in levels of literacy and above all the invention of the book provided fertile ground for the further germination of the idea.

The form, medium and greatest impetus for its mass dissemination — or at least the potential for its mass dissemination —

was provided by print capitalism, the invention of the newspaper and the novel. Once a model of nation was imagined, and the means of transporting it far and wide became more and more securely established, it had become available for what Anderson shrewdly calls piracy. By the second decade of the nineteenth century if not before, the idea could readily and widely be borrowed, reinterpreted, or appropriated for new purposes. And in the process newly imagined histories of states, newly formed and re-formed in the name of nation, could be created to become fixed as museum displays. Novel measures of a person's nationality in the census could be devised and re-invented boundaries became lines on re-drawn maps.

My crude summary of Anderson's sophisticated political and economic history of the idea serves, I hope, to indicate the manner in which nation has to be regarded as manufactured. For Anderson, nation is invented not as a deliberate fabrication or untruth [14], but as an act of imagination. Thus it is closely akin to the imaginative act enshrined in W.I.Thomas' famous dictum that "if men define situations as real they are real in their consequences".

Thus far, I have studiously avoided offering a definition of national identity. In part this is because my concern is precisely not to take it as given — a category used to explain other phenomena — but to begin understanding how it comes about. Mostly, it is because here I am interested in time and place as elements within its history. And this is why I have selected Anderson's work on which to concentrate, rather than other scholarly contributions. Others do, in the nature of things, identify some of the same features of the history of the idea that Anderson does. For instance, Newman (1987) points to the role of the literati in the construction of notion's of Englishness and the diffusion of the notion enshrined in their work via popular education. And in his recent major contribution, Smith's (1991) is eloquent on the ubiquity and import, the various functions and possible primacy, of national identity among the various collective identities to which nowadays we are heir.

Anderson's analysis casts time and space in a light that allows identification of their different manifestations, the while treating them as related to the whole. It is not only that Anderson, in common with many other scholars in what could be called the "invention" tradition (c.f. Hobsbawm 1983), treats time (and space) as a matter of history in tracing the origins of the idea itself. His analysis goes further, revealing additional refractions of time and place. The creation of the idea of nation becomes possible once mediaeval apprehensions of time are loosened giving way to more modern conceptions of linear time. Most particularly, he provides for a ready distinction to be made between two conceptions of history: the history that is authenticated as a disciplined intellectual activity committed to scholarship and the folk histories, the ethno-history, embedded into one or other remodelled version of nation and national identity.[15]

All these contribute to what makes Anderson's work so valuable in thinking about food as an expression of national identity. Centrally, it is the brilliance of his insights that the idea of national identity is modular; malleable and portable over time and across space. He has appreciated to the full the overwhelming significance of the rise of print capitalism (and its electronic successors) in providing a fluid means of making it available for re-use, remaking and remodelling, in principle, any time, anywhere. If, as I suggested earlier, we can indeed regard food as a medium of communication, then it can perhaps take its place, along with print capitalism as a another fluid means of transporting the modular idea of nation. In just the same way that the printed word — along with pictures and museums — is available for inscription with one or other version of nationhood, so food and the sociality of eating are available for proclamation of national identity.

Food may perhaps be as potent a medium of communicating an idea of nation as words and pictures. Novels, newspapers, the mass media of communication are ever more universally available, accessible and, at some level, unavoidable. These means whereby representations of national identity may be purveyed are inserted into the interstices of daily life of all of us — almost whether we like it or not. As a biological necessity, food is equally impossible to avoid. And whatever messages it conveys are thereby carried, in principle at least, into as many interstices of day-to-day life.

Food as an expression of national identity: variations on a theme

In this final section, the previous parts of the paper come together again to inspect different variants of the use of food to express national identity a little more closely. As far as is known, work deliberately designed to investigate the matter remains to be undertaken.[16] So for now, we have to be content with examples mostly based on selected quotation, anecdote and ephemera.

It has to be acknowledged that national identity and food, each in their own fashion, are capable of evoking deep attachment and can represent the focus for powerful sentiments. After all, as Anderson reminds us, the idea of nation can mobilise us to ultimate lengths; people are ready to die in the name of their nation. And as for eating, novel or unfamiliar foods can provoke physiologically measurable revulsion on the one hand, while, on the other, the enjoyment of the especially prized foods seems able to send people into ecstasies of sensation. While we are unable to do no more than grant that this is so, we can consider the different manifestations of sentiments and attachments. Indeed, Anderson's analysis provides for variants on the theme: nation is a *modular* cultural artefact. What, then are the different modes of expressing nationhood via food?

The examples with which this paper began, suggest that expressing nationality in terms of food is both widespread and long-standing. Regarding the leek as a badge of the Welsh is as recognisable in Britain today as it was to Shakespeare's audience. Modern theatre-goers might have to be reminded that his reference contains a sly political joke, an ironic allusion to the Welsh origins of the Tudor monarchs then on the English throne.[17] But the association lives on four centuries and more later. Leeks are an essential ingredient to *cawl*, the Welsh version of peasant stew, not just a mainstay of post-war school dinners in Wales, but extolled in modern recipe books variants as redolent of Welshness.[18] Although they can opt for a daffodil (the national flower) in their buttonhole, some Welsh people instead pin a little leek sewn out of coloured material on their coat to proclaim their national identity on St David's Day.[19]

Using foods as a badge (at times, quite literally) is one, seemingly long-standing, mode of expressing national identity. Name-calling, as we saw at the outset, is another. The emotions connoted are obviously various, depending on the circumstances. Badges may well be worn with pride[20]. Rude nicknames, "dog-people", "Frogs", "raw-flesh eaters", are intended to insult[21]. They express disparagement if not outright antagonism. Naming nationals in terms of their supposed eating habits is not confined to the Western world and shades into popular theories of national traits and character. Once differences in emotional style, manners and tastes become associated with nationality, they can flexibly be incorporated with other folk psychological concepts involving correspondences between food and temperament as much as any others.[22] The modular nature of the idea of nation caters readily for transposing them into a national idiom.

Assertions of national superiority and greater capacity for civilised sensibility are at issue in a recent British "home news" story reported by the mass media. It concerns animal rights campaigners picketing small airports and demonstrating at sea ports in protest, initially at the export from Britain of live calves destined for crate rearing in the Netherlands and later extending to the export of live sheep.[23] In one television programme's coverage of the issue, a distraught protester was filmed asking "How can this happen in England? We're supposed to be the caring nation" and in the studio discussion that followed, Carla Lane[24] declared "This whole business is so barbaric, so unacceptable, so un-British" (*Newsnight* BBC2 February 7 1995).

A different, perhaps more complex, assertion of national sensibility and good taste is evident in the expression of exiled identity in the second quotation that prefaces this paper. The passage is taken from *A Book of Middle Eastern Food* by Claudia Roden (Roden 1970:11), who was born into a Jewish Family in Cairo.[25] Even though the dish of brown Egyptian beans is food of the poor, in her memory of Paris as a school pupil, it is divested of its inferior origins and elevated to the epitome of all that the expatriate misses about home. Indeed, later in the book, Roden declares it is "(A)n Egyptian dish which has become 'the' national dish" that is enjoyed by the rich and middle classes despite its peasant origins (Roden 1970:280). Of course, a diaspora commonly involves peoples' taking their national foods with them to alien lands. By the same token, those for whom the alien lands are home not only have an influx of foreign nationals come among them, but are faced with the accompanying national cuisines.

Here, once again, is fertile ground for the modular idea of nation. For some, a babel of national dishes provides an opportunity for expressing the worldliness of the cosmopolitan. In this version, awareness of national identity is incorporated into a self-conscious *supra*-national variant, making a virtue of fluency in different national styles. Most Western metropolises offer scope for this mode of national expression in eating. For instance, in one area of north London there are French, Vietnamese, Italian, Lebanese, Singaporean, Thai, Mexican, Japanese, Indian, Columbian, and Chinese restaurants within ten minutes walk of one another. Even an unfashionable inner-city area of Cardiff (which though the capital of Wales has long had a provincial, small town air about it) has, within fifteen minutes walk, two Chinese, an Italian, one self-styled Welsh [26] and three Indian restaurants.

The malleability of the idea of nation is evident when foods of a diaspora are coupled with a view of world current affairs. An example also concerns Claudia Roden. It seems that when she was interviewed for a Jewish American magazine about the book already cited, the journalist exclaimed "I cannot believe that Jews ate Arab food" (Castell and Griffin 1993:94). From an American vantage point, images of Jew and Arab conjure the realities of violent conflict between them, war waged in the very name of nationalism — just possibly underscored by a North Eastern seaboard image of Jewish eating represented by Middle European emigré bagels, chicken soup and strudel. A book detailing a Middle Eastern cuisine provokes disbelief in the light of those other, combative ideas of nationality, that prompt assumptions that conflicting groups must also differ markedly in the foods they eat.

The flexible idea of nation temporarily fixed assumptions of difference in eating, perhaps to be disabused by the origins of the cookery writer herself as well as her recipes. And the disjunction between folk history and origins unearthed by scholarly investigation, once again find an echo.

Not only do all these examples illustrate different modes of expressing national identity, they also illustrate the suggestion that food, eating and cuisine is readily available for the imprint, the expression of nationality. I turn now to a final group of examples provided by the titles of an assortment of cookbooks: *Italian Food, The Finnish Cook Book, Portuguese Cookery, A Taste of Wales, The Cooking of Greece & Turkey, Le petit livre de la Cuisine Canadiennne, Russian Cookery, Basic English Fare, Dutch Cooking, Japanese Cookbook, British Cookery.*[27] Presumably aimed in part at a cosmopolitan market, they also fit neatly into what has sarcastically come to be called the "heritage industry". This is a trade that has become especially prominent in our own times; a trade in badges of difference between peoples and places, in reconstructions of the past; a trade designed to appeal both to the fantasies of other times and other places of those who are local as well as those, the visitors and tourists, who pass through. The marketing of heritage, of preservations and re-creations of its history, plays an important part in modern tourism industries (Urry 1990).[28] Here, then is an instance of the modular expression of nation via food whose invention is almost transparent. But being deliberately commercially contrived does not disqualify it from inclusion in the present discussion. On the contrary; though Anderson's study goes way beyond it his analysis nonetheless neatly provides for such representation (and re-presentation) of a nation's history in commercial form in just the same way that he argues it is celebrated in the form of museums.[29]

My very short conclusion returns at last to the questions I posed at the beginning. Why do we use diet or eating habits to describe national identity? What is it about food that lends itself to such expression? Cautiously, I suggest we might have moved some way towards thinking about how we may start to answer them, briefly summarised as follows.

As the first section of this paper indicates, food may be analysed as a means of communication; eating is analogous to speaking. Language — its conventions of grammar, pronunciation, vocabulary and so on — has to be learned. Unless a person is reared bilingually, acquiring a second and subsequent language demands a deliberate act of study, effort and attention. Eating too has to be learned — its conventions of combinations and transformations of foodstuffs, the suitability of foods matched to occasion, the manners and etiquette of the table and so on. Just possibly, the study, effort and attention of learning to speak a second and subsequent language of eating may turn out to be of a different order from that required to learn to speak a second and subsequent language. But even if it proves to be just as demanding, eating (or refusing to eat) an unfamiliar dish can serve as a further means of communicating (or refusing to communicate) across boundaries, over and above learning to speak a foreign tongue. Eating is marvelously flexible. The conversation over a meal composed of unfamiliar dishes can still be conducted in a familiar tongue. Tourists carry back with them acquaintance with an unfamiliar dish recreated at home. Equally, though unable to converse in the same language, eating the same dishes offers a commonality amongst those assembled at the table. The two sets of parents of a Czech and English couple incapable of exchanging a word in each other's language, can still express a recognition of their offspring's coming together for meals held to be typical of one another's national origins.

Taking neither national identity nor food's expressive, symbolic character as givens, it appears that each element has, as it were, double connotations. Food, already capable of expressing, among other things, profoundly deep seated emotional reaction is, like print, available as a vehicle for the transmission of modular phenomena. National identity is just such a modular cultural artefact that also happens to convey powerful attachments and sentiments. Phenomena that have in common the property of being potentially heavily emotionally laden, may, by that very token, have a strong affinity. But it is the second of the other two connotations of each phenomenon that suggests a possible answer to my initial questions: we use diet and eating habits to express national identity as a result of the conjunction between the malleable, modular nature of national identity and the flexibility and ubiquity of food as a medium of communication.

Notes

1. I should like to record my appreciation and gratitude to the organisers of the Symposium for their invitation to present this paper; and to thank both discussants, Christina Fjellström and Johan P.Olsen for their astute observations and Phil Strong for many discursive thought-provoking conversations as well as his comments on earlier drafts of this paper.

2. So saying verges on the disingenuous, for common to both is a Marxian inheritance. Though space does not permit development of the point, these bodies of work, nonetheless, offer much that is thought provoking for (ex-) Marxists and non-Marxists alike.

3. It should, incidentally, be noted at this point, that for the purposes of this paper, I shall mostly talk of food and eating, cooking or cuisine, meals, dishes and so on with little attention to the analytic distinction between them they otherwise deserve.

4. At this point, sceptical British readers are advised to put themselves through the test of imagining themselves in Belgium, hungry and in search of a meal, and weigh up whether they would go into a restaurant with a horse's head sign outside it.

5. If the reader is in some doubt, the following comparison can be made. Consider someone brought up in Japan, where fish is available and a cuisine based on raw fish is well developed, who is free to decide whether they like it or not and happens to prefer Japanese dishes based on cooked meat. Then consider someone else brought up in the North East of England for whom eating fish uncooked is to eat a raw ingredient and be "no better" than the cat, but for whom beef tastes "nicer" than lamb or pork. For both these imaginary people, expressing individual preferences is (ideologically) legitimate and materially possible. For others, the material circumstances preclude or the prevailing ideologies rule out the expression of individual preferences, as in the case of those facing extreme food shortage on the one hand, or one who has joined a self-denying monastic order on the other.

6. Once again, Farb & Armelagos' book proves to be a goldmine of appealing examples. They observe that "(F)or most Chinese, social

transaction are almost inseparable from eating transactions. The giving and sharing of food is the prototypic relationship in Chinese society, as if the word were literally made flesh ... No important business transaction and no marriage arrangement is ever concluded without the sharing of food. The quality of the meal and its setting *convey a more subtle social message than anything that is consciously verbalized; attitudes that would be impolite if stated directly* are communicated through the food channel" (emphasis added) (Farb & Armelagos 1980:4–5).

7. C.f. also DeVault's discussion of "cooking discourse" (1991:215).

8. "Structuralist" and "cultural" are used only as rough approximations, following Goody — a usage of which he drily remarks that "(T)hese are ... terms of art that are used to break up the continuities of ... enquiry in ways that are often more necessary as crutches for the commentator than as guides for the practitioner" (Goody 1982:29).

9. Atkinson (1978) offers a development of Lévi-Strauss famous culinary triangle (Lévi-Strauss 1966) to analyse the rationales for advocating a "folk" use of "honegar" (a proprietary mixture of honey and vinegar) to restore and promote health, where health is held to be an imbalance between humankind's natural and cultural elements. He notes that the modes of transformation entailed in the production of both honey and vinegar are ambiguous with regard to natural and cultural categories; honey is produced not by human but by animal/natural agency; the human manufacture of vinegar relies on the natural process of fermentation. A combination of the two, he argues, is therefore ideal as concrete resolutions of associated contradictions and imbalances in human beings. James (1982) turns Douglas' analyses of the place of sweets as threatening to interfere with the next meal neatly on its head. By detailing features of certain types of sweet to show that they represent deliberate contradictions and inversions of what is conventionally held to characterise and define food, she argues that, for children, it is meals that interrupt the eating of sweets.

10. Although many problems have still to be sorted out in investigating the meanings of food; for example, deciding whether we are to study the meanings of a single foodstuff, such as sugar, coffee or indeed fish, or whether we are to study roasting, boiling or other

71

modes of transformation rather than dishes, meals or whole cuisines, or whether we should concentrate on group arrangements for eating.

11. For instance, he notes: "... the Revolution may not have altered Chinese cooking itself, but it did significantly modify the enormous meals and banquets of earlier times." (Goody 1982:35).

12. *Pace* Smith (1991) among others, I am assuming for present purposes, that images of region and/or ethnicity are analysable in the same way that we may treat the idea of nation.

13. E.g. those such as Deutsch, Gellner and Hobsbawm, whom Hutchinson (1994) describes as "modernists".

14. Anderson himself is at pains to indicate that in aligning himself with Gellner's observation that nation is invented, he does not mean that it is a fabrication or falsity. It is puzzling, then, that Scheff criticises Anderson's formulation for failing to specify "under what conditions does one feel closer to unknown than known persons? Why is an imagined community chosen over an actual one?" (Scheff 1994:278–9). It would seem that despite Anderson's efforts, Scheff is taking "imagined" to mean "imaginary".

15. That these two conceptions of history are related — insofar as the rise of scholarship itself has a history and in some fashion the former arises from a grounding in the common-sense world of the latter, and the latter borrows from the former — is the more clearly grasped.

16. An on-line bibliographic search of the last 15 years' publications yielded only studies food, diet, and eating which took "national" as a given. I am most grateful to Laura McKenzie, for her help in this part of the work.

17. The footnote provided in *The Riverside Shakespeare* (1974:956) explains "On October 1 the Welsh wore leeks in their caps to commemorate a victory over the Saxons, as ordered by their patron saint, David". In the modern calendar, St David's Day falls on March 1.

18. e.g. Freeman (1980) Not only does she quote Richard Llewellyn's description of the dish in his novel *How Green was my Valley*— a book commonly used to epitomise Welshness. She is also at pains to stress how even the newly initiated react to *cawl* with special gusto — "(t)his food is soul food" — quoting others who refer to it as so important that it was "an unspoken part of life".

19. And when the designers of one of the British coins currently in use were required to signal Scotland's and Wales' membership of Great Britain as well as England's, they used the thistle as the Scots national flower, but chose the leek not the daffodil for the Welsh.

20. Pride can give way to fervour and, metaphorically, threaten violence: the author of a history of Scots food and cookery published in the 1930s began cautiously by enumerating the hazards of "venturing upon a book on Scots aliment" (MacClure 1935:1). He observed that the "touchy fervour of the Scot by profession" meant that "(O)ne hint from the author that there may be better food or cheese in the world than keilbrose and 'Dunlap' — neither of which your said Scot may ever have sampled — and scores of knuckles will whiten with tension" (McClure 1935:4–5).

21. No wonder the politically correct demand we use the word Inuit rather than Eskimo.

22. C.f. the discussion of humoural theories in Mennell, Murcott and van Otterloo (1982).

23. It was a widely covered story, with a series of newsworthy events. Running from about November 1994, it had seen the revelation that the Minister for Agriculture himself sold calves from his own farm, with export as their likely destination and the death, "crushed under the wheels of a lorry carrying calves to Coventry airport" (*The Independent* February 4 1995) of a young woman, of whom it was reported "her fellow protesters ... have begun to speak of ... as a "martyr to animal liberation" *The Independent* February 3 1995. The story was sufficiently newsworthy that it was covered in the BBC's second television channel prestige late night current affairs programme from which the quotations in the text are taken.

24. A well-known television script writer who has publicly and energetically taken up the cause of animal rights.

25. In the second edition Roden reasserts similar sentiments. By then resident in London, she describes how important the book has been to her: "(I)t has meant a continuing involvement with the area which holds my roots and for which I have a special tenderness" (Roden 1985:19).

26. It has to be said that though serving for instance laverbread, a seaweed still gathered along the less-polluted parts of the Welsh coast,

some dishes eg Sirloin Lloyd George seem only to be distinctively Welsh in the name written on the menu.

27. It is also possible to find small local area variants, often produced by voluntary rather than commercial effort: eg *The Leeds Cookery Book* from the northern English city, *The Terrace Times BALMAIN Cookbook* a cosmopolitan area of Sydney, *The Islington Cookbook* in north London.

28. It is hard to forget Hewison's acid comment that, given its economic and geo-political decline, "increasingly, instead of manufacturing goods, Britain is manufacturing heritage" (quoted in Urry 1990:109). And, it might be added, it is also manufacturing Britishness. It looks as if "essence of Britain" is being distilled, bottled and packaged in much the same way that Trevor-Roper (1983) argues that the kilt is a manufactured badge of ancient Scottishness invented comparatively recently in the second half of the eighteenth century by an Englishman.

29. The tour for visitors to the only American museum in Britain (near Bath) ends up in the kitchen with free, freshly baked brownies ...

References

Anderson, B. (1991), *Imagined Communities: reflections on the origin and spread of nationalism*, London: Verso (2nd edition).

Atkinson, P. (1978), "From honey to vinegar: Lévi-Strauss in Vermont", in P. Morley and R. Wallis (eds.), *Culture and Curing*, London: Peter Owen.

Atkinson, P. (1980), "The symbolic significance of health foods", in M. Turner (ed.), *Nutrition and Lifestyles*, London: Applied Science Publishers.

Baldwin, E. (1977), "Israeli Food", in J. Kuper (ed.), *The Anthropologists' Cookbook*, London: Routledge & Kegan Paul.

Bourdieu, P. (1979), *La Distinction*, Paris: le Minuit (English translation, 1986, *Distinction: a social critique of the judgement of taste*, London: Routledge.

Caplan, P. (1992), "Feasts, fasts, famine: food for thought", Inaugural Lecture, mimeo, Goldsmiths' College, University of London.

Castell, H. and Griffin, K. (1993), *Out of the Frying Pan*, London: BBC Books.

Charles, N. and Kerr, M. (1988), *Women, Food and Families*, Manchester: Manchester University Press.

Delamont, S. (1995), *Appetites and Identities: an introduction to the social anthropology of Western Europe*, London: Routledge.

DeVault, M. L. (1991), *Feeding the Family: the social organisation of caring as gendered work*, Chicago: University of Chicago Press.

Douglas, M. (1972), "Deciphering a meal", *Daedalus* 101(1): 61–81.

Douglas, M. (1984), "Standard Social Uses of Food: Introduction", in M. Douglas (ed.), *Food in the Social Order*. New York: Russell Sage Foundation.

Douglas M. and Nicod, M. (1974), "Taking the biscuit: the structure of British meals", *New Society* 30 (637): 744–7.

Farb, P. & Armelagos, G. (1980), *Consuming Passions: the anthropology of eating*, Boston: Houghton Mifflin.

Freeman, B. (1980), *First Catch Your Peacock: a book of Welsh food*, Griffithstown, Gwent: Image Imprint.

Giddens, A. (1985), *The Nation-State and Violence*, Cambridge: Polity.

Goody, J. (1982), *Cooking, Cuisine and Class: a study in comparative sociology*, Cambridge: Cambridge University Press.

Gusfield, J. (1987). "Passage to play: rituals of drinking time in American society", in M. Douglas (ed.), *Constructive Drinking: perspectives on drink from anthropology*, Cambridge: Cambridge University Press.

Harriss-White, B. (1994), "Introduction", in B. Harriss-White and R. Hoffenberg (eds.), *Food: multidisciplinary perspectives*, Oxford: Blackwell.

Hobsbawm, E. (1983), "Inventing Traditions", in E. Hobsbawm and T. Ranger (eds.), *The Invention of Tradition*, Cambridge: Cambridge University Press.

Hutchinson, J. (1994), *Modern Nationalism*, London: Fontana.

James, A. (1982), "Confections, Concoctions and Conceptions", in B. Waites *et al* (eds) *Popular Culture: past and present*, London: Croom Helm.

Lévi-Strauss, C. (1966), "The culinary triangle", *New Society*, December 937–940.

Lévi-Strauss, C. (1969), *The Raw and the Cooked*, London: Jonathan Cape.

MacClure, C. (1935), *Scotland's Inner Man: a history of Scots food and cookery*, London: George Routledge.

Mennell, S. Murcott, A. and van Otterloo A. (1992), *The Sociology of Food: eating, diet and culture*, London: Sage.

Mintz, S.W. (1979), "Time, sugar and sweetness", *Marxist Perspectives* 2: 56–73.

Mintz, S. W. (1982), "Choice and occasion: sweet moments", in L.M. Barker (ed.) *The Psychobiology of Human Food Selection*, Westport, Connecticut: AVI Publishing.

Mintz, S.W. (1985), *Sweetness and Power: the place of sugar in modern history*, New York: Viking.

Mintz, S. W. (1994), "Eating and being: what food means", in B. Harriss-White and R. Hoffenberg (eds.), *Food: multidisciplinary perspectives*, Oxford: Blackwell.

Monod-Becquelin, A. (1977), "Three recipes from the Trumai Indians of Brazil", in J. Kuper (ed.), *The Anthropologists' Cookbook*, London: Routledge & Kegan Paul.

Murcott, A. (1982), "On the social significance of the "cooked dinner" in South Wales", *Social Science Information* 21(4/5): 677–95.

Murcott, A. (1983a), "'It's a pleasure to cook for him ... ': food, mealtimes and gender in some South Wales households", in E. Garmarnikow *et al* (eds.), *The Public and the Private*, London: Heinemann.

Murcott, A. (1983b) "Cooking and the cooked", in A. Murcott (ed.), *The Sociology of Food and Eating*, London: Gower.

Murcott, A. (1986), "You are what you eat — anthropological factors influencing food choice", in C. Ritson *et al* (eds.), *The Food Consumer*, Chichester: Wiley.

Newman, G. (1987), *The Rise of English Nationalism: a cultural history 1740–1830*, London: Weidenfeld and Nicolson.

Richards, A. L. (1964) [1932], *Hunger and Work in a Savage Tribe*, Cleveland, Ohio: Meridian.

The Riverside Shakespeare (1974), Boston: Houghton Mifflin.

Roden, C. (1970), *A Book of Middle Eastern Food*, Harmondsworth: Penguin (2nd ed 1985).

Scheff, T. (1994), "Emotions and identity: a theory of ethnic nationalism", in C. Calhoun (ed.), *Social Theory and the Politics of Identity*, Oxford: Blackwell.

Smith, A. D. (1991), *National Identity*, Harmondsworth: Penguin.

Trevor-Roper, H. (1983), "The Invention of Tradition: the Highland tradition of Scotland", in E. Hobsbawm and T. Ranger (eds.), *The Invention of Tradition*, Cambridge: Cambridge University Press.

Urry, J. (1990), *The Tourist Gaze*. London: Sage.

Whitehead, A. (1994), "Food symbolism, gender power and the family" in B. Harriss-White and R. Hoffenberg (eds.), *Food: multidisciplinary perspectives*, Oxford: Blackwell.

by Aleksandra Ålund,
Department of Sociology,
University of Umeå, Sweden

The Stranger: Ethnicity, Identity and Belonging

The place of ethnic minorities in contemporary Europe discloses dilemmas and ambiguities of modern society. In a world where the search for roots has become widespread — from national identities to identity politics — the multiple expression of exclusion has spread. A new kind of European citizen — inside yet outside, a "stranger" — is being constructed. Strangers, usually people dispersed geographically from the place of their birth, join distant places and times. Memories, dreams and the contacts of the lived life interrelate; they build the web of diaspora crossings. These are the people of diaspora. Here to stay. Near yet distant, close but far away.

Home, an often imaginary "home" — this central, heavily loaded metaphor of diasporic existence — expresses the grief of not belonging, here and now. This goes beyond the pain of separation from, or the absence of, the (usually imagined) warmth of communities, places or socio-cultural spaces of "origin." Other times and places are echoed in the ongoing struggle to enter new communities, to become a member — thus pointing to the lack of jetties, the missing links, stormy seas around the boat, not being allowed to anchor ...

The metaphor of the boat expresses disconnection from the

homeland, the uncertainty of floating about the world, the feeling of dispersal permeating diasporic biographies. The boat symbolises the typically stormy journey from a place of exclusion to a (one hopes) welcoming asylum. The place where you can hope to find open doors, or to build connecting bridges. Ships, doors and bridges are metaphors through which I will try to illustrate the tragedy of exile, the tragedy binding Jewish passengers on the "St. Louis" at the start of the Second World War with the people divided by broken bridges in Sarajevo and Mostar, and with the divided people of the united multicultural Europe. I will then interconnect the politics of ethno-national exclusion in the Balkans with related tendencies in Western Europe. All this has to do with the search for identity and belonging in an age of not belonging.

The jews of the "St. Louis" on the way to Havanna

Let us begin with the film about the ship "St. Louis," in which we follow the desperate journey of German Jews on their way to Havanna. In the shadow of the realities of the Second World War and of German concentration camps, the passengers of the "St. Louis" hope to find a refuge in Havanna. They are informed, however, that they are not welcome there. The ship is forbidden to anchor and turns back towards Germany. Only after a nerve-breaking interlude and intensive diplomatic activities on the part of American Jews are the passengers of the "St. Louis" rescued from a return to their homeland and to death. Great Britain and some other European countries give them asylum.

I would like, however, to recapitulate the moment just before when the passengers are informed of the Cuban government's refusal. It is in the evening before Havanna is reached. A party with a dance and carnival is arranged on the ship. Suddenly, in the middle of the dance, a lady singer starts singing a famous German melody of the time. All the dancers stop dancing, and they all take off their masks. Tears fall down faces with a far-away look — as if all were trying to cross the sea, trying to hold on to the memories of a lost home.

Two German ship officers then make the following comments;

"Strange," one of them says, "these Jews seem to miss Germany." "Why not," answers the other, who is the captain of the ship — "after all they are Germans." This short discussion among the crew, and the moment when the passengers take off the masks — as if trying to reach into themselves — these expose the naked cynicism of exclusion, and the deep split of diasporic identity as well — the search for belonging, between naked feelings and hiding masks.

A way out from a split existence — a successful way home — requires inclusion, anchoring, bridges that join. Here we approach the tragedies of our own time — the time of broken bridges, the time of new mass exclusion, destruction and murder in the name of blood and ethnic purity. This is the case, for example, in the battlefield of ex-Yugoslavia, where authoritarian populism, nationalism and racist ethnicism act in the murky waters surrounding the construction of new communities, the underlying logic of which is ethnic fragmentation and the burning of bridges. The units to which people are considered to belong become smaller and smaller, in a process accompanied by the growth of ambiguous identities. A type of fraternity results which leads to fratricide, to use the expression of Richard Sennett (1977).

I believe most people in Scandinavia have at least seen the poster announcing the theater performance by the name of "Sarajevo." It pictures a divided city with its bridges covered by blind spots. The heavily loaded metaphor of the missing bridges symbolises the death agony of Sarajevo; bridges broken, covered, closed; a symbolic severing of connections and relations. The performance itself centers strongly on the agony of isolation inside the high walls, a life under siege, socially and physically. But it centers as well on the soul of Sarajevo as expressive of the complex interconnections and mixtures within a culture and a people once belonging to a truly transethnic and transcultural society and city. Stari Most — the Old Bridge of Mostar — has been destroyed, and its white ruins rise above the deeply parted shores of the blue Neretva. Beyond the traumas of exile — in a situation where old mixed-multicultural Bosnia has turned ethnically divided — identity crises follow the refugees, in the footsteps of a new ethno-nationalist consciousness.

Broken bridges symbolize ethno-nationalist regression into the exclusiveness propelled by *Blut und Boden* ideologies. Such ideologies entrench themselves in mini-fortresses of racial purification expressed in religious and ethnic terms. This exposes divided Bosnia as the perfect example of a world riven by cultural and biological racism. It brings into focus the paradoxical priority of the rights of ethno-cultural separatism over individual dignity and civil rights, not least in view of the mixed marriages of Bosnia-Hercegovina (now being called into question publicly by the Islamic clergy in allegedly multicultural Sarajevo). The possibility of building a future life in what once was Yugoslavia depends on a preparedness to recognize the reality of composite cultural identities traversing separate regions and so-called "cultures." At the same time, this challenge represents a connection between Sarajevo/Mostar and us, for it brings to light Europe's choice between a bridge-building, multicultural, transethnic community and a fortress Europe that builds new walls around and inside its imagined cultural territories.

Some imaginative reflections from Georg Simmel's essay "Bridge and Door," written at the beginning of the century, may deepen our understanding of this separation. "Bridge and Door" came to influence my conceptualization of modernity's antagonisms expressed through processes of alterity; closed doors and fragile bridges between different "others." "Belonging," through the accentuation of "home-space," is a fundamental human social and cultural marker. The symbolic home has symbolic doors and, following Simmel (1994), *door* signifies, in addition to a necessary psychological and cultural demarcation, the possibility of stepping outside its limitation. A door is a metaphor for the connections between social actors, for the public discourse, for the organization of solidarity and resistance. Modern society's limits — its programmed way of separating in order to connect — is expressed symbolically as a bridge. The multicultural society increasingly stands out as a system of bridge-building between separate parts which are regarded discursively as "finite" cultural products, with culture regarded as unchanging, as essence — as "roots." Understood in this way, bridges of multiculturalism are political and theoretical constructions of petrified structures of connection between human populations in terms of simplified and statically defined culture and ethnicity.

This seem to be the common problem uniting Europe. Not least Sweden, famous in Europe for its Multicultural Politics, is fenced in according to ethnic "boundaries," and the transethnic is still in its infancy (Ålund and Schierup, 1991). We can also see similar tendencies in, for example, France. Analyzing the French context, Michel Wieviorka (1993: 61) argues that "tendencies to refer to different kinds of boundary creating roots have been stronger than efforts to participate in the birth of new forms of collective actions." These tendencies reflect contemporary processes connecting the crisis of the welfare state, fundamental societal transformations and a deterioration of social conditions with anxiety over the future European Union, migration, and the spread of racism and its relationship with contemporary nationalism(s). The situation is a hot-bed for the growth of populist movements, localism and boundary-making, the separation of the connected, the simplistic singling-out of "parts" from the dynamic of the whole, the division of people into Us and the Others, Europeans and Strangers.

I have found the sociological notion of the stranger particularly important in this context.

The stranger: two paradigmatic approaches

Scientific discourses have helped to create the "stranger" and the "non-stranger." I will now discuss two classical lines of thought which discursively have branched off in modernity. The one is Alfred Schutz's conception of "the stranger," which he formulated in the US during his exile from Nazi Germany and Austria. This "stranger" appears to be a autobiographical reflection of being forced to seek refuge and to live in another world; a stranger who can "cease to be" and "gear into," hiding himself in order to avoid being the undesirable "other." Schutz's stranger develops a self-effacement in exercising the skills of adjustment towards total assimilation as the only possible way of saving himself. But between the stranger and the "group" he meets yawns an insurmountable gulf — a naturalized breach of cultural and psychological difference.

An alternative line of thought in the discourse of the "stranger" can be found in the work of Georg Simmel from the turn of the century. Simmel was also, like Schultz, a sociologist of Jewish background. Simmel, however, lived in a kind of inner refuge specific to the Jewish experience of the time. His analysis was a precursor of today's interest in the "global city" and globalizing "cultural flows." From his contemporary "Metropolis," Simmel reflected over the linkage between the inner and the outer. Proximity and distance, connection and separation — these are the different dimensions of human interaction. A stranger, a *potential* wanderer, is an important sociological category for the study of the process of interaction. In contrast to Schutz, however, Simmel does not see the stranger as a person outside the perceived natural continuity of the group. Rather, Simmel's stranger takes part in a dialogue. Being a stranger is "a very positive relation: it is a specific form of interaction. The inhabitants of Sirius are not really strangers to us, at least not in any sociologically relevant sense: they do not exist for us at all; they are beyond far and near" (Simmel, in Wolff 1950: 402). The stranger is the person who comes today and stays tomorrow. His "position is determined, essentially," according to Simmel, "by the fact that he has not belonged to it (the group) from the beginning," but "he imports qualities into it, which do not and cannot stem from the group itself" (ibid).

This specific form of interaction can, however, create special tensions. The stranger, Simmel says, is "fixed within a group whose boundaries are similar to spatial boundaries." Thus he calls attention to how the stranger is an element of the group itself — "like the poor and like sundry 'inner enemies.' His position as a full-fledged member involves both being outside of and confronting it" (ibid: 402–403). Addressing the peculiar unity of the stranger's position ."..composed of certain measures of nearness and distance" (ibid: 408), Simmel focuses on the problematic character of this relational peculiarity; "a special proportion" of specific conditions behind "its uniform life," which are then related to "reciprocal tensions." Together these processes produce the particular and formal relation to the "stranger" which goes beyond general "human commonness." The stranger is not really thought of as an individual, but rather becomes "itself" — a constructed human category, a "strangeness." Through the specificity of the relationship between proximity and distance, Simmel attaches a positional category with an identity and a cultural dynamic. "There arises a specific tension when the consciousness that only the quite general is common, stresses that which is not common." This ."non-common element is once more not individual, but merely the strangeness of origin" which in turn becomes "common to many strangers" (ibid: 407).

This understanding goes beyond incompatibility between cultures, beyond a perception of cultures as well-defined modules, and even beyond limits in the mainstream discourse of cultural bridging in the real multiculturalism of the present — where, to use Simmel's terms, bridges are seen as connecting "the finite within the finite" (Simmel, 1994: 8). Hence, instead of perceiving bridging as "the line stretched between two points" (ibid) which connects isolated entities, interaction and the relationship between the social and the cultural are emphasized. At the turn of the century, accordingly, modern life was perceived as an "open door" — "life flows forth out of the door from the limitation of isolated separate existence into the limitlessness of all possible directions" (ibid: 8).

While bridging seems to represent an attempt to connect solid points in a search for "unconditional security and direction" (ibid), the door displays an agency encompassing both entering and exiting. Closing the door is (culturally) a separation from "the uniform, continuous unity of natural being" (ibid: 9), which at the same time means that "a piece of space was thereby brought together and separated from the whole remaining world" (ibid: 7). After that, however, a kind of demarcation takes place, "its limitedness finds its significance and dignity only in ... the possibility at any moment of stepping out of this limitation into freedom" (ibid: 10). The door subsequently becomes a central metaphor for agency; it represents a subtle dialectical relationship between humankind's need to demarcate its unique being culturally, and the ability socially to transgress borders between human beings. The human being is "the bordering creature who has no border" (ibid).

The contemporary search for roots reflects the kind of bordering of which Simmel speaks, and it mirrors our contemporary social crises and cultural delusions as well. The latter seem to have more to do with the difficulties of connecting "the finite with the finite" culturally, as discursively formulated in the phenomenology of Alfred Schutz in his essay on "The Stranger." Cultural essentialism is becoming widespread, and it finds resonance in neo-liberalism's celebration of the private and the particular. The culturalization of modern life that should be "liberated" — in an academic and political sense — from social relationships of dependence (on the institutions of the welfare state, and on the "structural" in general) goes hand-in-hand with the spread of market styles and the celebration of the full expression of our natural instincts. The "natural" and the "authentic" form the frame of reference for the national, regional and local. Like a contemporary echo of Schutz's words (1976: 95), "thinking as usual" appears to be based on a "relatively natural conception of the world." The naturalization of a cultural "us" is accompanied by a demarcation of a "them"; an immigrant's atavistic ethnicity and a discursive banishment to its pre-modern roots. Boundaries are drawn, and the question is *whether* rather than *how* separate cultures can be connected.

"The Stranger," Schutz (1976: 103) writes in his classic essay, "constructs a social world of pseudo-anonymity, pseudo-intimacy, and pseudo-typicality. He is outplaced from his "home" and uprooted both geographically and culturally, which renders him invalid in the dialogue on the new social environment. The stranger lives on in an "unbroken" connection with "the cultural pattern of his home group" which becomes an unquestioned, *natural* frame of reference. In his lecture on "The Cultural Construction of the "Stranger" in Social Scientific Thought," Jonathan Schwartz (1994: 6) argues: "This is Scheler's phrase. Scheler spoke of 'the opening and closing of the sluice gates of the spirit' to describe the 'relatively natural' ideas and cultural styles." According to

Schwartz, the phenomenological core of Schutz's stranger is an abstracted essence — "Home" or rather *Heimat*; nostalgia for the *Gemeinschaft* of a rural village, "Heimat." The notion has its roots in Romantic German philosophy and is readily evident in Schutz's essentialistic concept of culture. Paradoxically enough, Schutz — himself an immigrant in the US — creates the "stranger" for whom it becomes impossible to belong or feel at home, as a consequence of his own and others' Heimatization.

While the exiled individual stubbornly preserves an "ex-world," and thus a (self-inflicted) psychological trauma of pseudo-existence, the *Heimat* he encounters is perceived as embodied in the group that, as a stranger, he is to approach. Here he is stopped by the rules of "naturalness." The result of the naturalness of "thinking as usual" is again the cultural pattern excluding the stranger. He cannot share the "essence" owned by the group he meets. "Any member born or reared within the group accepts the ready-made standardized scheme of the cultural pattern handed down to him by ancestors, teachers, and authorities as an unquestioned and unquestionable guide in all the situations which normally occur within the social world" (ibid: 95). The group the stranger encounters appears to be monitored by the unwritten rules of culturally inherited recipes — that is, "recipes for interpreting the social world" (ibid). Cultural recipes aquire hereby "the function of the cultural pattern of eliminating troublesome inquiries by offering ready-made directions for use" (ibid). While helping group members avoid "undesirable consequences," recipes serve ultimately as guardians of a social order.

The preservation of the social order can thus be seen as the reason why ."... only members of the in-group, *having a definite status in its hierarchy* [my emphasis] and also being aware of it, can use its cultural pattern as a natural and trust-worthy scheme of orientation" (ibid: 99). This also seems to explain why the "stranger" can only live in a pseudo-world. He can never take part in the mysterious "belonging" to the deep roots surrounding graves not his own; "graves and reminiscence can neither be transferred nor conquered" (ibid: 97). This is also why the stranger, "a border case outside the territory" (Ibid: 99), only approaches the group superficially, and in vivid and immediate experience. While he remains excluded from the foundations of the past, he is also excluded from "home" and from "belonging."

Thus, as Schwartz (1994: 8) observes, "phenomenology, because it claimed to dig deeply into the roots of existence — to care for them, and not to tear them up — had natural affinities for *Gemeinschaft* and *Heimat* as ideals." This exposes, mediated through Schutz, the irony of the rootlessness of the stranger who is uprooted and who cannot — on account of his cultivation of old roots — be rooted in the new environment. He is instead to remain rooted as a stranger in the new plantations of latter so-called urban villages. *Gemeinschaft*, Schwartz argues (Ibid: 8–9), "survives in Chicago immigrant milieux and the research of the Chicago school." In Jewish ghettos, Little Sicilies, Little Polands and so on, Schwartz continues, we are confronted with research which — with "ethnographic detail and its fieldwork quality" (Ibid: 9) — represents a paradigm which "was not the blazing hot melting pot of Henry Ford's Americanization; it seemed more like an amalgam of rural community and emancipated urbanity" (ibid).

But rather than an amalgam, maybe, what is at stake here is the immigrants' second exile — to excluded and in turn exclusivist urban ethnic communities. In the face of the devastating effects of urbanization and modernization upon the old worlds, the little worlds of *Heimat* disappear. "The century of exile," as Schwartz calls it, then begins. The uncertainties which develop are "organized" through the intolerance of modernity and the various kinds of rigidity and inequality within the "Heimats" of the future — "havens in a heartless world." The social psychology of cultural encounters has been reduced to a psychology of the culturally absolute and impregnable. Schutz's phenomenology lays the ground for a type of psychologized and naturalized cultural fundamentalism, which in many ways traverses contemporary academic and popular discourses dealing with the stranger and with cultural "collisions."

In a world where the search for roots has become widespread — from new social movements to the building of new nation-states, from identity politics to national cultural identities — Alfred

Schutz's phenomenology can provide food for thought. A cultural panic has spread in the wake of a globalization of uncertainties. This essentially social crisis has become a worship of the cultural as it fosters a quest for pluralization and ethnicization in an implosive "roots" radicalism. "The explosion of invented communities and 'reactive' identities is taking place in a situation of hegemonic cultural homogenization and scattered revolt" (Karlsson, 1994). The doors are closing, while possible bridges seek to connect points of scattered ethnic separateness — along the route of prescribed multicultural security and direction (cf. Ålund and Schierup, 1991).

Ethnicity

New boundaries and barriers to the transgression of boundaries illustrate the inner tensions of contemporary multicultural society. We are faced with the choice between an open and a closed society. No modern open society can exist as ethnically pure. Modern identities are formed in a dynamic interplay of different cultural elements from the composite living world which stresses the meaning of the transethnic in the construction of modern identities and the process of belonging.

Still, more often than not cultures are classified and ordered in line with prevailing ethnocentric norms. This results, at our northern latitudes, in a Eurocentric system of hierarchical classification, in which the perceived cultural distance of the "others" from the (Swedish) center is decisive. (One example of this classification in Sweden may be found in Charles Westin's *The Tolerant Public Opinion* (1987)). How far apart *we* and *they* are is expressed in terms of cultural distance and collision. The periphery seems to be associated with the traditional, moreover, and the center with modernity.

The culturally classified and ethnocentrically ordered functions as a discriminatory standard — as when, for example, determining suitability within a labor market divided increasingly along lines of ethnic origin. Despite the egalitarian discourse of Swedish cultural pluralism, cultural segregation is constructed on a status-oriented basis, and in accordance with stereotypical and deterministic notions. It leaves the field open for social inequalities and intense tensions between population groups.

I believe that representing ethnic relations exclusively in terms of culture or attitudes does not lead to an proper understanding of integration and disintegration in modern multicultural societies. In this multifarious, sometimes mixed and often divided world of ours, the notion of ethnicity is a central one. What do we mean? How do we use it? Ethnicity has become a key question in the discussion of multicultural and immigrant policy in Sweden and all over Europe. What we have learned thus far is that ethnicity is an obscure concept — it is used, for example, in contexts relating not only to culture but also to structure, and it addresses both purity and mixture, both imagined closed communities and the imaginative processes through which culture is created and boundaries are transgressed.

Immigrant ethnicity is not now — if indeed it ever was — solely the expression of pluralism in the cultural sense. Whatever we mean by "the cultural" associated with ethnicity, the structural constraints of the societal majority are rapidly infecting it. Ethnicity is becoming an expression of specific reactions to the growing experiences of multiple exile among a majority of Scandinavian immigrants. The social petrification of a hierarchical ethnic division of labor and the social/political marginalization of immigrant populations are cardinal factors in the development of ethnicity.

The widespread static view of ethnicity, with its emphasis upon cultural difference, has come under increasing criticism as a deterministic view that portrays cultural preservation as a goal in itself while presenting social inequality as cultural deviance. Ethnicity, and indeed race as well, have come to be understood as social constructions (Gorelic 1989, Ålund and Schierup 1991). Different types of ethnicity always historically appear — to use the expression of Stuart Hall (commenting on race in *New Ethnicities*) — in articulation, in a formation, with other categories and divisions in society. Being closely related to socio-cultural tensions, ethnicity is "constantly crossed and recrossed" (Hall 1992: 255) by the categories of race, gender and class. The primordialist concept (and practice) of ethnicity seems to me to be related, both historically and at present (as in the new states of ex-Yugoslavia, for example), to the same type of theoretical and "empirical" problems of exclusion. Indeed, as Stuart Hall warns us, there can be no simple "return" or "recovery" of the ancestral past which is not re-experienced through the categories of the present. Modern history also teaches us that clean cultures are too often cleansed according to "blood," and sometimes also with blood. Distant or not, these "issues" are related to the problem of cultural analysis (i.e., the cultivation of differences), the present (harmonized) politics of immigration, (culturally exclusive) Eurocentrism, and the obscure multiculturalisms of Western Europe. Culture is obviously a battlefield, embodying contraditions in political and mainstream intellectual discourse, in which the rhetoric of the liberal democratic politics of recognition tends to neglect the hierachical dissonance of social inequality, and explains structurally conditioned pluralism (Gordon 1970) in terms of culturally derived ethnic stereotypes.

The problems with a culturally reductionist understanding of ethnic processes were brought to attention as early as 1974 in Abner Cohen's introduction to *Urban Ethnicity*. He argued that, even if the concept of ethnicity is usually associated with minority status, lower-class position or "migrancy," the complex socio-cultural dynamics of ethnicity are seldom the focus of analysis. Instead, the social and the cultural are cast in terms of static and discriminating stereotypes. In this way, the social-structural and class aspects of ethnicity are rendered invisible in favor of the perspective of "cultural conflict" predominating among both researchers and the general public. The social construction of ethnicity remains concealed, and many of its important aspects escape observation: e.g., the complex processes of group formation, inversion, boundary-drawing, myth activation, fusion and the symbolic representation of cultural markers. However, this neglect of the socio-cultural complexity of ethnic processes has increasingly attracted attention, particularly in contemporary migration research in Western Europe and North America.

91

Ethnicity is a concept derived from the construction of ethnic groups and their dynamic relations with each other and their societal environment. Ethnicity has two fundamental determining criteria. Cultural solidarity, to begin with, is required, i.e., members of the group must feel a subjective sense of belonging and of shared values, norms and patterns of behavior. In addition, certain structural preconditions must be fulfilled, i.e., objective material conditions must obtain which generate common interests, group organization and sometimes political action. In this interplay between the "structural" and the "cultural," one can in varying degrees find ethnicity expressed with political, religous or cultural overtones (depending on the platform of interests of the ethnic group in question). Ethnicity is often regarded as situationally and contextually determined, and as symbolically charged. If, for example, the platform for solidarity is defined and understood in structural terms — as in the case of "political Blacks" — the result may be transethnic identities and mobilization on the basis of politically articulated solidarities. Similar experiences related to oppression, discrimination and racism can, independently of conspicuous cultural differences, form the basis for solidarity and a broad social mobilization and construction of collective identity.

Ethnicity and class are not related to each other in any immediate or automatic way. We find many examples of how the invocation of cultural similarity can become an integrative factor for a range of social groups which are far from one another as regards class position. The "cultural" can function as symbolically integrative (through myths, signs, etc.) and as a basis for solidaristic mobilization, or against a collectively perceived threat or commonly experienced degradation. A culturally defined religious sense of belonging — e.g., Muslim, Jewish, Christian — are clear examples of the integrative force of the "cultural". At the same time, many contemporary forms of ethnic mobilization and conflict point towards a complex interplay between structural tensions (local, regional, national and global) and culturally expressed forms of mobilization (e.g., reactive strategies in connection with inclusion/exclusion). A complex and dynamic perspective of ethnicity is therefore necessary and relevant if one is to analyze the fundamental social conflicts associated with ethnicity and culture. The social dimension has too often been overshadowed by cultural stereotypes in both scientific and popular discourse.

Culturalism, culturalization and ethnicization are notions that have been used to criticize a type of disguised hierarchizing ideology which is premised on a simplified antinomy between civilized/modern and primitive/traditional. Cultural differences are cultivated and polarized. Fuel is furnished for the increasingly common political and popular argumentation focusing on whether various groups among refugees and immigrants are suitable or unsuitable, or adaptable in higher or lower degrees, or "foreign" to a greater or lesser extent. Here is the basis for a differentiation and selection among people in cultural terms; its extension supplies the basis of legitimacy for what has been termed "Fortress Europe" and the "Mediterranean wall."

The structural processes must be explained if the underlying tensions in the social construction of ethnicity are not to be masked. Thus we see an interconnection between reinforced external barriers (Fortress Europe) and internal constraints like the discrimination on the job market, segregation in housing areas, political maginalization and growing racism in everyday life. Behind the labels of refugee, immigrant ("invandrare") and the New Underclass, a new kind of second-class citizen is appearing in Europe.

The risk that the culturalization of social disparities will become a type of "new racism" has been pointed out. While differing from a compromised racial-biological discourse, the "new racism" focuses on cultural differences, in a simplified and naturalized form. Culture is made to function as nature. "New Racism" appeals to notions of cultural apartheid and repatriation.

In the mid-September 1993 issue of the Swedish newspaper *Expressen*, a new lift-the-lid politics finds clear expression — "Kör ut dom" — drive them out. This seems rather symptomatic of the present ideological climate — in the whole of Scandinavia, I believe — where, in a rough interplay, the extreme right, new populist movements and the mass media join in announcing the character and type of exclusion. The process of constituting ethnicity behind the popular rhetoric about the refugee (and purportedly Muslim) "invasion" is — to use the expression of Stuart Hall — dividing the West from the Rest.

In this historical setting, the making of "home from home" (Phil Cohen 1991) has to be done under the besieged conditions of multiple exile. I would now like to connect the question of exile with that of the integration of society, and to relate this to the processes of identity-formation in modern, polyethnic society.

Identity

The question of social integration appears to be as loaded today as at the beginning of the century. Academic representations of this issue seem today to be polarized between, on the one hand, the theoretical heritage of the "lonely crowd" — the massification of publics, the undermining of collective morality, growing anonymity, modern individualism, etc.; and on the other, the recognition of new forms of cohesion, social bonds, and identity-building. These latter aspects have usually been associated with the meaning of cohesion on the micro-social level.

The notion of community has been fundamental in this context, even if not unproblematic. It frames the wide area of the potential of civil society, another notion with multiple resonance. The position of civil society has usually been placed in the conflicting perspective of center-periphery tensions, and explained in the context of power relations, autonomy and identity-forming processes. Emerging associations, networks and new social movements have been discussed as a zone of mediation and a buffer between the family and the state. Not seldom has this led to overestimating the potential of institutions and movements on the level of civil society (in contrast to the alleged suppressiveness and hegemony of the state). In the discussion of new social movements especially, the meaning of coherence becomes problematic. It relates increasingly to the particularism of identity or place, and celebrates differences and uniqueness in a world of migration, globalization, cultural amalgamation and merging.

During the 1980s and 1990s, the quest for identity — and its complex relationship to modernity as well — has become one of the most central characteristics of our civilization's transfor-mation. Crisis, the "end of history," the demise of the grand narratives of modernity, and the social and cultural meaning of life have come to dominate the academic debate. Transnational amalgamations in the shadow of a new international order, together with Eastern Europe's ideological and territorial transformation, have created the background for identity crises in both an individual and collective sense. We live in an epoch characterized by a parallelism between centrifugal and centripetal forces, where processes of transnational compression are accompanied by processes of frag-mentation. The latter are crucial in the construction of new and new-old individual, local, regional and ethnic identities. These often painful processes are increasingly influenced by wars and crises, as well as by public discourses pregnant with intolerance and exclusivism in relation to "the other." This is evident in the current conflicts between different ethnic groups in the new Baltic states and in former Yugoslavia. Russians in the Baltic states and various "minorities" in Serbia, Croatia and Bosnia no longer "belong." They are excluded in legal, cultural or religious terms. Irrespective of whether they define themselves as belonging to the "people" or traditions of the country in which they have lived — sometimes for generations — they are excluded from the newly formed com-munities, which are reserved for those considered to belong to the dominant national group. The fabrication of new national and often exclusivist identities — which are imbued with regressive ideo-logies based on an appeal to a "lost grandeur" in terms of sacrifice, *Blut und Boden* — frames a world of absolutism behind a myth of "imagined community." The "invention of tradition" in these constructed ethno-national histories often carries the vestiges of an instrumentality in the service of unscrupulous power struggles. The victims — the excluded, "the other" — which stand in the way of territorial, political or economic gains are often forced to join the ranks of the new "helots" in modernity's stream of refugees.

95

The quest for identity thus seems increasingly to be mediated through the fragmenting symbols and rhetoric of ethnicity, regionalism and localism, while the national shows tendencies of leaving the universal behind. Civic policies excluding "the other" are promulgated. The present also includes, however, the relaxation of social and cultural boundaries, the expansion of a "world culture," the fusion of cultures, and meetings across boundaries. New boundary-transcending cultures and lifestyles are emerging in the inner cities of Britain, in the Kreuzberg neighborhood of Berlin, in Sweden's multicultural suburbs, in Paris, etc. Parallel to the forces of exclusion and ethnic absolutism, the processes of merging present us with a multiplicity of answers to the crises of modernity, identity and integration.

It has often been pointed out that insecurities and crises in the West generally are created by the fragmentation of close social ties, the erosion of meta-social guarantees (Touraine), and the dissolution of the more or less homogeneous identities and ideologies of classes and nations. In addition to marginalization, discrimination, and the racism of structure and of everyday life, a more profound feeling of social and cultural erosion is most likely relevant, especially in diasporic immigrant settings.

Given the context of this crisis of modern consciousness in the course of the erosion of systems of integration, the turn to history is appearing, and it has shown itself to be both reflexive and reactive. On the one hand, we see the emergence of increasing societal reflexivity in the identity-forming processes on both individual and collective levels. On the other, we see new enclosures following ethnic lines. Processes of identity-formation around exclusion resemble what is going on in the so-called newborn democracies rising from the ashes of the Soviet Union, ex-Yugoslavia and eastern Europe.

While the nationalists of newborn states appeal to the glory of a purified ethnic past of old victories, heroes and other ghosts, thus demonstrating a sclerotic symbolism of old imperial dreams, the umbilical cord (or bondage rather) to the hinterland helps reflect these tendencies among immigrants in Europe. Thus, in the processes of identity- and community-building among immigrants in

European polyethnic settings, we meet an echo that in a way mirrors the hinterland type of ethic revival, but which also — and this needs to be stressed — frequently calls it into question.

Thus, janus-faced dynamics in the development of ethnic consciousness among immigrants include — besides the processes of purification — ethnic amalgamation and merging. This very often takes on, especially among youth, the character of wrestling with the ghosts of the past — in the present (Schierup and Ålund 1987).

The metaphorical expression of these processes, deeply enbedded in the autobiographical stories that I have collected during my current fieldwork in Rinkeby, a suburb of Stockholm, demonstrates the delicate character of modern ethnic consciousness. Present dilemmas and struggles are often expressed through the mediation of old ghosts. In the specific intersection between the old and new antagonisms faced by immigrants, novel insights are released and "amalgamated" into new forms of collective identity and social community — in which the symbols of tradition attain their place, not seldom in the service of modern solidarities. Emerging mixtures of cultures and cultural innovations, as well as a variety of identities (in an individual and a collective sense), illustrate the diversity of contemporary multicultural society and its potential for change. In Rinkeby, however, we do not find a "multiculture," i.e., a kind of "pluralist order of discrete patches of culture, all somehow, equally valid within the polity," as Roger Hewitt (1992: 29) has observed about Britain. Rather, we find here a variety of cultures which are "active together and hence bound up with change" (Ibid: 30). Rinkeby became famous for, among other things, its new language — Rinkebyska (or Rinkeby Swedish). This dialect consolidates a composite local identity and sense of belonging to a community which, ethnically speaking, also includes Swedishness. A widely announced Rinkeby "spirit" — a sort of transethnic collective identity expressed through the locally produced label "Rinkeby: a village in the world" — alludes to the manifold relationships between the local and the global, and to the inventiveness of the ways in which the people there make a home from home — their local sense of their place in the world. I also became aware of how centripetal forces of togetherness act beyond fragmentation, and of the political importance — beyond the social and psychological — of popular culture like rap music, hip-hop and samba-group, all of which have to do with the formation of new urban social movements and processes of identity.

Individual interviews repeatedly expose a destabilization of fixed ethnicities in the process. In contrast to the dominant Swedish stereotypes of rootlessness and ethnic conflicts in the "concrete ghettos" of the suburbs, young men and women there seem to share a tendency towards an extensive transcultural identity. Young people mediate experiences anchored in several social and cultural worlds. In their reflexive relation to the "self" and the "other," they expose a type of ethnic consciousness that relates in complex ways to present tensions in the countries of emigration, to major structural tensions in the society of immigration, to shared inequality, and to a common outsider identity among modern youths. Thus, to paraphrase Anthony Giddens (1991), social events and social relations "at a distance" are interlacing with local contextualities.

Referring to the society in which they are growing up, and which they want to consider their own, young people expose the traumas of modern diaspora — not by expressing feelings of displacement, but rather by referring to obstacles in the way of their wish to make a home of their actual homes. They do not belong to one single world, nor are they telling one particular history, or developing straightline cultural identities. Their stories are traversed by a multiplicity of histories, connecting their own memories and those of others with dreams of overcoming the experienced boundaries of the "multicultural" society.

The complex interplay between ethnicity, class, gender and generation forms the implosive force for a reflexive rejection of both old and new forms of oppression, and for the creation of new forms of solidarity and collective identity. Here we find a social force which has been neglected until recently. The reflexive relation to tradition to which Marshall Berman (1983) calls our attention, and the "recognition" binding time and space to which Paul Gilroy (1987) refers, places modern ethnic consciousness, syncretic culture and transethnic social movements at the frontline of research. New hybrid cultures are building upon history as the carrier of meaning in the diaspora present. Contemporary experiences are welded to life-forms in and through transcultural movements that transpose the historical symbols of tradition on to the symbolic decor of the contemporary inner city's public space.

The psychological, cultural and political importance of a world of mixture and boundary transgression is often overlooked in favor of a overwhelming scientific interest in differencies and boundaries. By crossing boundaries, in both a social and cultural sense, young people are throwing light on the complexity of lived realities. There are experiences of hybridity between social worlds and identities that must be heard — beyond the ongoing polarization between "us" and "them"; beyond the disparity between, on the one hand, the official rhetoric of tolerance and, on the other, the lack of recognition and the brutal reality of growing intolerance, marginalization, discrimination and racism; beyond the more or less clearly announced purification of the mainstream, of the majority and nowadays also of the minority. Otherwise, we run the risk not only of veiling the emergence of new ethnicities arising from interaction and merging, or of camouflaging "the inventive act itself," to use the expression of Werner Sollors (1989). We also run the risk of finding ourselves behind the Wall(s).

Latinos on the way to Stockholm

I will attempt to summarise the diasporic experiences of trying to belong in not belonging. Processes of belonging are filled with tensions between dreams and realities — realities of merging, exclusion and exile. Identity is not fixed or unchanging, of course, but given the character of the social experience of the majority of the migrant population in Scandinavia and elsewhere in Europe, there is a danger of the petrification of stigmatizing images of the stereotypical "other" based on the existing social order. This can contribute — further down the line — to releasing reactive or defensive feelings in the service of new forms of ethnic purification and absolutism. It can also effectualize a partition of the public space into separate ethnic territories. In that case, the broken bridges of Mostar and Sarajevo will not just be metaphors for distant barbarism ...

During the summer of 1993, a mosque and a Greek Orthodox church were set on fire in Sweden. Countless attacks on refugee centers, fires, and plundered ethnic businesses are seen on our TV screens. Politicians march in torchlight demonstrations against racist terror and the desecration of Jewish graves. The police mobilize massive force to meet the confrontations between racists and antiracists occurring in connection with the celebration of the great Swedish cosmopolitian and conqueror, King Charles XII. The racists celebrate, rather paradoxically, the memory of an adventurer who internationalized Swedish culture and political praxis. The racists, by contrast, want to rid Sweden of all "foreign races." The police meet them with the same irritation they show towards "unruly" antiracists (cf. Löwander, 1993). The most important goal on the part of the police seems to be keeping the streets of Stockholm clean, quiet and free of people (Ålund, 1992). Stockholm's streets and squares are no longer safe. The memory of the "Laser man" who killed and wounded a number of men of foreign appearance has spread terror throughout that part of the Swedish population with a "foreign" and "non-Swedish" appearance. Isolated "nutcases" are running amok at a time when organized racism is on the rise and cultural racism is spreading in insidious forms throughout society — from the street to the parliament.

At the same time, new voices are spreading like rings on the water. The local rapp artist, Lucco, sings, "Because they have the name of the country... no somos criminales no nos traten como animales ... fuck the gringo con el sabor de latino, Huh ..."

Gringos and Latinos meet in Sweden, and the history of colonial oppression relates to closed doors, disco security guards, and patronizing glances here and now. "Flows in space" of rhythm and resistance are televised to private rooms, redrafted to texts about the local and particular, and mediated through meeting places to embrace the unifying and common, as a collective insight of outsider status and as a challenge to resist. Young racists in the hardrock group, *Ultima Thule*, sing "out with the riff-raff" on a TV program about racism, while the TV camera zooms in on a Nazi flag. While Jan, a young member of this group, says that "we need very high walls around Sweden," the young immigrant rapp artist Dogge, from the group *Latin Kings*, answers: "Brown Latino with black hair, ten fingers and ten toes, just like you, here and now ..." In an interview on another occasion, Dogge explains, "skinheads and 'blackheads,' they are really the same," and adds, "we are all idiots who go against each other ... instead we should, skinheads and 'blackheads,' come together against politicians and all those damn big dudes that have money and power. First when we come together and do something together are we a threat" (Moe 1994, Ålund 1995).

Like the racist skinheads, Jan and Roger in *Ultima Thule*, the antiracist rapp artists Lucco and Dogge are children of their time, children of the same struggle. The former want to build walls, the latter want to build bridges. The former lock themselves in. The latter leave the door ajar and are on their way out. Both groups mirror the same world in the texts of their songs — where are we going?

The sociology of complex societies allows for no automatic answers. Amongst all of us who are more or less exposed to the expansion of "alterity," alienation and the search for identity, the different effects of the uncertainty caused by the demise of the welfare state, weakened collective identities, economic crises and the broken promises of universalism are ramified. In the face of transnational capital accumulation and hypernational political processes, anonymous forms of control, and legitimacy crises for the nation-state and its system of political representation, the conditions are created for uncertain identities and new ethnicizations. We are all ethnicized, at a rapid pace and in different ways — exclusively or inclusively. An increasingly common result of these processes is reactive flight into regional and local imagined communities.

"Culture" has become a universal ideological category in the political struggle, an indispensible tool for the techno-scientific administration and organization of differences, a general common-sense popular cliché celebrating the separateness of "cultural belonging" as a "natural" right. The cultural has acquired an independent role. Cultural explanations in a bare and distorted form have colonized the social by means of culturization. The social space has been reduced to a site for the production of identities or merely differentiated entities.

The conditions are developing for the emergence of collective identities which are ethnicized in a flora of variations (from exclusive ethnic absolutism to inclusive transethnic syncretism). This ethnization is "new" in that it assumes its form in relation to the social and cultural boundary-making of modern societies. That is, through inventive processes rather than repetitive practices governed by ritual or tradition — even if the latter can appear as old symbols (actual or invented) injected with new meanings for purposes other than traditional ones, albeit in the name of "tradition." The symbols of tradition often assume their place in the service of modern solidarities. Emerging mixtures of cultures and of cultural innovations, new boundaries and transgressions of boundaries, and a variety of new identities (in an individual and collective sense) illustrate the diversity of contemporary multi-ethnic society, its potential for change, and its inner tensions.

Among immigrant ethnic minorities the ambivalence is strengthened by a cross-breeding between the general cultural crisis and the specific discriminatory and stigmatizing practices of an increasingly racialized society. "Immigration" is developing into a dilemma joining far-flung times and places, Europe and America. It is a European dilemma resembling what Myrdal terms the "Negro problem," but without an automatic connection to skin color. It is a matter, in Balibar's terms, of "racism without race."

It should be stressed, finally, that in the wake of a consciousness of these processes, new transethnic identities are developing, not least among youth in the multiethnic environments of the cities. These new European identities are besieged, however. The social contexts and immediate life-worlds, with their inequalities and tensions, carry fundamental conflictual forces, which are particularly important for young people who still are called "immigrants" and strangers. The young contest their "not belonging" status more sharply than their first-generation immigrant parents do. Like Simmel's "stranger," they are near yet far away. They are, to paraphrase Simmel again, an element of the group itself, constructed not to be part of it fully. They are equipped to mediate but forced to struggle.

References

Berman, M. (1983), *All That is Solid Melts into Air: The Experience of Modernity*, London: Verso.

Chambers, I. (1990), *Border Dialogues: Journeys in Postmodernity*, London and New York: Routledge.

Cohen, A. (ed.), (1974), *Urban Ethnicity*, A.S.A. Monographs No. 12, London: Tavistock.

Cohen, P. (1991), "The Migration of Identity", (revised paper for the Conference on Racism, Das Argument, Germany), New Etnicities Unit, Polytechnic of East London.

Giddens, A. (1991), *Modernity and Self-Identity*, Oxford: Polity.

Gilroy, P. (1987), *There Ain't No Black in the Union Jack*, London: Hutchinson.

Gilroy, P. (1993), *The Black Atlantic: Modernity and Double Consciousness*, London: Verso.

Gordon, M. (1970), "Assimilation in America: Theory and Reality", in Hawkins and Lorinskas (eds.), *The Ethnic Factor in American Politics*, Columbus, Ohio: Merrill Publishing Co.

Gorelick, S. (1989), "Ethnic Feminism: Beyond the Pseudo-Pluralists", in *Feminist Review*, No. 32/89, (pp. 111–118).

Grillo, R. (1985), *Ideologies and Institutions in Urban France: The Representations of Immigrants*, Cambridge: Cambridge University Press.

Hall, S. (1992), "Introduction", in Hall S. and Gieben B. (eds.), *Formations of Modernity*, Cambridge: The Open University.

Hewitt, R. (1992), "Language, Youth and the Destabilisation of Ethnicity", in Palmgren et. al. (eds.), *Ethnicity in Youth Culture*, Stockholm University.

Karlsson, L-G. (1994), "Hegemonic Cultural Homogenisation", unpublished manuscript, Department of Sociology, University of Umeå.

Löwander, B. (1993), "Massmedierapportering om etniska relationer", in *Invandrare & Minoriteter*, 1/93.

Moe, A.M. (1994), "Intervju med Dogge", unpublished manuscript, Department of Sociology, University of Umeå.

Porter, J. (1968), *The Vertical Mosaik: Analyses of Social Class and Power in Canada*, Toronto: University of Toronto Press.

Schierup, C-U. and Ålund, A. (1987), *Will They Still be Dancing? Integration and Ethnic Transformation Among Yugoslav Immigrants in Scandinavia*, Stockholm: Almqvist & Wiksell International.

Schutz, A. (1976), (first published 1944), "The Stranger: An Essay in Social Psychology", in A. Brodersen (ed.), *Collected papers II*, The Hague: Martinus Nijhoff.

Schwartz, J. (1993), "A Century in Exile: Social Science as Witness", in *Rescue -43: Xenophobia and Exile*, Copenhagen: Munksgaard.

Schwartz, J. (1994), "The Cultural Construction of 'the Stranger' in Social Scientific Thought", Lecture at University of Umeå, Feb.

Sennett, R. (1977), *The Fall of Public Man*, Cambridge: Cambridge University Press.

Silverman, M. (1992), *Deconstructing the Nation: Immigration, Racism and Citizenship in Modern France*, London: Routledge.

Simmel, G. (1950), "The Metropolis and Mental Life", in Wolff, H.K. (ed.), *The Sociology of Georg Simmel*, New York: The Free Press of Glencoe.

Simmel, G. (1950), "The Stranger", in Wolff, H.K. (ed.), *The Sociology of Georg Simmel*, New York: The Free Press of Glencoe.

Simmel, G. (1970), *Kamp (Der Streit)*, Uppsala: Wikströms Tryckeri AB.

Simmel, G. (1994), "Bridge and Door", in: *Theory, Culture & Society*, Sage, Vol. 11.

Sollors, W. (ed.), (1989), *The Invention of Ethnicity*, Oxford University Press.

Taylor, C. (1992), *Multiculturalism and "The Politics of Recognition"*, Princeton N.J.: Princeton University Press.

Westin C. (1987), *Den toleranta opinionen*, Rapport Nr 8. CEIFO, Stockholms Universitet.

Wieviorka, M. (1993), in Wrench and Solomos (eds.), *Racism and Migration in Western Europe*, Providence: Berg Publishers.

Wolff, H.K. (ed.) 1950, *The Sociology of Georg Simmel*, New York: The Free Press of Glencoe.

Ålund, A. (1992), "Immigrantenkultur als Barriere der Kooperation", in Kalpaka A. and Räthzel N. (eds.), *Rassismus und Migration in Europa*, Hamburg: Argument.

Ålund, A. (1993), "Crossing Boundaries: Notes on Transethnicity in Modern Puristic Society", in *Rescue -43: Xenophobia and Exile*, Copenhagen: Munksgaard (pp. 149–161).

Ålund, A. (1995), "Vida's Metamorphosis to 'Immigrant Women'", in *Settlement for Warriors* (preliminary title: forthcoming) Esbjerg: SUC.

Ålund, A. and Schierup, C.U. (1991), *Paradoxes of Multiculturalism: Essays on Swedish Society*, Aldershot: Gower.

by Sandra Scarr,
University of Virginia, USA

Family Policy Dilemmas in Contemporary Nation-States: Are Women Benefited by "Family-Friendly" Governments?

Although mothers in the Western industrialized world have increased their economic activity, the gendered division of responsibility and work involved in childcare provision is still a foremost feature in families of young children. Men's collective choice of non-participation in child-care helps to maintain men's privileges position in society, and in relation to the market and the state (Leira, 1992, p. 175).

Women will not be truly liberated until men take equal care of children. If I had an affirmative action plan to design, it would be to give men every incentive to be concerned about the rearing of children (Justice Ruth Ginsburg, United States Supreme Court, April 17, 1995).

A universal problem

Nordic countries are renowned for their family-friendly policies, which recognize women's childbearing role and the child care needs of young children, while guaranteeing mothers' rights to return to their jobs after maternity and parental leaves and to work part-time when during children's preschool years. In principle, fathers are encouraged to accept some family and child care responsibilities by permissive policies toward which parent takes all or part of the parental leave and works part-time. In practice, however, men take only a small fraction of parental leave time and seldom work part-time. Until, and if, family responsibilities are shared equally between parents, women are caught in the dilemma of working full-time like men, using extensive child care, and balancing their greater family roles, or of accepting lesser roles in the society.

In a remarkable piece of social engineering, in 1994 both Sweden's and Norway's Parliaments passed legislation to require fathers to take one month of parental leave, or else the family loses the month's benefit. The goal of the new law is to increase fathers' child care responsibilities and to promote gender equality in the home. I hardly need tell you that such legislation is *unthinkable* in the United States or the U.K. Not only would nearly all Americans oppose such government interference with family decisions, most men would be horrified at being required to take major responsibility for infant care, and most women would not want fathers to stay home with an *infant*. In Norway, acceptance of the new law seems to be less than universal, in that only 1,200 fathers have taken the one-month leave in its first year (out of approximately 75,000 births; Borge, 1995).

Government policy requiring fathers to use some parental leave raises other possibilities to advance gender equality, such as whether credit toward career advancement and retirement should include home as well as employment history, which might be taken slightly more seriously in the United States than fathers providing infant care. The precedent of Veterans Preferences for employment and promotion seems to be a model that veterans of child care responsibilities could apply. The prevailing model in the U.S. is that mothers either stay home with young children and depend upon fathers' incomes, or they work full-time like men.

Despite emancipation of women and their increased political and economic participation in the Nordic countries, women are still not equal partners to men in politics or the labor force. Gender segregation of jobs and employment settings persists and political power is limited (Skard & Haavio-Manilla, 1984). Policies toward gender equality in Sweden, and proposed by some in the U.S., emphasize reduced labor market participation for mothers, to make it easier for mothers to combine work and family responsibilities. According the Nordic social scientists, Sweden emphasizes paid maternity and parental leaves, part-time work, and children's allowances. Only the entitlement to subsidized child care encourages mothers' investments in their careers. Truly "women-friendly" policies, suggested Spakes, foster both equality of opportunity and equality of outcome (Spakes, 1992), which for women must mean some kind of employment credit for their greater family responsibilities.

> The expanding Scandinavian welfare state changed the social division of labor, but upheld the gendered division of labor in the public domain and in the private sphere, and may even have strengthened it, More or less tacitly it was assumed that women would go on coping with care ... (Leira, 1992, p. 175).

Not all family-friendly policies are favorable to women's long-term interests or gender equality in the society, even if they provide short-term benefits. Most family-friendly policies in Scandinavia result in women's lower lifetime achievements, because they encourage women to shun full-time employment, which has profound impact on their earnings, promotions, power, and prestige. Disproportionate numbers of women are employed in the dwindling public sector, which has a further negative impact on women's long-term interests. Another family-friendly policy — subsidized child care — has the opposite effect, of increasing maternal employment and commitment to the labor force. This duality in family policies was described by Leira (1992).

> My analysis shows the welfare state relationship to women as "Janus-faced". Although contributing to women's decreased economic dependence on individual men, the welfare state nevertheless upholds men's privileged position in the labor market and in the welfare state reward system (p. 11).

In the United States, no family-friendly policies exist, which impels more women to work full-time, even when their children are very young, which creates excessive burdens on young families but does less damage to gender equality and women's lifetime achievements.

Caring and sharing (the economic burden)

In contemporary, Western nation-states, women face a Hobson's choice: To strive for independent achievement, with attendant social and economic rewards, or to focus their efforts on family development, household maintenance, and child rearing. To address women's dilemmas, enlightened nation-states, most notably the Nordic countries, have adopted policies to assist mothers to combine work and family responsibilities. Even Scandinavian policies reveal ambivalence about mothers' family and labor-force roles, through "a lack of coordination between the welfare state policies that more or less intentionally promoted the employed-mother family, and the childcare policies that did not meet the 'new mothers' demand, though Sweden and Denmark did better than Norway' (Leira, 1992, pp. 161–162). In this paper, I explore the causes and consequences of different policies and perceptions of family-friendly policies in several nation-states.

By promoting family-friendly policies, humane, well-intentioned governments have the *intended* consequence of promoting mothers' labor force participation by reducing conflicts between family and work responsibilities. But family-friendly policies have also had the *unintended* consequence of reducing mothers' years of full-time employment, thereby limiting their lifetime, career achievements. Less enlightened governments, which ignore mothers' conflicting work and family responsibilities, have the *intended* consequences of making maternal employment expensive to individual families and of keeping some mothers at home, and the *unintended* consequence of promoting *some* women's lifetime achievements. The Nordic countries have relieved some of mothers' daily struggles, but they have not fully addressed gender inequalities in power and status.

Despite extensive legislation and policies toward gender equality, equal status for women is elusive in all nations, in large part because of their disproportionate family responsibilities.

> After a hundred years of organized struggle against the discrimination of women, equality between the sexes has become a commonly accepted ideology in the Nordic countries, an acceptance reflected in the establishment of a public equality policy and in the implementation of reforms to promote the ideal and improve the situation of women. Nordic societies nevertheless continue to be overwhelmingly patriarchal: men still hold most of the leading positions and the essential power and control most of the resources, and the masculine mind-set clearly dominates the culture (Skard & Haavio-Mannila, 1984, p. 141).

Clearly, there are problems in women's societal status, even in nations that have ostensibly family-friendly policies.

Mothers' work

Around the world, women still shoulder most family responsibilities, especially onerous, routine, daily, repetitive, caregiving (Scarr, Phillips, McCartney &, 1989; Roby, 1975). In cross-national studies of women and men's home and labor force participation in Israel, Denmark, Finland, Sweden, Norway, and the U.S., fathers in all countries participate less in home responsibilities than mothers do. U.S. mothers of children under five years of age work an average of 90 hours per week in combined family responsibilities and full-time jobs. By comparison, fathers put in about 60 hours per week in home and full-time employment. The crushing load of combined full-time employment and home responsibilities leads some U.S. women with small children to leave the labor force until their children are in primary school, but most U.S. mothers cannot afford to leave the labor force for more than a few weeks. In 1993, 58% of mothers with infants under one year were working, 75% of them full-time. More than two-thirds of preschool children have employed mothers.

In the Nordic countries, mothers are more likely to return to the labor force after a year of leave and to work part-time — in 1986,

111

43% of Swedish women worked part-time (only 6% of men did), and they constituted 87% of all part-time workers (Leira, 1992). Some scholars refer to the organization of reproduction in the welfare state as merely "a shift from what has been termed 'private' to 'public' patriarchy" (Brown, 1981). Others see a partnership between mothers and the welfare state, which supports maternal employment with child care entitlement and employment policies that enhance mothers' part-time employment.

What are "family-friendly" policies?

Family-friendly policies come in three types, with respect to gender equality and women's lifetime achievements: Neutral, positive and negative.

Neutral. Family-friendly policies include provisions such as prepaid medical care and other social insurances that do not directly affect women's career achievements.

Pro-achievement. Family friendly policies include one major benefit that has positive impact on mothers' labor force participation: Entitlement to heavily subsidized child care. Affordable, available child care is *the* major policy to promote gender equality in the labor force and the society. Is government-supported child care an entitlement today? Certainly not in the U.S. or the U.K. Even the Nordic nations seem ambivalent, because there is not enough child care for all families in all municipalities, Swedish child care is the world's most expensive, and parents are being asked to pay ever larger proportions of the cost of child care. Increasing the cost of maternal employment reduces women's labor force participation, which has far more than economic consequences for the society. Historically, by reducing the cost of mothers' employment through government-subsidized child care, Nordic governments have achieved very high rates of maternal employment, but other family-friendly policies undermine the effects of child care on gender equality.

Anti-achievement. The list of family-friendly policies includes significant benefits that lessen mothers' lifetime earnings, limit their chances for promotion, and reduce mothers' probability of achieving the power and status that men of the same abilities and education routinely achieve. Mothers have jobs, not careers. Sweden provides child allowances; paid, job-guaranteed maternity leaves; paid, job-protected parental leave (mothers take more than 90% of the leave time); and part-time work during children's early years. Child allowances reduce the need for mothers to be in the labor force. Part-time work when children are young is nearly exclusively a mother's prerogative. With multiple children (2.3 on average), mothers may be out of the full-time workforce for 5 to 10 years. The focus of such policies is to make the balance of work and family responsibilities, which fall disproportionately on women everywhere, easier to manage when there are minor children in the household.

Moen conducted surveys of three cohorts of 1,445 working parents of Swedish preschoolers in 1968, 1974, and 1981. She found mothers more distressed than fathers in all three years. Mothers expressed lower feelings of well-being in all three years, but the gap narrowed by 1981 (Moen & Forest, 1990). Increased workplace supports benefited mothers in 1981 more than fathers, but mothers' increased well-being from 1968–1981 was not accounted for by workplace supports but by *permitted absences from the workplace*. Being able to take more time off from their jobs was directly related to mothers' short-term feelings of well-being. The longer term problem of lack of full-time, career-committed, labor force participation portends ill for Swedish mothers' lifetime achievements.

Years of maternity leave, parental leave, and part-time work make juggling family and employment less stressful for mothers in the Nordic countries than in the United States, for example, where family-friendly policies are unknown. In the U.S., President Clinton initiated the first, 12-week, *unpaid* maternity leave in January 1993. There are no job-guaranteed paid maternity leaves, no parental leaves, and no guaranteed part-time work while children are young. Most U.S. mothers either leave the labor force or work full-time. Those who leave the labor force temporarily probably take no more than 2–4 years out of full-time employment, with an average of 2 children. For U.S. mothers who are willing and able to work like men, there are *higher lifetime achievements.*

The payoffs for Nordic women are short-term improvements in their daily schedules during child rearing (and less frantic home lives for children and spouses). Taking advantage of maternity and parental leaves, and part-time employment can mean, however, that mothers do not work full-time for many years. Policies that reduce mothers' full-time, continuous employment sacrifice long-term gender equality in the search for short-term relief for mothers who work.

Full-time employment, and career commitment, are strongly related to career advancement in all industrial nations. Gender inequalities in income, power, social status and prestige result. Women end up being dependent on men (and the government in Nordic countries) for status and support. Welfare-state family-friendly policies can be seen as entrapment for women: "Motherhood models that imply doing formal work part-time, allowing for interruptions or discontinuous labor market participation, for example to care for young children, mean reduced access to welfare state entitlements ... (Leira, 1992, p. 172). Are family-friendly policies that reduce mothers' full-time employment in the true, lifetime interests of women? Are women willing to accept the consequences of lesser commitment to occupational achievements; that is, fewer female executives, professors, and members of the stock exchange? Or should policies be adopted to promote greater gender equality in women's and men's lifetime achievements?

Gender equality

What does gender equality mean, when women have disproportionate family responsibility? The same family-friendly governments that promote extended parental leaves and part-time employment also have passed laws to increase gender equality in the workplace and in the home. The major issue is how to combine work and family life without fostering gender inequalities in income, power, social status/prestige that leave women dependent on men for status and support. A recent review of family-friendly policies of the 12 EU countries (Bjornberg, 1993) showed that policies concerning child birth and care of small children increased women's dependence on men. Questions were raised about the joint effects of taxation schemes, allowance regulations, and chronic shortages of child care, which negatively affect women's equality in EU societies.

Whereas the United States and many EU nation-states have not addressed causes or consequences of gender inequalities in lifetime achievements, Nordic governments have manifestly concerned themselves with gender issues. The key is more equal sharing of family responsibilities, not providing special dispensations for mothers alone to reduce their participation in the labor force.

On average, women do not earn as much as men (about 74% of men's 1993 wages in the United States), are not given advanced job training as often, are not promoted as often to positions of power or prestige, and do not earn the retirement benefits that men enjoy. In Finland, Norway, and Sweden, women on average earn one half to one third what men do — and consequently have smaller social security benefits, since these are tied to income (Skard & Haavio-Mannila, 1984). The reduced labor force participation of women has resulted in job segregation and lower incomes, but may have enhanced women's entrance into the labor market, because women have not seriously challenged men's dominant positions or their "male preserves" of desirable jobs. In Scandinavia, men are still the "model workers" for whom contracts and benefits are written. (Leira, 1992, p. 106).

Carlsson (1988) and Hellberg (1987) both proposed that, from employers' perspectives, Nordic women employees are less stable, less interested in taking on management responsibilities, and less committed to careers (Hellberg, 1987). This dismal view may result from a combination of women's segregation in low income jobs and lesser participation in training schemes to advance to better paying jobs.

Despite the comparative advanced state of Swedish social legislation and the large percentage of women represented by trade unions, women remain at a disadvantage both in terms of job advancement and the quality of working life (Carlsson, 1988).

The considerable difference in the total income of women and men is attributable to the general downgrading of women's work, their relatively perfunctory job training, their briefer period of service, and the number of hours worked. The economic dependence of women is still with us (Skard & Haavio-Mannila, 1984).

Despite income inequalities, women's mental and physical health are better when they are employed (Harrell, 1993; Kessler & McRae, 1982; Scarr, Phillips, & McCartney, 1989). Although full-time employment is stressful for mothers of young children, combined roles at home and in the workplace are associated with better health and adjustment than roles that are limited to one sphere. Thus, family-friendly policies need to consider both the economic and personal benefits of women's participation in the labor force.

Employment discrimination or differential labor force participation?

What is responsible for this nagging gender gap in women's and men's lifetime achievements, including earnings, influence, and security? Many feminists suggest gender discrimination; others point to women's lesser participation and commitment to the labor force. In addition, women's segregation in the labor force by occupation, industry, and firm, is clearly responsible for women's income inequality and lack of promotion. There is also evidence that women choose "women's" occupations to lessen conflict with their greater commitment to family roles (Harrell, 1993).

Abundant literature shows that single women in the U.S. are more advanced in their careers than married women. Single women are more likely to be employed, to be working full-time, to have higher occupational status and higher incomes, and to be more highly represented in professional and technical fields and to hold higher-ranking academic positions (see Houseknecht, Vaughan, & Statham, 1987 for a review of this literature). Although many studies show that, on average, women do not advance in careers as far as men, when married women have continuous careers in which they work full-time, their incomes do not differ from earnings of single women (Schneer & Reitman,1993). In a study of 434 men and 421 women graduates of the Stanford Business School from 1973 to 1985, Harrell (1993) found men progressed faster than women in their careers. Single women progressed more equally with single men, whereas married women lagged far behind married men. Businesses prefer to advance married men and single women; a study of mentoring showed that women received more career help from mentors if they were single, whereas men received more help if they were married (Olian, Carroll, & Giannatonio, 1993).

Based on their study of women in the labor force in Denmark, Sweden, England, France, Norway, Poland and the U.S., Domanski and Sawinski (1993) concluded:

> Women show a weaker commitment than men to occupational and professional accomplishments. As a result, occupational position plays a less important role in determining the life chances of women. (Domanski & Sawinski, 1993).

A good example of women's lesser commitments to professional development comes from a large study of physicians in the U.S. Female physicians earned less than their male counterparts, worked fewer hours, and were five times more likely to be working part-time. Gender differences in marriage patterns among MDs were greater than among the general population. Fewer female MDs were married with children. 64% of male MDs (N = 882) had non-employed wives, whereas no female MD (of 1,159) had an unemployed spouse. Similar findings for physicians were reported in Sweden and Australia (Ulenberg & Cooney, 1990). The role of wives in the occupational success of male MDs is hard to calculate but very evident in husband's work commitment and income success (Hunt & Hunt, 1977). I often said, when my children were small and I was a full-time professor, that what I really needed was a wife.

Because most women are mothers, whose labor force participation is more sporadic and less committed than men or non-mothers, employers respond with lesser rewards for most women. There is good evidence that motherhood is more responsible than gender for reducing women's achievements. Not all employed women are mothers. Work histories of single women and married women without children, in the Nordic countries and in the United States, are more like those of men than are those of mothers, and higher incomes, career advancement, and achievements of non-mothers follow from long-term, full-time employment. Given multiple role responsibilities, women establish priorities for where to invest time and energy, according to internalized norms, which press mothers to put their children first.

> Given the high import that is placed on the family role for women in our society, it is not surprising that many married professional women curtail their careers in various ways (3 references) so that they can reduce role strain associated with carrying out their family responsibilities (Poloma and Garland, 1971). (Houseknecht, Vaughan, & Stratham, 1987, p. 255).

In a study of 663 29 to 65 year old professional women who received graduate degrees from 1964 to 1976, career patterns of divorced/separated women were compared to those of never-married women. Length of singlehood and timing of marriage were more important to career paths than singlehood per se. Being single (never married or divorced/separated) during and just after graduate education enhanced women's occupational achievements significantly throughout their careers (Houseknecht, Vaughan, & Stratham, 1987). Marriage and children are significant impediments to women's independent achievements.

Thomas Sowell, Stanford economist, claims that single, never-married women have the same job histories and income as men, but married women, particularly those with children, do not stay continuously in the labor force or earn positions or incomes as high as those of men. Gender differences in lifetime earnings and power/status result more from mothers' lesser commitment to employment and fewer years of full-time employment than from gender discrimination.

Attitudes toward job or career are crucial, and married women do not share the same high level of commitment to careers that many others (both men and other women) have. In countries not noted for gender equality, such as the U.K., Janman (1989) studied University College, London students' views of men and women's careers. When asked if one member of a couple was more successful than the other, students expressed negative views about women's greater success. Their stories had predominant themes of women who married and were willing to give up careers for family or husband's career. Undergraduate women at the University of Virginia express the same ambivalence about careers, believing that they should stay home with young children, and male undergraduates agree. Although most will be employed for economic reasons while their children are young, their lack of commitment to careers is obvious. Older, female undergraduates in the U.S., returning to university, were differentiated in career goals by marital status (MacKinnon-Slaney, Barber, & Slaney, 1988). Single and divorced women aspired to change careers, gain employment, and advance in employment; married women's primary goal was merely to gain employment, followed by changing careers and getting ahead. Married women were also more worried than single or divorced women that family issues would keep them from reaching their goals.

> Women who are reassessing their own career plans consider not only their own values, attitudes, abilities, and fears but also the values and attitudes of significant men in their lives (Mishler, 1975). Internal biases and self-expectations about life roles, as well as external biases and societal expectations, influence and complicate career development for women (Osipow, 1975). The salience of marital status as an influencing factor on the educational and occupations plans of women cannot be overestimated (MacKinnon-Slaney, Barber, & Slaney, 1988, p. 328).

Economic inequality

The number of hours worked predicts income for both American and Swedish mothers, but U.S. women pay a higher price in their later careers for having worked part-time (Rosenfeld & Kalleberg,

1990). Labor market location, that is, occupation, industry, job promotion opportunity, trade union membership, job autonomy, hours employed and tenure, all relate to women's income more powerfully in the U.S. than in Sweden (and even less in Norway; Rosenfeld & Kalleberg, 1990). U.S. Women pay a larger price than Nordic women for deviating from the male employment pattern, and fewer of them do. Although women do not earn as much as men, at comparable ages and levels of education, income transfers are often used in the EU and Nordic countries to prevent poverty in mother-headed households. Marriage dissolution brings poverty to many mothers and their children in the U.S. Although Sweden has the highest dissolution rate of marriages and cohabitations of any industrialized nation (Popenoe, 1987), income transfer programs prevent single-parent poverty. Child support payments are often enforced more effectively than in the United States, where 59% of the single-parent households are poor (U.S. Department of Labor, 1992).

In the U.K., U.S., and the Netherlands, women are also at a disadvantage relative to men in access to and utilization of social insurance programs, but not as much in Sweden (Sainsbury, 1993). Women earn less in old age pensions, sickness/disability and unemployment insurance for every country except Sweden. In other nations, married women's entitlements often derive from husbands'. Sweden differs from other nations in its larger female workforce, endowed with labor market entitlements, and regular income. Although retirement benefits are tied to earnings, there is less demand to earn benefits in Sweden, because many are given for residence alone. Thus, despite women's lack of full-time, lifetime employment, Sweden has policies to protect mothers and children from poverty. But are Swedish women protected from the effects of lower, non-monetary lifetime achievements?

Public versus private sector employment

Political representation of women in national governments is far greater in the Nordic countries than in the rest of Europe or the U.S.: In Norway, women hold 38% of the seats in Parliament, compared to only 22% in Germany, 6% in France, and 11% in the U.S. (Drozdiak, 1995).

In Nordic countries, women dominate public sector employment; the public sector employs 75% of all working women. This disproportionate public share of female employment seems to arisen in the 1970s from correlated, massive increases in public employment that arose in the same period as massive increases in female employment. The expansion of the welfare state created a large number of jobs that, although not specifically reserved for women, occurred in typical women's fields, such as child care, education, health, welfare, and lower and middle level administration (Leira, 1993). In addition, until the 1990s, the public/private distinction has been less important in social democratic welfare states than in free market economies, because the state intrudes into all aspects of the economy, thereby blurring the public/private distinction. In this era of privatization and downsizing the public sector, women workers are particularly vulnerable. Only 25% of women have been hired and retained in the private sector of Nordic economies.

In the U.S. public employment is also more typical of women, who are concentrated in education, health and welfare fields. Affirmative action programs for women and minorities, to improve access to desirable job opportunities, have resulted in greater female representation in pubic than in private employment. In federal and state governments, women occupy more than half of lower and middle management positions. Yet, women occupy only one of 15 Presidential Cabinet positions and few high-level management jobs.

In a study of actual promotion decisions for the U.S. federal government Senior Executive Service positions in cabinet-level departments, 438 applicants (88% men) were included. In fact, women were promoted preferentially over men with equal or superior qualifications (Powell & Butterfield, 1994). Although employees' own history in the department had the largest effect on promotion, women were given preference by gender. But this is government service, where affirmative action reigns. It is not necessarily the same scenario in banks and corporations.

The "Glass Ceiling"

Much has been written in the United States about a "glass ceiling" that permits women to rise in job status and income only so far before they hit an invisible barrier to further advancement (Mainiero, 1994). It is alleged that women are discriminated against in promotions to higher levels of management and the professions, such as corporate executive positions and partnerships in law firms (Morrison & von Glinow, 1990). Only 5% of top corporate management positions in the U.S. are held by women (Top management defined as within three positions of the Chief Executive Officer). Mainiero (1993) interviewed 55 successful women executives in America's largest corporations to find out how they broke through the purported "glass ceiling".

The women perceived themselves as largely non-political but extremely competent at their jobs. They negotiated their ways through patches of corporate intrigue but were largely uninterested in male competition and maneuvering for power. Their effectiveness lay in scrupulous attention to the business at hand and telling the truth about the enterprise. The author concluded that women executives need to develop political skills, build credibility, refine their styles of management, and shoulder responsibility *in the same ways that men do.*

Welfare reform in the U.S.

U.S. welfare reform can be seen as a barometer of public sentiment toward working mothers. Now that two-thirds of middle-income mothers are in the labor force (most of them full-time), the public will not tolerate paying poor mothers to stay home. Nearly universal agreement, regardless of political party, has fixed on the principle that work must be demanded of mothers on public support, because it will raise their self-esteem, give them feelings of participation in the society, and help socialize their children to an ideal of hard work. The old ideal of the one-earner, two-parent family, who currently constitute only 6% of all households, has been converted to a busy, two wage-earner family where both mother and father share responsibility at home and in the workplace. Thus, welfare mothers are being pushed into the labor force because it is good for them and their children.

Recent, welfare-reform legislation in Massachusetts and Virginia present models of what will be national policies. Mothers on welfare, mostly unmarried women with young children, must find work within one to three months and cannot stay on welfare supports for more than two years in total. Medical care and *child care costs* will be subsidized by the government for one to two years after they find employment. The poor-family-friendly policy of subsidizing child care for poor mothers is not new. Low-income families have been eligible for (not entitled to) government subsidized child care since 1987, but there has never been enough money to support all the families who need the subsidy.

At present, work does not pay as well as welfare for most low-income mothers, unless their wages and the costs of medical insurance and child care are subsidized. Full-time employment at the minimum wage rate ($4.25/hour or about $8,500/year) will not support a mother and two children above the official poverty level (Bergmann, 1994). The solution to low earnings is not to reduce welfare benefits to a comparable level of poverty but to raise the benefits of employment. The typically low wages of former welfare recipients are supplemented by Earned Income Tax Credits (EITC) for parents with children under 18 years. Welfare-reform proposals also supplement medical and child care costs.

When welfare-reform goes nationwide, child care services of good quality for 19 million preschool children would cost $36 billion, if child care is free to the lowest-income fifth and partially subsidized on a sliding scale to next two-fifth. After-school care for 29 million children between ages 5 and 12 would add $39 billion. Additional costs will be incurred in EITC and unemployment insurance, because welfare mothers will displace some other workers. Additional costs will be offset by some decline in food stamps (currently $32 billion) and in welfare (AFDC) payments (approximately $15 billion; Bergmann, 1994). Nonetheless, welfare reform that sends mothers to work will cost many billions of dollars more than current policies that keep them at home.

The increased costs of welfare reform are being accepted because Americans have decided that no one is entitled to income support without working to the full extent of their capabilities. This major change in values occurred because most U.S. mothers are in the labor force, full-time, and they are unwilling to pay taxes so that other women can enjoy an easier life at home with their children. Most American mothers are working like men, at great cost to the quality of their lives when children are young, but at great benefit to their lifetime achievements. It is expected that women currently on welfare will benefit from new-found independence and self-esteem, and their children will take pride in their mothers' accomplishments.

Conclusions

- Do family-friendly policies make it easier to combine work and family life? Yes, during the period of children rearing.

- Do family-friendly policies that support women's lesser participation in the labor force make women less self-sufficient and more dependent on men's earnings and the government's largesse? Yes.

- Do these family-friendly policies make it difficult for women to achieve the prestige, power, and self-esteem that men earn in the course of their careers? Yes — to all of the above.

- Are some family-friendly policies needed to protect the economic interests of women and children. Yes, enforced child support from noncustodial fathers and sometimes income transfers to supplement low wages.

- Is there one family-friendly policy that truly promotes gender equality and women's lifetime achievements? Yes, publicly-supported child care that encourages maternal employment throughout her lifetime.

- Social welfare nations have policies that address income supports, which the U.S., U.K, and some EU nations have not, but none has policies that call upon men to share more equally in family responsibilities and give women credit for child care.

No policies have yet been successful in addressing the major problem of gender equality: That fathers must take more responsibility for child care and routine maintenance of household (the repetitive, time-consuming responsibilities of daily life). Historically and at present, men do less than half of all child and family care.

> No modern industrialized society has managed as yet to attain real equality between the sexes — nor will any, until the sufficient ideological and theoretical groundwork necessary to bring about equality is developed and insight into the concrete modes of operation of patriarchal societies gained (Skard & Haavio-Mannillo, 1985, p. 157).

Nordic women have made more political than economic strides toward equality; in the workforce, they lag far behind men in all areas of achievement. Family-friendly policies can narrow the income gap but it cannot give them power, prestige, and self-esteem.

The United States is committed to *Equality of Opportunity*, and in that vein has myriad affirmative action laws and policies that level the achievement playing field for minorities and women who are equipped to take advantage of the same opportunities white men enjoy. Subject to intense national debate at this time, affirmative action is not supposed to mean *preferential* treatment for any group, including women. U.S. policies do not guarantee equality of outcomes. Thus, women who can work like men — single women, childless married women, and mothers who are willing to take on nearly unmanageable burdens for some years while children are young — *can* achieve like men. There are no family-friendly policies in the U.S. to encourage, or even permit, mothers to stay at home or work part-time. The lack of subsidized child care makes maternal employment expensive for individual families, but maternal employment increases family income in nearly all cases.

To encourage greater gender equality in lifetime achievements,

women need more subsidized child care and more male participation in the home. Choosing to subsidize mothers to take time
out of the full-time labor force and to stay at home is supporting
gender inequality. If women accept and encourage policies that
lessen their full-time participation in the labor force, they must
also accept lesser roles in political, economic, and cultural life. Is
that what contemporary women in Western, industrialized nation-
states really want?

References

Bergmann, B.R. (1994), "The economic support of child-raising: Curing child poverty in the United States", *American Economic Association Papers and Proceedings*, 84(2), 76–80.

Björnberg, U. (1993), "Family policies in the EC countries from a female perspective", *Sociologisk Forskning*, 30(3), 3–29.

Borge, A. I. (1995), "Personal communication", *Folkhälsa*, April 22.

Carlsson, B. (1988). "The organization of work in Sweden", *Women and Health*, 13(3–4), 159–165.

Domanski, H., & Sawinski, Z. (1993), "Social mobility of women from an intercountry perspective: Theoretical context and methodological difficulties", *Social Science Information*, 32(1), 87–109.

Drozdiak, W. (1995), "Young voters, women seen as keys to French election", *Washington Post*, April 12, A31.

Ginsburg, R., (1995), "Justice Ginsburg takes on affirmative action", *Washington Post*, April 17, p. A4.

Harrell, T.W. (1993), The association of marriage and MBA earnings. *Psychological Reports*, 72(3, Pt 1), 955–964.

Hedman, B., & Herner, E. (1988), "Women's health and women's work in health services: What statistics tell us", *Women and Health*, 13(3–4), 9–34.

Hellberg, I. (1987), "Labor mobility at the Gothenburg belt factory 1892–1977", *Sociologisk Forskning*, 24(1), 37–55.

Houseknecht, S.K., Vaughan, S., & Statham, A. (1987), "The impact of singlehood on the career patterns of professional women", *Journal of Marriage and the Family*, 49(2), 353–366.

Hunt, J.G., & Hunt, L.L. (1977), "Dilemmas and contradictions of status: The case of the dual-career family", *Social Problems*, 24(4), 407–416.

Janman, K. (1989), "One step behind: Current stereotypes of women, achievement, and work", *Sex Roles*, 21(3–4), 209–230.

Kessler, R.C., & McRae, J.A. (1982), "The effect of wives' employment on the mental health of married men and women", *American Socio-logical Review*, 47(2), 216–227.

Leira, A. (1992), *Welfare states and working mothers*, Cambridge: Cambridge University Press.

Leira, A. (1993), "Mothers, markets and the state: A Scandinavian model?", *Journal of Social Policy*, 22, 329–347.

MacKinnon-Slaney, F., Barber, S.L., & Slaney, R.B. (1988), "Marital status as a mediating factor on career aspirations of reentry female students", *Journal of College Student Development*, 29(4), 327–334.

Mainiero, L.A. (1994), "On breaking the glass ceiling: The political seasoning of powerful women executives", *Organizational Dynamics*, 22(4), 5–20.

Mellinger, J.C., & Erdwins, C.J. (1985), "Personality correlates of age and life roles in adult women", *Psychology of Women Quarterly*, 9(4), 503–514.

Mishler, S.A. (1975), "Barriers to the career development of women", In S.H. Osipow (Ed.), *Emerging woman: Career analysis and outlooks*, (pp.117–146). Columbus: Charles E., Merrill.

Moen, P., & Forest, K.B. (1990), "Working parents, workplace supports, and well-being: The Swedish experience. Special Issue: Social structure and the individual", *Social Psychology Quarterly*, 53(2), 117–131.

Morrison, A.M., & von-Glinow, M.A. (1990), "Women and minorities in management. Special Issue: Organizational Psychology", *American Psychologist*, 45(2), 200–208.

Myers, D.L. (1993), "Participation by women in behavior analysis: II. 1992", *Behavior Analyst*, 16(1), 75–86.

Olian, J.D., Carroll, S.J., & Giannantonio, C.M. (1993), "Mentor reactions to proteges: An experiment with managers", *Journal of Vocational Behavior*, 43(3), 266–278.

Osipow, S.H. (1975), *Emerging woman: Career analysis and outlooks*. Columbus: Charles E., Merrill.

Poloma, M.M., & Garland, N.T. (1971), "The married professional woman: A study in the tolerance of domestication", *Journal of Marriage and the Family*, 33, 531–540.

Popenoe, D. (1987), "Beyond the nuclear family: A statistical portrait of the changing family in Sweden", *Journal of Marriage and the Family*, 49(1), 173–183.

Powell, G.N., & Butterfield, D.A. (1994), "Investigating the 'glass ceiling' phenomenon: An empirical study of actual promotions to top management", *Academy of Management Journal*, 37(1), 68–86.

Roby, P.A. (1975), "Shared parenting: Perspectives from other nations", *School Review*, 83(3), 415–431.

Rosenfield, R.A., & Kalleberg, A.L. (1990), "A cross-national comparison of the gender gap in income", *American Journal of Sociology*, 96(1), 69–106.

Sainsbury, D. (1993), "Dual welfare and sex segregation of access to social benefits: Income maintenance policies in the UK, the US, the Netherlands and Sweden", *Journal of Social Policy*, 22(1), 69–98.

Scarr, S., Phillips, D., & McCartney, K. (1989), "Working mothers and their families", *American Psychologist*, 44(11), 1402–1409.

Schneer, J.A., & Reitman, F. (1993), "Effects of alternate family structures on managerial career paths", *Academy of Management Journal*, 36(4), 830–843.

Skard, T., & Haavio-Mannila, E. (1984), "Equality between the sexes — Myth or reality in Norden?", *Daedalus*, 113(1), 141–167.

Spakes, P. (1992), "National family policy: Sweden versus the United States", *Affilia*, 7(2), 44–60.

Ulenberg, P., & Cooney, T.M. (1990), "Male and female physicians: Family and career comparisons", *Social Science and Medicine*, 30(3), 373–378.

U.S. Department of Labor (1992), *Employment and Earnings*, 39(5). Washington, D.C.: U.S. Department of Labor.

Part Two | INSTITUTIONS

by Richard Pipes,
Harvard University

The Historical Evolution of Russian National Identity

Speaking in general terms, the phenomenon of nationalism consists of two discrete elements. One is the feeling of community with individuals who belong to the same group, as defined by language and other criteria, mostly of a subjective nature. The other is a sense of uniqueness, of distinction from all strangers, that is, those outside one's own group. Thus it is both inclusive and exclusive. When the historical conditions are favorable, the feeling of community loyalty may evolve into patriotism, which is the belief in the supreme value of the community. The sense of uniqueness, for its part, can lead to xenophobia and end in genocide. The two emotions — patriotism and xenophobia — coexist in an uneasy relationship, with the balance shifting now in one direction, now in the other, depending on the circumstances. It is certainly as possible to be a patriot without feeling hostility to outsiders, as it is to feel hostility toward outsiders without having a corresponding sense of loyalty towards one's own community. It is my contention that in Russia, animosity toward foreigners has always prevailed over national loyalty, and it is my task to explain the reasons for this fact.

The issue is not only of theoretical interest. Historical experience indicates that the modern state attains effectiveness to the extent that it accomplishes two things: gives its citizens the opportunity of individual self-fulfillment and, at the same time, retains the ability to persuade them to sacrifice some or all their private interests for the sake of the common good — whether by paying taxes or risking their lives in war. Community loyalty is a *sine qua non* of proper functioning of the modern state with its integrated society and interdependent economy. During the past two centuries, this loyalty has largely centered on ethnic identification. All successful states, whether England — the first to develop a sense of nationhood — or the United States, Japan and Israel, have been distinguished by strongly developed ethnic loyalties. By contrast, most of the Third World countries, where small communities have been stronger than the national community, have failed to create viable political and economic structures. This could change in the future when bonds other than ethnic ones may well take precedence. But in our times, ethnic bonds have turned out to be by far more effective social integrators than either loyalties to the supranational empire or a shared ideology.

Xenophobia has an ancient lineage in Russia. Russian dislike and contempt for foreigners has been noted by travellers to Muscovy as early as the sixteenth century. In some respects, it was rooted in the most primeval sensations of fear and hostility to strangers, observed by anthropologists among many primitive peoples. But in Russia's case it had also a specific cause, namely religion. Pre-modern Russians, like pre-modern West Europeans, identified themselves by their religious affiliation which was Orthodox Christianity. But whereas Catholicism, and, since the sixteenth century, Protestantism, were transnational faiths — that is, faiths which embraced all their adherents regardless of ethnic affiliation or state allegiance — Orthodoxy was a national religion, inseparable from the Russian people and their monarch. After the Turks had captured Constantinople and conquered the Balkans, Russia remained the only Orthodox state in the world, for which reason it was natural for Russians to equate their religion with both their nationality and state. To a sixteenth century Frenchman, being French and being Catholic were affiliations intimately linked but not identical. The English could break with the Church of Rome and not only remain English but feel more strongly so. But for the sixteenth century Russian, such a distinction was inconceivable: for him, to be Russian was to be Orthodox, and to be Orthodox was to be subject of the tsar.

The source of Russian xenophobia seem rooted in this historic idiosyncrasy. Surrounded by Catholics and Protestants in the west, and by Muslims in the south and east, the Russians developed a sense of uniqueness combined with antagonism toward other faiths, i.e. other nations. These attitudes survived into the twentieth century. They were secularized by Communism which inculcated in Russians the perception of being history's chosen people because they were the first to make the transition to an allegedly "classless" society.

I do not mean to suggest that Russians are hostile toward foreigners. In fact, they are a very hospitable people, and curious about the outside world. But their sense of identity is determined more by what they are not than by what they are: more by the awareness of being different from others than of being one with their own kind. Russian governments have found it easy to mobilize anti-foreign feeling among their people when it served their interest to do so — but very hard to rouse patriotic sentiments for the sake of the national community.

Evidence for this contention can be found in military history because warfare provides the supreme test of a people's devotion to their nation and state. Russians have always displayed great tenacity in expelling foreigners who threatened their lands and homes. They have been slow to respond when called upon to carry out broader national tasks, to bear sacrifices when their immediate interests are not so clearly affected.

In World War I, whose purpose was quite obscure to the mass of Russian soldiers, Russia's performance was markedly substandard. Russians surrendered in droves, at a rate well beyond anything seen on the western front. Thus, if the British, French and German armies, for every 100 battle fatalities lost between 20 and 26 men to enemy capture, in Russia for every 100 battle fatalities there were

300 prisoners of war — a figure which indicates that Russians surrendered at a rate 12 to 15 times as high. Only the Austro-Hungarian
army, with its ethnically mixed population, came close to that figure.

In 1917, after the tsar had abdicated, the army quickly fell apart.
Deprived of the visible personification of statehood, and led by
officers whom the socialist intellectuals in the Petrograd soviet had
deprived of disciplinary authority, the troops turned into rabble
whose sole concern was to rush home to join in the looting of
privately-owned land. When in 1918–19, White generals sought to
rebuild the army in order first to continue the war on the Allied
side and then to dislodge the Bolsheviks, their appeals to patriotism
fell on deaf ears: we have testimony to this effect from both General Denikin and Admiral Kolchak, the principal White com-
manders. Their volunteer cadres consisted mainly of secondary
school students and junior officers. The Bolshevik appeals to class
hatred and xenophobia, by contrast, proved very successful, as
were their exhortations to plunder. Once the Civil War was over
and the Bolsheviks tried to arouse their people to socialist construction, they, too, found little response.

In the initial phases of World War II, Russian troops were even
more willing to surrender than in World War I. The Germans
managed to capture nearly three million Soviet soldiers in the
opening months of their invasion, before their massacres and other
brutalities aroused mass resistance. In general, in all the wars
waged away from their homes — against the Western powers in the
Crimea in 1854–55, against Japan in 1904–05, or, more recently,
against the Afghans and even Chechens, Russian troops seemed to
lack strong motivation.

Reasons for weakly developed national consciousness of Russians

The question now arises what accounts for the apparent lack of
patriotic feelings on the part of the Russian population: why did
the Russian people fail to undergo the evolution from religious

identification to ethnic identification, such as experienced by the other European peoples?

To answer this question it is useful to turn to the history of England, the earliest country to develop the sentiments of nationalism.[1] In nearly all respects, the differences between England and Russia are extremely sharp. It is always instructive to compare the two countries, because by noting what England had and Russia lacked one finds explanation why Russia's course turned out to be so different from that of the rest of Europe.

To begin with, early modern England was a small, compact country with an ethnically homogeneous population: an extended community, as it were. Russia, by contrast, was an immense realm, spanning Eurasia, with a population which almost from the foundation of the state included other ethnic and religious groups. In the sixteenth century, when Tudor England took shape as a nation-state, Russia was already an empire: inchoate, unintegrated, and boundless. Implausible as it may seem today, in the middle of the seventeenth century, England's population was roughly the same Russia's (some 5 to 6 million): but whereas the English lived in a compact mass, on a territory that from east to west measured at most 500 kilometers, Russians were scattered over a continent that extended from Poland to the Pacific, a distance of some 6,500 kilometers. As the frontiers of the Russian Empire expanded through ceaseless conquest, the proportion of Russians shrunk until by the end of the nineteenth century they accounted for no more than 40 percent of the population. This reality found reflection in linguistic usage. Over time, the Great Russian people came to be designated "Russkie," whereas their state is "Rossiiskii". The tsar was not "Russkii Imperator" but "Imperator Vserossiiskii" — a distinction which cannot be adequately translated into English but which conveys the non-ethnic character of the pre-revolutionary Russian state (Kristof, 1968:349–50). Adjusting to this fact, the tsarist government fostered an imperial — *rossiiskaia* — rather than a national (*russkaia*) ideology. Neither Russian schools nor the Russian army inculcated patriotism, stressing instead loyalty to the person of the tsar — this in striking contrast to most west European countries as well as Japan.

137

Perhaps even more decisive for the weak development of ethnic identity in Russia was the absence or underdevelopment of institutions capable of implanting in separate social groups the sense of common destiny. Historians have identified, on the example of such West European countries as Norway and France, a number of institutions which served to transform an amorphous population consisting mostly of peasants into modern citizens (Redfield, 1956:42–64; Weber, 1982: *passim*). Prominent among these were churches, schools, political parties, and the market, and, I would add, and effective judiciary and secure private property. In an hour-long address it is, of course, impossible to discuss to what extent such institutions were absent or underdeveloped in Russia, and what effect this had on the country's political culture (Pipes, 1990:110–13). I shall, therefore, deal with them selectively, using England as my standard.

In early modern England, the concept of nationhood was intimately connected with the sense of civil and legal rights. A community can tolerate inequalities of wealth, social status and even political rights, but not unequal treatment of life and property. Members of a community — and a nation is a community — must feel that they receive the same treatment from justice, that they can be as confident of the security of their person and belongings as the mightiest and richest — or else they are without a bond to hold them together. Inequalities in this respect create a gulf among members of a society which renders coalescence into a community impossible.

The evolution of law is closely connected with the institution of property because historically civil suits have mainly concerned property claims and disputes: in England, it is said, as late as the beginning of the seventeenth century, lawsuits were almost exclusively preoccupied with this issue (Pound, 1931:53). This is not surprising in view of recent researches which indicate the remarkably early development of private land ownership in England. As Alan MacFarlane has demonstrated, already in the thirteenth century England knew a great deal of individual landed property which the owners, women included, could dispose of at will. Even much tenant land was held in *de facto* ownership (MacFarlane, 1978).

The prevalence of private property in the main productive asset, agricultural land, and the protection extended to it by the courts, provided England with an economic and judiciary system that helped forge the majority of inhabitants into a working community — a community of individuals who, in addition to speaking the same language and professing the same faith, enjoyed the same civil rights. And from this sense of community grew, no later than the sixteenth century, pride in nationhood.

In Russia, these prerequisites were missing

To begin with private property. The medieval Russian principalities did know property in land, for both nobles and commoners, but by the time the centralized Russian state came into being in the late fifteenth century — at the same time when the Tudors ascended the throne — it was effectively wiped out. The tsars of Moscow, beginning with Ivan III, insisted on regarding all the land of their realm as their own. They dispossessed the noble proprietors by a variety of violent means, including mass deportations, and replaced them with servitors who held the land as royal fiefs, conditional on proper service to the tsar. From then until the end of the eighteenth century, all secular landowners in Russia were what in England was known as "tenants in chief," that is, tenants holding land directly of the sovereign. The Russian Crown also took into the state treasury for distribution to servitors the so-called "black lands," freeholds tilled by independent peasants. In sixteenth and seventeenth century Russia, ownership of land was, for all practical purposes, the monopoly of the Crown (Pipes, 1994:524–30).

This meant that one basic ingredient of national solidarity was missing: the inhabitants of Russia were not linked by a common concern for their private landed possessions. It further meant that legal institutions were weakly developed since all disputes over land, so critical to the development of the judiciary in England, were resolved in the tsarist chanceries.

But the single most important factor impeding the emergence of a national sense among Russians was surely serfdom. Human bond-

139

age, which disappeared in England by the fourteenth century, was only introduced in Muscovite Russia at the end of the sixteenth: it survived for over two and half centuries, into the age of the railroad and telegraph. This was not, as in the United States or the British Empire, servitude of a captive minority from a different race, but of a majority from the same race and origin as its masters. On the eve of serf emancipation in 1861, in the central provinces of the Russian Empire, populated by Great Russians, the incidence of serfdom ranged from 50 to 70 percent. The vast majority of today's Russians are direct descendants of serfs of the crown or the nobility.

The status of the serf differed in several important respects from that of a slave but the two had in common a complete absence of legal rights. Like the slave, the serf could own no property: all his personal effects belonged to the landlord. He could not testify in court. He could not even lodge complaints against his master to the authorities. The master could punish him at as he saw fit, exile him to Siberia or send him to the army, marry him against his will, and even sell him.

The serf was thus entirely outside the *pays légal*: his only protection lay in custom, which his master could violate only at a certain risk to himself, and in a highly refined spirit of cunning. Naturally, a person in this status could feel no common bond with those who, for all practical purposes, owned him. How hard it is to integrate people raised in such conditions over generations is evident in the United States where notwithstanding the abolition of slavery in 1865 and the various governmental and judiciary steps taken since the 1950's to assure the descendants of the slaves of genuine equality, the black population still feels itself and is widely perceived to be a community apart.

Hence it is not surprising that even after the Emancipation Edict of 1861, the Russian peasant felt part neither of the Russian state nor the nation. Leo Tolstoy wrote on this subject as follows:

> I have never heard any expression of patriotic sentiments from the people, but, on the contrary, I have constantly heard the most serious and respectable men from among the people give utterance to the most absolute indifference or even contempt for every manifestation of patriotism (Tolstoy, 1956:52).

These "people", by which are meant peasants, constituted in Russia until sixty years ago fully 80 percent of the population. They felt alienated alike from the government and the westernized social elite, including the radical intelligentsia which believed itself committed to their welfare. They lived in a world of their own, a world which had more in common with that of primitive man than with nineteenth or twentieth century western culture, dominant among the Russian elite. Lenin's ambitious plans to westernize Russia by brutal crash methods ultimately broke against the stubborn resistance of the peasantry whom, toward the end of his life, embittered by the sense of failure, he cursed as Asiatic savages.

Obviously, with four-fifths of Russia's population estranged from the political, economic and social elite, no sense of nationhood could emerge. Russia, until well into the nineteenth century, offered the majority of her population neither guarantees of property nor protection of law, such as England had known since the Middle Ages. Society was structured along rather rigid caste lines. One's status, and the obligations that went with them, were determined by inscription in the rolls of either the gentry, or the clergy, or the tax-paying estate, and little else but territorial proximity connected the three groups. The only communities the peasants knew were small ones, embracing their neighbors, with whom they formed the *mir* or *obshchina*. Their horizon stopped at the boundaries of the *volost'*, the smallest rural administrative unit.

Nor did Russia have self-governing cities which in medieval Western Europe gave birth to civil and political liberties: as its etymology indicates, citizenship originated in the *cité*. Russia, of course, had urban settlements, but these were primarily administrative centers and military outposts, the inhabitants of which enjoyed no special rights but only such duties as their respective estate affiliation carried with it.

Next, let us turn political parties and their corollary, representative institutions, the principal agents of politization. The outstanding fact is that until 1906 Russia was ruled autocratically: she had neither a constitution nor a legislature, nor even a cabinet of ministers. Political parties were strictly forbidden and all attempts to organize them, severely punished. Such political activities as took place in defiance of the autocracy, therefore, had to assume illegal forms, which, in the case of radical elements, verged on the criminal.

The result was that Russians were deprived of the opportunity to become politicized, that is to acquire the conviction that political institutions and practices had direct bearing on their lives: in other words, that they mattered one way or another. For just as the possession of property brings people in contact with the law, so the right to organize parties and to vote gives meaning to political allegiance. For the majority of Russians living under an autocratic regime, the state meant the person of the tsar, God's vicar on earth and the owner of Russia. Russia's historic development subsequent to the abolition of tsardom only deepened this alienation from politics, since under the Bolsheviks independent political activity was even more savagely persecuted than under the tsars and voting became a meaningless ritual. Is it surprising that Russians are political fatalists, who feel that they can no more influence politics than change the climate?

What a difference from England! While the English parliament until the late nineteenth century was chosen on a restricted franchise, and, for a time, limited its membership to persons with substantial income, it was from the earliest a symbol of national liberty. From the time the English state came into existence, kings could impose direct taxes only with the consent of the House of Commons. It was also tradition that every new law required parliamentary sanction. Writing in the middle of the fifteenth century, Sir John Fortescue in his *In Praise of the Laws of England* singled out parliamentary authority over taxation as the foundation of English liberty and glorified his country above all others for prohibiting kings from legislating without authorization of the Commons. By 1610 it was formally established in England that the locus of sovereignty was neither the king nor "the king-in-council" but "the king-in-parliament." There can be little doubt that this perception of the state as a partnership of the Crown and its subjects, as represented by parliament, played a crucial role in consolidating the English nation: for whenever kings tried to overstep their customary authority and rule on their own, they met with parliamentary resistance backed by popular support. Thus the growing might of parliament contributed to and accompanied the growing sense of national unity.

As a result of the above mentioned factors, positive as well as negative, such patriotic sentiments as succeeded in gaining a foothold in Russia — they emerged rather late, mainly in the nineteenth century — were confined to the small educated minority. For members of the Imperial Establishment as well as conservative intellectuals, it derived from pride in Russia's vastness and military might. An important factor in the collapse of tsarism in 1917 was the anger of the conservatives over the humiliations suffered by the Russian Armies in World War I and the loss of the extensive and rich western provinces to German occupation. It was the conservative, nationalistic assault on the monarchy for mismanagement of the war that opened the floodgates of rebellion first to the liberals and then the radicals.

As for the intelligentsia, it lived very much in limbo, isolated equally from the Establishment and the mass of the population. Its patriotism was a compound of resentment, disgust, and boundless hope. They resented the West, even as they admired it, because they felt inferior to it. They were disgusted with the present condition of their country even as they entertained unlimited hopes for it in the future. They were just as alienated from the population at large as that population was estranged from them. When they spoke of serving the "people", the radical intellectuals meant not the Russians as they actually were but as they believed they should be and would be after being liberated from oppression and ignorance. This attitude found the clearest expression in the doctrines of the People's Will and its successor, the Bolshevik Party, which construed the will of the people to be what, in those parties' leaders' judgement, was good for them.

While they loved their country and gloried in its literature, by and large, the intelligentsia did not take pride in Russia as she actually was and at the decisive moment in 1917, when her destiny was being decided, failed to rally to defend her. In the 1930's they paid for this passivity with their lives.

Implications for the future

Such has been the record of Russian national consciousness until now. We may next ask what does this record portend for the future now that Russia has finally gained the opportunity of creating a law-abiding and democratic society? Will the absence of strong national sentiments inhibit the development of Russia or will the new conditions finally make it possible for these sentiments to emerge? And if they do emerge, will they express themselves in imperialism and xenophobia or patriotism?

To begin with, some relevant facts. With 82 percent of her inhabitants consisting of Great Russians, Russia is today, for the first time since the sixteenth century, a national state rather than an empire. Moreover, the proportion of Great Russians is steadily growing because of the continuing influx from the ex-Soviet republics, especially Inner Asia. The ethnic minorities of the Russian Federation are made up of small groups: only the Tatars and Bashkirs constitute sizeable minorities, and even they, in their own autonomous republics, are outnumbered by Russians. The one and a half million Volga Tatars represent less than half the population of the Tatar republic. As for the Bashkirs, Soviet Russification policies, combined with famines, have done their work: today there are one-third fewer Bashkirs than there were one hundred years ago. The one million Bashkirs residing in the Bashkir Autonomous Republic represent but one-quarter of the republic's population. Both these Turkic republics are surrounded by ethnic Russian lands. Moreover, many of the non-Russians inhabiting the Russian Federation — notably, the Jews and Ukrainians — are culturally and linguistically Russified. In sum, the Russians now have their own national state and the traditional confusion between nation-state and empire, one of the major obstacles to the emergence of nationalism, no longer obtains.

Unfortunately, there is no evidence as yet that this changed reality has had much influence on the way Russians think and feel. It is striking that during the political turmoil of the recent past, neither the communists, nor the nationalists, nor the democrats have appealed to patriotic sentiments. Die-hard communists have centered their propaganda on the argument that in the old days Russia had been a mighty and feared super-power, capable of protecting her citizens and guaranteeing them satisfaction of their basic needs, whereas today, under democracy, it is held in contempt and neglects its people. The nationalists, for their part, are appealing to xenophobia, inciting now against the West, now against specific minorities such as the Caucasians and Jews. This, perhaps, was to be expected. Puzzling is the fact that the democrats have also not had recourse to patriotic slogans. This failure can be explained either by the conviction that such slogans would once again, as during the Civil War, fall on deaf ears, or else by the opinion, which some Russian democrats share, that nationalism spells xenophobia and hence is inimical to democracy. I have heard one Russian intellectual with an impeccable liberal and pro-Western record declare that if forced to choose between nationalism and imperialism, she would, without hesitation, opt for the latter.

Regrettably, Russian reformers have recently been increasingly keen on reconstituting the vanished empire — as if to demonstrate that mastering others is easier than mastering oneself. President Yeltsin and his minister of foreign affairs have more than once given utterance to imperial aspirations. Especially disturbing is the insinuation that the Russian government has responsibility for the security and well-being of ethnic Russians who happen to be citizens of sovereign states that once had been part of the Soviet Union: a claim reminiscent of Hitler's insistence that the Third Reich had the duty to intervene in the Sudetenland to protect ethnic Germans from non-existent Czech persecution. Pressure is being exerted on the ex-Soviet republics to re-merge with Russia. The pressure so far has been mainly economic, but in the instance of Georgia it has also involved deliberate provocation of ethnic strife which ended only when Russian troops were invited to intervene. (In this context, I do not refer to Russian military action in Chechnia, which however brutal, concerned a region that is part of the Russian Federation: failure to prevent it from seceding would have further discredited democracy in the eyes of Russians for whom defense of the homeland is a basic criterion of government legitimacy). In the case of Latvia and Estonia, Moscow has demanded that the Russian minority, consisting mostly of colonists brought in by the conquering imperial power, be given the right to vote. All these are troublesome symptoms of a lingering imperialist mentality.

They are troublesome for two reasons

Any effort to reconstitute the Russian Empire as a political and military entity will certainly require the use of force. Just how strong the resistance of the minorities can be to attempts at reintegration was recently demonstrated in tiny Chechnia. One can expect it to be no less fierce and even more effective in the Ukraine, Central Asia, and the Baltic countries. A protracted military conflict along the borders of Russia would inevitably undermine the precarious democracy in that country. Pressures would be exerted on the political opposition and the media to support the government and its armed forces on the grounds that criticism aids and abets the enemy. The political repercussions of the recent events in Chechnia certainly lend substance to such fears.

No less important are the potential effects of an imperial drive on Russia's political culture. Imperialism will once again abort the development of healthy national sentiments by equating patriotism with xenophobia. Once again, Russian national self-consciousness will dissolve in great power consciousness; once again the Russian will see himself first and foremost as the subject of a large, mighty empire, and only secondarily as an ethnic Russian — the master of other nations rather than member of his own. This, too, will be harmful to the cause of democracy.

It is quite possible that the nation-state is a transient phenomenon which in time will yield to other forms of allegiance. Europe has had experience with such transformation once before. After the barbarian tribes had conquered the Roman Empire and settled in the midst of Rome's one-time subjects, they enforced not the laws of the land but their own, tribal laws: thus Franks were judged by Frankish codes, and Visigoths by Visigothic ones. Gradually, however, they merged with the other inhabitants of their territory, with the result that the territorial principle triumphed over the tribal or ethnic one. This development provided the basis for the emergence of the modern European state. It may recur. In some respects it is already recurring in contemporary Western Europe with the formation of a transnational union which allows the free flow of people, goods, and capital. Here, territorial allegiances, as happened one thousand years ago, are once again superseding ethnic allegiances.

Nevertheless, it is difficult to see how such transnational units can be constituted before their component elements, namely nations, are fully shaped. It seems that the nation-state, although neither the beginning nor the end of the historical process of state formation, is a necessary stage through which peoples have to pass before being ready for supranational arrangements.

Russia faces this prospect with great handicaps. Her history has not been favorable to the formation of a sense of national cohesion, and her ethnic identity is poorly developed, ever ready to express itself in xenophobia and imperialism. She faces an arduous process of nation-making. For this she needs, above all, democracy and guarantees of human rights and private property. The failure to take advantage of a unique opportunity to develop a strong sense of ethnic cohesion, of communality, can have only two consequences, both of them tragic: anarchy and civil war, or revived despotism and renewed aggression.

We, in the West, who are putting nationalism behind us, must bear in mind that the historical clock runs differently in different parts of the world. From the point of view of ethnic cohesion, Russia finds herself approximately where England stood in the late Middle Ages. What is regressive in Western countries, is progressive in Russia and other regions of the world which have not yet developed viable nation-states.

Notes

1. On this subject see the opening chapter of Greenfeld (1992).

References

Greenfeld, L. (1992), *Nationalism: Five Roads to Modernity*, Cambridge, Mass: Harvard University Press.

Kristof, L.K.D. (1968), "The Russian Image of Russia", in Charles A. Fisher (ed.), *Essays in Political Geography*, pp. 345–387, London: Methuen and Company Limited.

MacFarlane, A. (1978), *The Origins of English Individualism: the Family, Property and Social Transition*, Oxford: Blackwell Press.

Pipes, R. (1990), *The Russian Revolution*, New York: Alfred A. Knopf.

Pipes, R. (1994), "Was there private property in Muscovite Russia?", *Slavic Review*, Summer Issue, 1994: 524–30.

Pound, R, (1931), in *Encyclopaedia of the Social Sciences*, IV. New York: The MacMillan Company.

Redfield, R. (1956), *Peasant Society and Culture*, Chicago-London: University of Chicago Press.

Tolstoy, L. (1956), "Khristianstvo i patriotizm", in *Polnoe sobranie sochinenii*, Vol. 39. Moscow: Gosudarstvennoe Izdatel'stvo.

Weber, E. (1976), *Peasants into Frenchmen*, Stanford: Stanford University Press.

by Alan S Milward,
London School of Economics
and Political Science

The Frontier of National Sovereignty

Now that Sweden has joined the European Union seems a particularly appropriate moment to ask what exactly is the nature of the
organisation which it has joined. Is the European Union, as so many
of its more ardent supporters believe, the inevitable future for each
separate European state? Swedish membership gives the question
particular emphasis, because when the European Communities, as
they then were, were created in the 1950s, Sweden rejected the
idea of membership as an infringement of its national right to
maintain the long-cherished principle of neutrality. Not only
that, but neither the European Economic Community nor the
American government which promoted and supported it wanted
Sweden as a member (af Malmborg, 1994).

The issue only came forward for serious debate in Sweden in
late 1961, with the United Kingdom's first, rejected application for
membership. It took Tage Erlander's government only two months
to decide that Sweden could not follow the United Kingdom into
the EEC, in spite of the commercial disadvantages of not doing so.
But had the decision gone the other way, Sweden would still not
have been able to join. The six member-states of the EEC in 1961

refused to contemplate a neutral member.[1] The American Under Secretary of State responsible for European Affairs, George Ball, quite explicitly refused even to help a Swedish application for some form of commercial association with the EEC. For Ball, Sweden was a free rider on the European state system.[2] Its long neutrality, he thought, was but a series of lucky historical chances. The western world must present a unified policy response to Khrushchev's Soviet Union. Swedish membership of the EEC would make that impossible. This was not mere power politics; Ball's opinion coincided with, and may even have been formed by, that of European federalists like Monnet, Kohnstamm and Hallstein. They too were actively opposed to Sweden's joining the European Community with the United Kingdom.

Where neutrality for the Swedish government was a fundamental expression of national sovereignty, for European federalists and their friends in Washington it was an anachronistic and doomed assertion of an independence of national policy in an area where independence was no longer possible. The independent defence of the nation state's territory was, they argued, by 1961 beyond the economic means of all but the two superpowers. Sweden's national defence policy weakened the western world because Sweden's national territory in reality could, in any war that was actually envisaged, only be defended by NATO, which in effect meant by the USA. It was at everyone else's expense that Sweden was refusing to face its ineluctable destiny.

The defence of its citizens and its territory has probably been the primary function of the nation-state in history. It is on its frontier that its sovereignty is defended and it is sovereignty that frontiers demarcate. If effective national defence by the nation alone had indeed been impossible, something which most European countries in 1961 would have as vigorously refuted as did General de Gaulle, Sweden's position would indeed have been that of a free-rider. But the argument that national defence had become impossible for the nation-state takes its place in a succession of similar arguments about other aspects of the activities of nations, all of which have, at least so far, proved great exaggerations.

There exists a considerable body of theory whose implication is that the nation-state must inevitably be rendered functionally inadequate by the process of modern economic development. The argument that it can only fully carry out its extended range of twentieth-century functions by sacrificing some part of its separate national policy-making capacity is heavily influenced by theoretical analyses of the state as a functional political and administrative unit. It has been common in economic theory since the late eighteenth century for example to regard the state as a barrier to the maximisation of income or other satisfactions. Its frontiers and tax collectors restrict the size and limit the perfection of markets. In a theoretical world without frontiers and national taxes satisfactions would be more efficiently maximised. This was not just a capitalist argument. Marx, even more than other economists, saw the nation-state as the captive creation of socio-economic interest groups who until the full course of capitalist economic development had been run would impede the attainment of that world of liberty in which the state would finally be transformed into an organisation of universal benevolence. From the mid-nineteenth century to now economists and other commentators have forecast that the course of international economic development will eventually render the state's frontiers meaningless and its functionaries powerless.

The intervention of the railway train gave rise to the first outburst of such forecasts in the 1850s. It took a fast passenger train only forty minutes to traverse the territory of some of the German states. Since the intention of the constructors was frequently to link two major cities, neither of which was in the state's territory, the opposition between the German states' own survival as functional entities and technological innovation was plain. The British general staff identified the same problem when they forbade the building of a railway tunnel between France and Britain on the grounds that it would make the national frontier less defensible. The invention of the fast-flying aircraft has raised this opposition in starker clarity, for most modern aircraft traverse a country the size of Belgium in less time than it took the train to traverse Saxony. Spy satellites, of course, traverse it even more quickly. The nation-state's response, no less strongly in Europe than elsewhere, has been to nationalise the sky, its "air-space" (Naveau, 1989).

Coupled with technological innovation in transport has come the greater ease and more rapid growth of foreign trade. When European integration first became a serious issue in 1950 rich countries like Belgium and the Netherlands already depended on foreign trade in commodities for more than a third of their national income. The trend it was argued, was for countries to become so increasingly dependent on both exports and imports to satisfy the wants of incomes of their citizens that the growth of foreign trade would dissolve the capacity of the state to formulate its own economic policies. With the expansion of international capital flows between states in the mid-nineteenth century, much of which was at first related to the new railway technology, the levels of economic interdependence increased. Even before the liberalisation of trade and of capital movements in the 1960s about 60 per cent of Dutch national income was earned outside the frontiers of the Netherlands, and for every western European country there has been a steep increase in the percentage of national income so earned since 1958. The rise to dominance in international commodity trade of the multinational enterprise has also been seen as a final indication of the inadequacy of the nation-state in the face of modern economic development to assert any meaningful concept of national sovereignty. The concept of "national income" on which that great nationalist Keynes relied as one conceptual basis of his economics, has ceased, it is commonly said, to have the meaning he gave to it; it is no longer national. National general elections will not therefore be won by the economic defence of the national frontier. On the contrary, they will be won by minimising the controls over goods and capital on that frontier, because, to take but one example, citizens would prefer to enjoy their "national" pension on the Costa Brava in part of the property development in which they have invested their life-cycle's savings, rather than in Umeå or Aberdeen.

Much of the political theory of European integration has tried to encapsulate the weakening of the idea of the national frontier as the line of transition from one sovereignty to another. In the 1950s

Karl Deutsch based his analyses of what he called "The North Atlantic Community" on the growing permeability of its frontiers, particularly to people and ideas (Merritt and Russett, 1981). The political circumstances of the Cold War tended, he implied, to generate a common stance in the west on the nature of political society and in such circumstances the frontiers were more permeable. This, he argued, was reflected in the sudden post-war proliferation of international organisations linking western European countries.

The ideas were vague, and like much political writing in the Cold War tended to support the objectives of American foreign policy, strongly in favour of some form of western European unity, and to play down the existence of dissent from the kind of consensual North Atlantic politics which Deutsch was describing. Furthermore, although the observation that the number of international organisations linking western European countries underwent a sudden proliferation from 1947 onwards was correct, it made little sense to see this as an aspect of European integration when the great majority of these organisations was in no sense integrationist. Most, like OEEC, were organisations in which fully sovereign states, as Sweden believed itself to be, met in a forum which was only cooperative and, like Sweden, intended to keep it that way. Nor was it the case that there was any demonstrable connection between this intensification of contacts at the governmental level and the intensification of contacts at a lower level. The greatest contribution by far to the increase in persons crossing western European frontiers was made up of tourists. Increasingly their most favoured destination was Spain, which was excluded from almost all the new international organisations and whose frontiers were still the least permeable in western Europe to the movement of goods, capital and ideas (Romero, 1994).

The proliferation of international forums was taken by other scholars as the outcome of a different process, but one which nevertheless drove the states towards integration. It was frequently argued that the nature of international contact between states had changed as the nature of the state itself had changed. In earlier periods, so writers like Haas argued, the contacts between states had been only on the level of "high" politics, the regulation of questions of war, peace and defence (Haas, 1964). As the extent of state intervention in and regulation of economic and other questions had grown, so, it was argued, had the need for states to regulate between themselves issues of "low" politics grown. As a consequence, it was claimed, international organisations where national bureaucrats could organise a national, functional solution to the problems which arose had grown. Integration was seen therefore as one response to the increasing range of functions which the state undertook. If we believe the state to exist only because of its capacity to carry out a range of functions for its citizens, it becomes a plausible explanation of the European Union that the increasing range and complexity of those functions will require trans-frontier functional cooperation to carry them out, or to carry them out better.

Of course, Sweden is the classic case of a nation-state whose functions expanded into an intimate range of social and personal activity. It has only joined the European Union as the state has begun to withdraw from some of those functions. The profound difficulty which functionalist theories of this kind have in explaining the European Communities and the European Union is that they only explain why states should cooperate in carrying out their functions. They do not explain why they should surrender elements of national sovereignty, as they have done in the Community and may do in the Union. They do not explain why integration was the only possible response to this change in the functions of the state, nor indeed why it was the consequence of the growing importance of a lower-level functionalism at the expense of higher-level grand politics.

Most studies have shown that in so far as the widening range of functions which the state undertook did require some action beyond its borders in order to make them effective, a sufficient level of effectiveness could often be attained by the same type of merely cooperative action which had developed in the nineteenth century. The regulation of international road transport for example needed nothing more complicated than the international railway "clearing-houses" of the nineteenth century or than the cooperative agreements on postal services of the 1860s. And where anything more complicated was required the problems almost always proved incapable of being settled at the merely functional level. They were then elevated by national governments to the "high" political level. This was the case, for example, with the international regulation of air transport. It seems evident therefore that the links between the growing policy ambitions and domestic powers of twentieth-century states and the process of European integration are explained in too simple a form by this functionalist argument. In exactly what circumstance would the state's growing interventionism lead to European integration, rather than just cooperation? Without an answer to that question it could certainly not be argued that European integration is the inevitable historical goal.

This has been largely accepted by neo-functionalist theorists. They, however, have undiminished faith in functional bureaucracies as an expression of the rational mind, as well as a teleological faith in the surrender of the state's national sovereignty as a rational response to the path of economic development. From the beginnings of the European Communities the crucial process, for neo-functionalists, has been that of "spillover". One institutionalised bureaucratic solution to a functional problem, no matter what the motive for the solution, will lead to another. Thus, the European Single Act in creating a unified market led, functionally, to the clauses in the Treaty of Maastricht setting out the goal of a monetary union, because one unified market could function only with one unified currency (Pryce and Wessels, 1987). It is inherently difficult to test such a theory other than by detailed historical examination, and because of the secrecy still so severely enforced by the allegedly weakening national governments, most detailed historical examination is not possible after 1964, at the latest. All that can be said is that up to 1964 the detailed history of European integration has not recorded one single instance of spillover.[3]

What do historians say which might actually help us to answer the questions with which we started? Why have European states, now including Sweden, surrendered parts of their long-cherished national sovereignty? If the reasons do not self-evidently lie in the nature of economic and technological development, or in the implementation of those functions which electors require from their governments, what other explanations are on offer?

One prime cause of European integration, all historians are agreed, has been the "German problem", the post-war division of Germany and the need to integrate West Germany into the western political framework. (Herbst, Bührer and Sowade, 1990, But the point has been made by every general history of the federal Republic.) The Treaties of Paris and Rome, in this view, had immediate, chronologically specific political and diplomatic causes. The Treaties provided both a practical basis and an ideological cement for the Franco-German alliance. They satisfied American demands that western Europe should serve as a coherent defensive bulwark of the United States and eliminated the most serious security problem *within* the western world.

Beyond that strong scholarly agreement, there has developed an increasing tendency to see the Treaties of Paris and Rome, not as landmarks in the progressive weakening of the nation-state but as landmarks in its post-war reassertion. This is much more disputed territory, but practically no historians accept the argument that, at least before 1964 in which year their accurate knowledge expires, the nation-state became weaker. And some, including myself, now believe that states surrendered parts of their national sovereignties to the European Communities in order to strengthen the nation-state system (Milward, 1993).[4]

Studies of policy-formulation in the post-war western European state reveal the crucial importance of certain policies to the reassertion of the nation-state as the basic political organisational unit in Europe after its disastrous experiences in 1929–32 and in 1939–44. Over a brief period of time most European states had failed in the primary tasks which their citizens expected them to fulfil, to provide economic and personal security and to defend their frontiers. The increases in unemployment and the falls in personal income of 1929–32, in some cases lasting much longer, were followed by invasion and collapse over the period 1939–44. The reaction in almost all states was to search for new policies which would regain the allegiance of citizens. They found them in a strikingly similar set of policies; the search for growth, the drive to "modernisation", the pursuit of high employment, the supplementation of agricultural incomes, and the welfare state.

Of this policy mix, some policies were better advanced through an international framework than solely within the confines of the nation-state. This was obviously so, for instance, with policies of agricultural income support. Inevitably, the subsidisation of agricultural production induced output surpluses, even in Sweden where alone in Western Europe genuine efforts were made to avoid this outcome (Duchêne, Szczepanik and Legg, 1985). The disposal of overpriced food surpluses clearly required some form of international framework, unless they were to be simply destroyed or given away, and already from 1949 the French and Dutch governments were exploring the possibilities of a general West European agreement to provide a market for these surpluses, which would have been too expensive to sell, other than at a continuous substantial loss to the exchequer, elsewhere in the world (Noël, 1988).

The international framework of interdependence which western European states inherited from the pre-war world was by no means satisfactory for advancing all these policies. It could be described as an agreement on the principles of economic interdependence which had increasingly turned into disagreement and a renunciation of some of these principles after 1929. Some of the new policies could be advanced through this framework as it was inherited. Others could not, and were more effectively advanced and supported through a new concept, integration. The close similarity between the domestic policies which emerged generally in the period after 1945 in western Europe meant that integration was a path which could be chosen with reasonable hopes of agreement and success on several occasions. The choice between the inherited order, interdependence, and the new concept, integration, depended firstly, however, on the appropriateness of either concept to advance and strengthen particular domestic policy choices.

To take an example where integration failed to serve this purpose, we might focus on the migration of people, which Deutsch saw as a cause of integration. It seemed in the period 1945–55 to

Italian governments that any solution to the problems of unemployment and underdevelopment in Italy required a high rate of emigration. It was soon clear that the emerging concept of integration would provide no help with that problem. During the negotiations for the European Coal and Steel Community the other five countries took a very restrictive view of the freedom of movement of labour. Where Deutsch's college professors crossed European frontiers in blithe liberty, Europe's coal miners and steel workers could only do so if they had first secured an offer of employment in exactly the specialised trade they were already pursuing. The Treaty of Rome, for all its ringing words, did no better in this respect than the Treaty of Paris, so that the EEC labour market was much more restricted and controlled by national immigration laws than the Nordic Labour Market, which was in no way intended to lead to a political union. Italy solved its problems within the inherited framework of interdependence; Italians migrated to all regions of the world, as they had done since the mid-nineteenth century, and not especially within the European Communities.

To take an example where the inherited framework of interdependence could not serve the objectives of national reassertion and where something new was needed, we could turn to the connection between economic integration, growth and commercial policy. In an age when the growth of foreign trade appeared to explain the rate of growth of the national economy, and when winning national general elections was thought to depend on a high rate of economic growth, national policies sought to combine a high rate of growth of foreign trade with the effective protection of selected industrial sectors and also with agricultural protection.

The main protectionist instrument before 1929 had been national tariffs. The events of 1929–32 had shown that they were not adequately protective of new or of declining and uncompetitive industrial sectors unless they were so high as to severely restrict the expansion of trade. They called forth heavy retaliation, which could normally only be avoided in a complex pattern of international tariff bargaining. They were intimately linked in many countries to the parliamentary process, because in an age when parliamentary parties had not been as responsive to economic and social demands from the broad mass of citizens as they were after 1945 the national tariff rates could be adjusted as a way of forming a national consensus. Although the task of forming such a consensus was taken over by parliamentary parties after 1945, historic links to the parliamentary process, still visible in every American election, made tariffs a cumbersome and slow-moving device subject to widespread national debate. The alternative form of protectionism to which countries had resorted in the Great Depression, quota limitations on imports, although highly effective as a protectionist device had had the effect of driving down the volume of world trade in the 1930s and was unsuitable for a period when all governments sought trade expansion as an aid to economic growth.

In the immediate post-war period an increasing willingness to reduce tariffs by multilateral bargaining in western Europe always encountered protests from countries whose tariffs were already low, Sweden for example, that it was unfair to them because their tariffs too had to come down in proportion. Of the smaller countries only Austria and Norway were seriously trying to use tariffs as instruments of selective industrial policy. Any way forward which would effectively combine selective protection and trade expansion clearly needed to deal at least as much with non-tariff barriers as with tariffs. The OEEC trade liberalisation programme was an imperfect way of dealing with them. It was concerned only with the removal of quotas. Furthermore, as the programme of action within OEEC developed, it failed entirely to deal with the problem of quotas on agricultural trade.[5] Maintaining agricultural incomes had become a basic policy in the reassertion of national government.

An effective international solution was only found with the Treaty of Rome. The aspect of the treaty which has always been most stressed is that it guaranteed the progressive and orderly removal of tariffs between the six signatories. This is because the tariff union was seen by federalists and their allies as a step towards a political union. In fact this was one of the easiest aspects of the treaty to negotiate, because tariffs were coming to be regarded as an outmoded instrument for regulating trade between a small cluster of contiguous, highly industrialised, trade-dependent economies, all of whom sought trade expansion as a means to economic growth. Equally important was that the Treaty of Rome established a common set of working practices for regulating the new wider market by non-tariff barriers, leaving the common tariff as an instrument for bargaining against the rest of the world. It thus created the wider market that would stimulate the growth of foreign trade, while at the same time allowing the participants to regulate unwanted competition within the market by the same methods they had been using since 1945.

Having achieved satisfactory arrangements for industrial trade, the Treaty of Rome committed its signatories to solve the problem of quotas on agricultural trade and the disposal of their agricultural surpluses through a common agricultural policy which would systematise the rules of agricultural income support and the regulation of foreign trade in agricultural products, by centrally agreed and enforced rules on non-tariff barriers. By Europeanising their policies of agricultural income support nation-states were able to win the allegiance of the most disaffected group within the nation during the inter-war years, farmers. Their allegiance typically was given to the "governing party"; the Social Democrats in Sweden, the Christian Democrats in Germany and Italy (Tracy, 1982, is the best overall account of the politics of the Common Agricultural Policy).

The surrender of sovereignty in this case was a gain to the participant nation-states. It allowed them to substitute for the system of inter-dependence which, as far as foreign trade was concerned, depended on policy instruments which were clearly inadequate. In this light of course European integration was a response to changes in the nature and ambitions of the nation-state, which, although they were strengthened by the Cold War and the competition with the Communist system, did not depend only on the diplomatic circumstances of post-1945 Europe for their force.

The creation of the Coal, Iron and Steel Community fits neatly into both historical accounts of European integration. It was the substitute for the peace treaty with Germany that was not signed, and thus the start of the Franco-German alliance. But it was also a step in the reassertion of national policy. National plans in France to increase the total output of French steel as the basis of an industrial modernisation programme were incorporated in 1946 into the Plan for Modernisation and Re-equipment. They were dependent on a greater supply of German raw materials than France had obtained in the inter-war period. Once it proved impossible to guarantee this supply by occupation and exploitation, once an increase in output in the German economy became a priority for America and Britain, Monnet produced the European Coal, Iron and Steel Community in order to guarantee equal access to German coal resources to both countries. The intention was to make more realisable the national planning objective of rebuilding and modernising the economy, a direct programme for enhancing national strength.

If we turn to the state which entered the Coal, Iron and Steel Community most reluctantly, Belgium, we can see an equally strong national foundation for integration.[6] Coal was the largest industrial sector in the post-war Belgian economy, measured either by numbers employed or by its contribution to the national income. Yet from 1929 onwards, except in the period of rearmament and war, most of this large industry had been uncompetitive internationally. It was preserved in the 1930s by protection through quotas on imports, by government subsidisation, and by low wages. Its problems were made much more acute in 1945 by the steep increases in wages and welfare in the Belgian economy, even steeper in coal than elsewhere. In the interests of employment and welfare policies the coal-mining sector was nevertheless preserved through the process of integration almost unchanged in size until 1958. The cost was high. In direct subsidies to the collieries alone, discounting the additional costs to Belgian industry of using Belgian coal when over more than half the time cheaper American coal would have been available, amounted to $141.4 million from February 1953, when the common market in coal opened, to the end of 1958. Of this direct subsidy, $50 million was paid by other Community members, most of it by Germany, a remarkable benefit of Europeanisation to set beside the income transfers that France received under the Common Agricultural Policy. Would Belgian taxpayers alone have been ready to contribute so much to preserve welfare and employment levels in the coal industry? The question has particular force because that part of the industry which could not have survived without European Community subsidisation was entirely francophone, whereas the northern Belgian mines, entirely Flemish-speaking, would have been all that was left of the industry. Would Flemish tax-payers have paid so much for Walloon industry without the Europeanisation of policy?

Until the end of the great European boom, in 1968, the process of nation-state building was supported by the process of integration and the European Communities came into existence as an additional support to the nation state. Without them, the post-1945 reassertion of the nation-state as the fundamental unit of European political organisation might well have been impossible. The European Communities were to the nation-state what the great flying buttresses are to gothic cathedrals; they helped to support an ever more complicated and ambitious edifice.

Whether there would be further integration depended, nevertheless, on who would control the nation-state and for what purposes. At any moment when there might occur a sufficient level of consensus on policy-choice a further stage of integration could be envisaged. Provided such a policy choice did not call into question the solution of the German problem, it did not necessarily have to conform to the pre-1968 model of the interventionist, centralising, welfare state. Theoretically, the Europeanisation of the privatisation of nationalised industries, or of the decentralisation of political power, is as possible a basis for integration in the European Union as were the policies that historians have analysed in the earlier period. It is this that raises serious, if as yet unanswered, questions about the validity of forecasting the future of the European state in the light of evidence from thirty years ago. If political theory has failed to explain the European Union, and therefore can hardly be regarded as a reliable guide to mapping the future of the nation-state, history has only explained integration in the past.

The western European nation-state of 1995 is not that of 1964. It is governed in the interests of social groups whose income over their life cycle has different origins from thirty years ago. Its voters are wealthier and older; the inflation that spelled full employment to their parents directly threatens their own status as rentiers. As for the farmers, they are too few for politicians to worry at night over their votes. The democratic political parties on which the reiteration of national governance was built in the 1950s no longer have the same relationship to electors as they did then. Then, they served as conduits through which the demands of electors for security reached the floors of national parliaments. Now, about a third of the representatives who electors send to parliament become at once members of the executive. The tendency now is for policies not to come from local grass roots, but to be handed down to local parties and to the electorate and then sold to them through media management; the conduits work in the reverse direction.

That, of course, may also reflect the fact that electors do not necessarily now see national parliaments and national governments as the sole possibility of satisfying their ambitions. Partly, that may be because the technological determinism which so repeatedly but mistakenly rang the death-knell of the nation-state now has better grounds for doing so. What the railway train, the aeroplane and the spy satellite failed to achieve, the computer might succeed in doing. It may have made the control of capital on the frontier impossible. And one consequence of that, given the changing structure of personal fortunes, may be that the revenue of the nation-state will become more uncertain. It is not improbable that direct taxation will disappear, because where it can be collected accurately its yield will be too small, and where its yield would be handsome it will be easily evaded by the internationalisation of income sources and holdings. And the logical consequence of that trend is that electors will be concerned to influence decisions in various loci of political power, perhaps even in the European Parliament.

In spite of its massive use of symbolism, and in spite of the advantages of military conscription, few European states, if any, retained the allegiance of most of their populations in the nineteenth century. About 150 million Europeans voluntarily changed the state in which they resided, between 1815 and 1914. Political and economic success did not alter that; the rate of emigration from the United Kingdom was exceptionally high throughout the whole period, and not only because of heavy emigration from Ireland. We may well come to think of the period 1945–68 as the only period of any length when the west European nation-state did successfully retain the allegiance of most of its citizens. Partly because doing so became too costly, but partly because citizens no longer wished to remain so confined once the deep post-war sentiments of insecurity had been allayed, multiple allegiances began to develop. It is only in Denmark, of the European Community member states on the eve of the Community's present expansion, that a majority of the population did not express, when asked by pollsters, an allegiance to the Community. The Union satisfies some of the life cycle economic aspirations of national voters that were satisfied before 1968 by national policies, and in some member-states, like the United Kingdom, it promises to satisfy them better than national government. All that stops the European Parliament now from playing some of the role of national parliaments after 1945 is that the member-states make sure that it has nothing to do. Where allegiance is so fickle, and where technological change strikes now at the very foundation of the nation-state — its ability to levy and collect taxation — it would be foolish to suppose that historians have had the last word.

Notes

1. U.S. National Archives, State Department Records, Office of Atlantic Political and Economic Affairs. Records Relating to United Kingdom Negotiations for Membership in the EEC, Box 1, Conversation between Russell Fessenden and Michel Gaudet, 26 October 1962.

2. Ibid., Box 3, Memorandum of lunch meeting of Under Secretary of State George Ball with Tage Erlander and Gunnar Lange, 27 January 1962.

3. Doubters may read the official history of the European Coal Iron and Steel Community, Spierenburg and Poidevin 1994.

4. See also the pertinent remarks in Hoffman 1995, *The European Sisyphus: Essays on Europe, 1964–1994*, Boulder, Westview Press.

5. Diebold 1952, impressive pioneering work though it is, is confined to the Marshall Plan period and gives too optimistic an account of the possibilities of simultaneously lowering tariffs and removing non-tariff barriers, perhaps because 1950 was the one year in which some progress was made in both directions. From late 1951 "trade liberalization", in the sense of removing both types of barrier, effectively ceased, eventually becoming concentrated in the OEEC programme on the task of the removal of import quotas. When that programme had reached the limits of acceptability states turned to other forms of regulating trade, of which the European Economic Community was the most comprehensive example.

6. Motivations on the French and German sides have been most recently set out by Gillingham 1991. For the Belgian motivations, Milward, 1993.

References

Diebold, W. Jnr. (1952), *Trade and Payments in Western Europe. A Study in Economic Cooperation 1947–51*, New York: Harper Brothers for the Council on Foreign Relations.

Duchêne, F. / Szczepanik, E. / Legg, W. (1985), *New Limits on European Agriculture. Politics and the Common Agricultural Policy*, London: Rowman and Allenheld, Croom Helm.

Gillingham, J. (1991), *Coal, Steel, and the Rebirth of Europe, 1945–1955. The Germans and French from Ruhr Conflict to Economic Community*, Cambridge: University Press.

Haas, E.B. (1964), *Beyond the Nation-State: Functionalism and International Organization*, Stanford: Stanford University Press.

Herbst, L. / Bührer, W. / Sowado, H. (1990), *Vom Marshallplan zur EWG. Die Eingliederung der Bundesrepublik Deutschland in die westliche Welt*, Munich: R. Oldenbourg Verlag.

Hoffman, S. (1995), *The European Sisyphus: Essays on Europe, 1964–1994*, Boulder: Westview Press.

af Malmborg, M. (1994), *Den Ståndaktiga Nationalstaten. Sverige och den västeuropeiska integrationen 1945–1959*, Lund: Lund University Press.

Naveau, J. (1989), *International Air Transport in a Changing World*, Brussels: Bruylart.

Merritt, R. and Russett, B.M. (eds.) (1981), *From National Development to Global Community: Essays in Honour of Karl W. Deutsch*, London: Allen and Unwin.

Milward, A. S. (1993), *The European Rescue of the Nation-State*, London: Routledge.

Noël, G. (1988), *Du Pool Vert à la Politique Agricole Commune. Les tentatives de Communauté Agricole Européenne entre 1945 et 1955*, Paris.

Romero, F. (1994), "Migration as an Issue in European Interdependence and Integration: The Case of Italy", in Milward, Alan S.; Lynch, Frances M. B.; et al., (1994), *The Frontier of National Sovereignty*, London: Routledge.

Pryce, R. and Wessels, W. (1987), "The Search for an Ever-Closer Union: A Framework for Analysis" in Pryce, Roy ed., *The Dynamics of European Union*, London: Croom Helm.

Spierenburg, D. and Poidevin, R. (1994), *The History of the High*

Authority of the Coal and Steel Community. Supranationality in Operation, London: Weidenfeld and Nicolson.

Tracy, M. (1982), *Agriculture in Western Europe. Challenge and Response 1880–1980,* London.

	The Strength of
by *Beate Kohler-Koch,*	Weakness:
Universität Mannheim,	The Transformation
Germany	of Governance in
	the EU*

Introduction

Reflecting on the transformation of governance in the European Union is motivated by the desire to know more about the actual changes that take place in "governing" and by the assumption that, bringing together concepts from international relations and integration theory with those currently debated in policy analysis and state theory, we may gain a better understanding of the nature of the transformation process.

The essay starts from the premises that the European Union is not an "emerging state" in the sense federalists have conceptualized the Community as a "not yet completed federation"(Hallstein, 1969).[1] It is rather assumed that the present state of a multi-tiered system of government will last at least for some more decades to come. After all, the Community as a political system "sui generis" has been with us now for more than 40 years and should not longer be conceptualized as a "system in transition". Furthermore, the distribution of allocative authorities to different levels of policy-making is not singular to the European Community. It is a phenomenon that is considered to spread and gain importance in the international system, too (Czempiel, 1981; Walker/Mendlovitz, 1990). Therefore it is of general interest to know more about the interpenetration of political systems and the effects this process will have on the future of governance.

There is already a well established academic discussion on who governs the European Community in terms of the relative power of the member-states as compared to that of the Community institutions, above all the Commission. Two opposing schools of thought dominate the stage and according to the dramaturgical rules of intellectual debate, political scientists have put their arguments (or at least the contributions of the opposing camp) in the framework of either neo-realist or neo-functionalist writings. From a neo-realistic perspective, "states are here to stay", they do and will also in the coming future dominate the political fate of Europe, whereas from a neo-functionalist point of view there is a "dissemination" of power and supranational institutions, in particular the Commission, will become central actors, transgressing national boundaries by forging influential transnational policy communities. I will not recall this long and lively debate, ranging from Hoffmann (1966) to Moravcsik (1991;1994) and from Haas (1958) to Sandholtz/Zysman (1989). My intention rather is to draw the attention of the reader to the limits of the present debate. Mixing domestic politics with international cooperation produces effects that go in two different dimensions and not just one: It does not only affect the distribution of power between different levels of government and between the public and the private, but it changes the nature of governance which prevails in the polity at the makro as well as the meso-level.

To develop my argument I will sketch the state of the management of interdependence which has brought about a very particular combination of losing and pooling of sovereignty in the European Union. The ensuing loss of control by member-state governments, however, did not curtail their capacity to act. Evidence is presented which puts into question the conventional assumption that the redistribution of authority between states and the Community is a zero-sum game. A similar lesson may be drawn from analyzing the development of the public-private relationship.

It will be argued that the very specific properties of the European polity as a multi-tier negotiating system allow national administrations as well as the Community institutions to turn their weakness into strength.

To conceptualize "governing" as an exchange relationship between distinct and independent actors determined by their relative bargaining power provides, however, only a limited understanding of the effects the political practise of the Community has on the transformation of governance in Europe. There are new forms of public-private interactions which have developed at the national and sub-national levels, and which run parallel to strategies of governing in the EC. Elements of a new mode of governance have evolved. These disseminate through system boundaries. Developments in the EC tend to promote a broader trend and give it direction not in the sense of implementing a preconceived masterplan, but by inducing actors of different kinds and at different levels to take advantage of opportunities offered. By taking it up in bits and pieces, actors contribute to a new "practise" and a new understanding of governance.

Integration today: The management of interdependence

From peaceful co-existence to common problem solving

The impetus of the post-war years which started the adventure of West-European integration certainly has been lost. It faded away not only due to changing external conditions but just because it has been so successful. Still it has to be remembered what it was about, because it entailed a concept that shaped material relations as well as our way of thinking about the organization of the "political". It was more than a technocratic enterprise in economics. It was aimed at the transformation of that anarchical system of states which had led the neighbouring states of Europe to get trapped by their security dilemma. The anarchy that had provoked the ruinous power struggle between self-assertive nation-states was to be transformed into a "society of states" (Bull, 1977) bound together by common norms and rules of behaviour. From the very beginning, integration was more than an economic strategy to open up markets by dismantling all the different types of trade barriers which had been built up during the depression and the war. It was a political programme to strengthen peace by ensuring cooperation which was supposed to increase welfare. "A Working Peace System" (Mitrany, 1943) was to be established which would build on parallel interests to be transformed into common expectations and efforts. The effectiveness of joint problem-solving was expected to lead from competition to cooperation and to ensure peaceful conflict-resolution in the long run.

The threat of the cold war has certainly strengthened West-European cooperation. Communism was a challenge to the concept of democracy and civil liberties prominent in the societies of the West. The pooling of resources to meet the diplomatic and military threat supported the belief that the "West" had many things in common: A common political history that had brought about a specific civic culture and congenial political and economic systems. The "imagined community" (Anderson, 1991) of the West thrived on the contrasting image it produced from its adversary. As soon as the adversary vanished, the integrating force of drawing and defending the boundary against the external threat weakened. But the Western Community did not fall into disarray because it is tied together through institutions. The common belief in the overarching principles and norms of joint problem-solving is firmly embedded in numerous international regimes and regional organizations. Both channel political behaviour, establish firm practices and consolidate mutual expectations.

The transformation process induced by the European Communities was slow, incremental, but effective. The policy of "negative integration" opened up markets and steadily increased the interconnectedness and mutual dependence of the formerly independent "national economies".[2] More important, interdependence was not just considered a fact of life, but has been welcomed as a beneficial state of affair. The image of the world one lives in has changed from a system of competing sovereign nation-states to that of a regional "Community" and a "Common Market". This holds true for elite as well as for public opinion; surveys show a declining but still overwhelming "diffuse" support for the European Community.[3] The member-states of the Community have moved well beyond the stage of open markets and peaceful coexistence. They have established an organisation for joint problem-solving and have agreed on strategies of "positive integration". When talking about governing in the European context, it is first of all the institutional system of the EU, and especially that of the EC, which comes into mind. But the institutional framing of political co-operation is only part of the picture. The substantial changes in economic exchange, and material interconnectedness, as well as shared conventional wisdoms and outlooks, are important context variables for supra-national governance.

Loosing and pooling of sovereignty

This is not the place to enter into the multifaceted debate about the nature of the European polity[4] nor to tell the long story of the successive inroads into the regulatory and allocative powers of the member-states in detail. The following chapter will briefly sketch the four different aspects that should be taken into account when trying to judge what integration has done to the autonomy and capacitiy of states to act. First, some evidence is presented to indicate in what respect member-states have lost sovereignty. The second point is that there are mechanisms at work which further restrict their autonomy despite the fact that the states still retain a high level of formal authority over many policy issues. The third aspect is the role member-states play in the institutional system of the Community and the fourth is about the relevance of market integration. A particular feature of European integration is that states have indeed lost formal authority over many policy issues, but only some has been transferred to the Community as a new decision-making authority, while other competences fell prey to the supremacy of market allocation.

Sovereignty is the supreme power over a body of politic, the freedom from external control, the right to discriminate in favour of one own's citizens. Being part of the European Community implies a loss of sovereignty in terms of being "independent of legal control by any other community". Member-states accepted the supremacy of EC-law, they have lost their right of autonomous decision-making and jurisdiction. Supranational law is executed by lower courts and EC regulations are implemented on the sub-national level without the expressed agreement or even the right to interfere by the central government of the state.[5] No member-state can limit benefits to its own citizens or insist that these are to be consumed within the state's own territory. National policy-makers are bound by law to give equal treatment to the citizens of other member-countries when residing within the borders of the state and even give them protection abroad. Most spectacular in terms of sovereign rights is that states have lost their right to close their borders to "foreigners" as long as they come from within the European Union (Leibfried, 1996).

From a legal point of view the member-states still have control over any further loss of sovereignty. The signatories to the treaties are "Herren der Verträge", which means that any formal transfer of competence has to be agreed upon by the governments and ratified according to the constitutional procedures of the member-states. The formal barriers against any shift of authority from the state to the Community level are high, but an expansive logic of integration has been written into the EEC-Treaty: The fundamental principle is that the Community may intervene whenever it is necessary to further the development of the Common Market. To control the ensuing tendencies towards a centralization of powers at Community level, the principle of subsidiarity has been inserted into the Treaty of Maastricht. This, however, is open to varied interpretations and the phrasing chosen rather sounds like an invitation for Community intervention.[6] (Dehousse, 1994)

There are numerous other factors which push and pull into the direction of an even closer integration. The "acquis communautaire", that is the extensive array of secondary EC-law which any state wanting to join the Union has to suscribe to, is de jure and de facto an entangling commitment. EC regulations will persist even if a national legislature will later decide otherwise; any alteration has to be agreed upon in the Community framework. As each follow-up decision will be path-dependent, the policy options may not be to the liking of a particular government. With the deepening of integration, however, the costs of non-decisions increase to such an amount that most actors rather accomodate with a second to best solution than with no decision taken at all. The logic of "spill-over" already described in early investigations of the European integration process (E. Haas, 1958) may not work in such an automatic way as later authors may have assumed, but it has a visible effect.

Those authors that call the period prior to the Single Market initiative the "dark ages" of integration history (Keohane/Hoffmann, 1991:8) are quite mistaken. It is undisputed that in the 70s and early 80s no formal transfer of authority took place. It was rather a time in which a gradual adjustment to the two enlargements of the Community and to the turbulence in international economic affairs took place. This, however, was done in close cooperation between member states and by deepening supranational policy collaboration. There was an incremental expansion of the scope of integration, as more and more policy areas became directly or indirectly connected to the Community. It was not just the persuasive strategy of the Commission derived from its institutional self-interest or the pro-integrative rulings of the European Court of Justice that contributed to deepening the integration, but the member states themselves, that considered joint problem-solving more attractive than preserving their national autonomy.

The dynamic of integration is bound to become even more salient due to the broadening of Community responsibilities agreed upon in the Maastricht Treaty. In the past, national policies were a viable alternative to an agreement at Community level. In the meantime "... the increasing reach of Community law makes it evermore difficult for Member States to conduct their own regulatory policies separately." (Dehousse, 1992:397). As a consequence, governments may accept a further transfer of authority to the Community if it supports the policies they want to pursue.

The most obvious feature of the European Community is that it is not just an international regime embodied in a regional organisation, but a political system with an institutional core which serves for the "joint exercise of pooled sovereignty".[7] It is widely acknowledged that governments play an eminent role in the policy-making of this system, even after Maastricht. Nevertheless, it is the collective weight of member-states that counts. Unanimity is required for decisions on key issues. The same is true if the Council wants to override the opinion of the European Parliament and the Commission.[8] Both institutions as well as the European Court of Justice are beyond the direct control of member-states and endowed by the treaties with special rights to give the "Community interest" a voice in EC policy-making. On many occasions, the Commission has effectively used its right of initiative to give the integration process new momentum, and the European Parliament has already used its new rights of co-operation and of co-decision to build "advocacy coalitions" (Sabatier) between Parliament, Commission and a Council majority.[9] The Court has proved to be a "motor of integration", ruling many times in favour of an expansive interpretation of the Community's authority as well as non-interference with the functioning of the common market (Everling, 1993; Zuleeg, 1994). The Community institutions are not strong in the sense that they are insulated from the reach of member-state governments. They rather gain strength from being so closely integrated in the whole process of exchange of information, negotiating and bargaining which finally leads to a Council decision. State governments seek to reign the European Community, but they have accepted that they have to share power with one another and with the Community institutions as well. Above all, they have acknowledged that the Community will not function without a joint commitment to a "shared exercise" of authority.

The limits of joint decision-making are quite obvious. Rules of unanimity preserve sovereignty rights, but these rights can only be used as a power to obstruct, and not as a capacity to shape a policy. Majority rule lowers the costs of cooperation which stem from the danger of non-decision; but for the opposing minority it means to be subdued to foreign will. Decisions taken by "consensus", that is coming to an agreement without taking a vote, have been introduced a long time before majority rule was expanded by the Single

European Act bridging the demand for control and for efficiency in policy-making. From a legal point of view, decisions taken by consensus do not encroach on state-sovereignty. In practice, however, norms of behaviour ensue which in an international setting that is characterized by institutionalized cooperation become binding, too.

Talking about sovereignty in terms of joint-decision-making only, would miss a major point, because integration has advanced in recent years especially through market integration. It went parallel to strengthening the collective decision-making authority of the Community. In total, however, the policy making capacity of the Community has not been strengthened as much as the capabilities of the member governments have declined. Partly this has been done on purpose because it was propagated over and again and finally became conventional wisdom that building up an economic community is above all a matter of deregulation and strengthening the market as a central institution of allocation.

The persistent strength of the state

Shifting targets and flexible adaptation

The statement that "in the European Union, both member state sovereignty and autonomy have diminished in tandem" (Leibfried/Pierson, 1995:22) expresses very well the conventional wisdom concerning the state of the state in European integration. But there is some irritating evidence which gives proof of an unrestricted vitality of national governments in shaping the social and economic environment according to their own individual preferences.

It should be recalled that the single market initiative was launched just because member-states had been so successful in undermining the Common Market rules with a multitude of nontariff barriers (Kommission 1985:5). Following the completion of the customs union at the end of the 60's, the history of the Common Market is a fascinating story of how ingeniously governments have invented new instruments to protect markets and keep off unwanted competition.

Decentralization of economic policies was one way to circumvent EC rules without obstructing openly the functioning of the Common Market. It was a response to the EC's increased control of state aids to implement conditions of equal competition throughout the Community.[10] By shifting state intervention from the national to the sub-national level EC interference could be avoided. Another strategy was to change policy concepts. This took place in particular in the field of industrial policy, especially with respect to research and development. Instead of supporting the innovative capacity of industry by subsidizing its research activities, state interventions took more subtle forms like those of public-private partnership in technology transfer. It was geared in particular to promote the innovative capacities of small and medium enterprises.[11]

The conclusions to be drawn from this kind of evidence are compelling: State interference did not vanish away. It changed its outer appearance, different instruments were applied, and other actors at different levels became responsible. Being member of the European Community did above all not curtail the spending for public activities at state level. It was widely assumed that the Common Market would cut public spending because state aid to private firms and other forms of state support run counter to EC law. Cross country comparisons, however, tell a different story.[12] State expenditures for industrial policies stayed as high in member-countries of the Community as in other OECD-countries. Some of the better off EC-countries like the (old) Federal Republic of Germany and the Netherlands which were comparatively less plagued with declining industries and underdeveloped regions, high rates of unemployment or other structural problems even increased their spending. State aid was not channeled any longer to firms directly, and public attention notibly shifted from declining sectors and firms in need towards other targets. Industrial policy became more future oriented and by this more in line with the strategy propagated by the Commission.

The level of expenditure as such tells little about the autonomy of a government to design the economic policy which suits its own national preferences. In a cross-country comparison (Corbey, 1993) the broad economic policy orientation of the core EC-member countries looked more or less the same. A closer analysis of particular policy areas like social policies, regional policies, and state subsidies, however, revealed that each member-state follows a particular path. On the one hand there was a variation in policy instruments, on the other hand quite diverging policy objectives had been pursued: export-promotion in the Irish case, strengthening regional infrastructure in the Federal Republic of Germany, support to small and medium sized firms given by the Dutch government.[13] Kurzer (1995:1) comes to the conclusion that there is a surprising "... lack of evidence of direct immediate constraints flowing from the structural changes wrought by the Single European Act and the Maastricht Treaty".[14]

The conclusions to be drawn from these empirical findings are twofold. First, losing formal authority is not synonymous with losing the actual capacity to act and to pursue individual political preferences. Therefore, it is not so much the transfer of regulatory competences and the loss of legislative prerogatives that should be taken as an indicator for the change in power of member-states.

Second, integration is not a zero-sum redistribution of actual political power. Member states have managed to pool their sovereignty for joint problem-solving and strived to adapt in a flexible manner to new context conditions. However, further empirical research would be needed to draw general conclusions about the kind of learning process that has been brought about by the restrictions imposed by Community law. Governments have been induced to redefine their policies and to open up new rooms for manoeuvre. They have done so "in the shadow of the market"; in other words after a period of competitive protectionism they shifted away from non-productive policy competition.

Taken together, the establishment of the Single Market and the treaty revisions of Maastricht certainly have curtailed the competence of member-governments to regulate markets and frame social conditions on their own territory. This weakness, however, may be turned into a source of strength. By agreeing on a particular path to be followed in EC policies, member governments can set the course for their own national policy.[15] They are able to commit external actors in order to mobilize internal support. It is a process of "institutionalized learning": governments are forced to stay flexible, to adapt instruments and strategies, and to shift targets in constant exchange with their internal and external environment. There is some evidence that living under such conditions of institutionalized interdependence has turned out to benefit particulary the smaller states. They have a long experience in adapting to external dependence, the public is more aware of having to live up to external challenges than in the larger member states. The joint management of interdependence is to them rather a gain than loss of autonomy. Furthermore, they enjoy the advantage of having well established practices of mobilizing internal forces in order to live well under changing external conditions and vice versa to make use of international or European restrictions to pursue a strategy of "flexible adaption" even against vested interests at home.

Escaping capture

Another argument deploring the gradual loss of state power follows a different notion of the "state". Not the fate of the nation-state — that is the discussion among international relations specialists — is what they are worrying about, but the changed relationship between the proponents of public and private interests. The authors are not so much concerned with a possible shift of power from one level of public policy-making to another than with an undue influence of private interests. Their concern is that the state as advocate of public interests is pushed back by well organized groups representing only partial interests.

There has been, indeed, an explosive growth of interest representation at the European level in recent years. New European federations of interest organizations have been established. In addition, a multitude of national associations, firm representatives, public interest representations etc. from inside and outside the Community have established liaison offices; professional lobbyists, i.e. private consultants specialized on European affairs have joined the crowd (Kohler-Koch, 1992, 1994a; Tiedemann, 1994). To draw the conclusion, however, that the mushrooming of interest representations may be equivalent to an undue influence of private interests on EC affairs seems to be premature. The growth of European interest representation may as well be interpreted as a consequence of the accelerated speed of integration that state governments have brought about since the launching of the Single Market Programme[16]. In trying to evaluate their political relevance, European interest groups have to be seen in relation to the power organized interest used to exercise within the individual member states. Neo-corporatist entrenchment rather than countervailing pluralist pressures, intricate clientelistic dependencies or even a situation of capture characterize the reality of public-private relationship at the national level. Shifting competences to the EC in many cases was welcomed by national administrations, because it liberated them from the suffocating embrace exercised by well organized interest groups like agricultural associations or by the uncontested demands of privileged "national champions" in industry.

Another argument which is less easily refuted is that the very properties of the EC political system invite partial interests to gain access and voice. Its most outstanding characteristics are the complexity of the political issues and the segmentation of the policy process as well as the fragmentation of the policy outcome produced.[17] If partial interests are able to take advantage of this state of affairs, "capture" would not fade away. Instead, a European dimension would be added to the existing dependence of policy makers on guidance given by interest groups.

Policy-making in the Community is at its heart a multilateral inter-bureaucratic negotiation marathon. Complexity results not so much from the material content of a problem to be regulated. Rather it is due to the fact that any problem that has to be dealt with also is a political issue. It is embedded in a particular economic and legal setting, benefits and preferences are attached to it. To get a deeper insight into the setting of the problem, to assess the rationality and acceptability of a policy pursued, the administration has to call in external advice. This is already true for any national administration. It is indispensible for the European administration which has to cope with 15 different types of legal regulations being part of different systems of law and legal practises, quite divergent economic situations and political preferences. There are good reasons to assume that in such a situation the exchange relations between public and private interests become unbalanced.

It seems to be a paradox that the administration should gain independence when it is to such a degree dependent on societal actors and in a setting where it has to share decision-making power with Community institutions and other member-states. That it can, however, recover autonomy and get a better chance to ward off unwanted demands has its roots in the very same institutional structure of policy-making in the EC, which is by nature a multi-tier negotiating system. Throughout the different phases of agenda-setting, policy formulation, implementation and evaluation, issues are dealt with sometimes even simultanously at the national, subnational and supranational level. Depending on the issue and the respective Community procedure of decision-making which has to be applied, the arena shifts from the national to the European level and back again. At the European level representatives of the national administrations are omni-present during the preparation of a Commission proposal as well as during the deliberations of the Council. Both national and Community representatives work together closely.[18] Private actors that want to take account of what is going on and make their voice heard have to be present at both the European and the national level. Arenas develop at both levels and change in importance in the course of the policy-making process. Rather than being neatly separated, these arenas are linked through transnational networks. These networks break up established national policy communities and form new transnational clusters. Private interest representatives are in a less advantageous situation than members of the administration. First, there is no longer "the" point of access for efficient lobbying. Instead multiple channels of contact have to be used at once in a most complicated two-level strategy. Second, it is in particular the Commission that enjoys a competitive advantage compared to any European coalition of interests. It is constituted as a Community body, whereas European interest associations are mostly federations. Even when they have been working together for more than thirty years up to this day they are still divided in clearly discernible subgroups.[19] Last but not least the Commission enjoys a privileged position as the "process manager" (Eichener, 1996).

But it is not only the Commission which profits from the particular characteristics of the European policy-making system. National administrators frequently make strategic use of the paradoxical logic of self-commitment in a "two-level game" (Putnam, 1988). At the European level a government may turn its weakness in terms of being dependent on domestic pressures into strength in terms of an improved position vis à vis its national negotiating partners. Having lost its autonomy as being part of the European policy-making system, it will turn this weakness into strength when dealing with domestic interests. It is the centrality of the administration in interlinked, multi-tier systems that makes them a central player.[20]

Once and again, the EC has been used as a plausible excuse for denying favours asked for or for giving up long established practices that in the course of events were no longer in line with political preferences, but hard to change against protected resistance by formerly privileged and still strong partners. Just because the national government was no longer exclusively in control, a change of policy was possible. In addition, the dynamics of multilateral negotiations in a multi-tier system force policy-makers to follow a strategy of temporary closure in terms of cutting off information to and consultation with external actors. In his empirical investigations on the European research and technology policy, Grande (1994) discovered a consistent pattern of sequential phases of closure and aperture. Such an alteration seems to be necessary in order to come to an agreement in a joint decision-making situation which involves a multitude of actors each of which is embedded in dense political networks (Grande, 1996). In a first preliminary phase the administration is open to external advice and demands. It is getting engaged in an issue network which supplies information, and channels demand and support. In a second phase of intra- and interadministrative negotiation, external actors are excluded and even have difficulties to follow the development of an issue. In a consecutive third phase, the administration again gets engaged in external consultations to improve its own proposal, test and assure its acceptability. At this stage it will be difficult to achieve any substantive changes, however, because the proposed policy is the product of a long and complicated process of internal agreements.

Such a proceeding is accepted because it is deemed necessary to avoid the "joint decision trap" (Scharpf, 1985) and because a non-decision at Community level is many times equivalent to no decision taken at all, with the consequence of the prolongation of an undesired situation. Grande has summarized his findings in what he calls "the paradox of weakness": it is not the strong state, but rather the state that has lost part of its autonomy to a supra-national decision-making system, which has gained the power to pursue its own (public) interest against strong pressures from societal actors.

Another argument has to do with the role governments play in the fragmented system of EC policy-making. The functional segmentation of the system allows for a strong representation of sector specific interests. Narrow interests find it easier to form trans-national coalitions, than more encompassing interest associations. If such a coalition is matched by the command of superior expert knowledge they might find it easy to influence the way in which a problem is defined and what is considered to be the apt problem-solving strategy. As soon, however, as matters become highly disputed, the debate is bound to move up from the level of inter-bureaucratic negotiations to higher levels within the administrative hierarchy. Controversial issues tend to get politicized, and political decisions then will be taken on political grounds. Actors involved will have to take a broader view because of their more encompassing responsibility and because the logic of politics will prevail as soon as an issue is drawn into the public debate. This still is the original domain of the national political systems, whereas the Community still is a "polity without politics" in the sense that partisan political battles are not fought transnationally by Europe wide political parties. In such a moment even interests that may be highly influential in their own limited domain have to step back.[21]

To draw a preliminary conclusion it can be said that some ana- lytical approaches are less promising than others. It certainly is misleading just to look for quantitative aspects, such as the number of interest groups, their growth rate over the years in terms of number as well as resources (Tiedemann, 1994). It is equally mis- leading to draw conclusions from just taking stock of policy processes at one level of the multi-tier European policy making system as was the case with many EC-policy studies. A close analysis of the interwoven multi-level and multilateral negotiating system gives a more pertinent view of those mechanisms which allow member state governments and administrations to gain autonomy and allow the Commission to play a central role as broker, enjoying a considerable room of manoeuvre to pursue interests of its own. In particular, if a controversial issue turns into a matter of politics and decisions have to be taken on political grounds, it becomes an affair of responsive and responsible gover- nance, which still is the "domain reservé" of member state govern- ments.

The transformation of governance

A changing view of governance

The preceeding chapters leave us with a puzzle. The general assumption about states losing sovereignty and autonomy in the course of the integration process is confronted with empirical evidence and plausible arguments which tell a different story. In addition it became apparent that the question of whether states lose their autonomy will find a different answer depending on whether it is raised from an international relations scholar's point of view, whose main concern is with the future of the international state system or from a policy analysis perspective, which rather looks at the respective power of public and private actors. In the following chapter, I will take yet another approach which will focus neither on the state as "actor" in international affairs nor on the capacity of the state to keep private and public interests "in balance". I will rather discard those two approaches because I consider them as attached to an outmoded conception of governing centered on the "state" and of its role in politics. My argument will be that in order to gain a better understanding about the changes that take place in the European polity as a whole — that is the European Union and its member-states — one should rather look at the transformations that take place in the nature of and conceptions about governance. They certainly cannot be attributed only to the dynamics of the integration process and the properties of the EC system alone. Both, however, contribute to a large extent to that transformation of governance and in this respect to the role of the state in Europe.

The still prominent discussion about the supranational "rescue" or "decline" of the nation state (Wildenmann, 1991; Milward, 1992; Moravcsik, 1994) certainly no longer starts from the presumption that the state can be modelled as "unitary actor", as the "one and indivisible" body of unitary policy making based on parliamentary majorities and the undisputed right and capabiliy of the executive to implement whatever decision is taken thanks to the "monopoly of the legitimate use of physical force" (Max Weber). This concept of the modern state has always been an ideal type with limited descriptive accuracy even in the second half of the last century when it was developed (Ellwein, 1992). But dividing political actors into national and European executives on the one hand and societal groups on the other, attributing to them "distinct and independent sets of preferences" and modelling their relationship as an "ongoing set of bargains between principals and agents" (Moravcsik, 1994:4) means to uphold a concept of governing which is synonymous with political control and in this way still is very much in line with the traditional model of the state: Governing is what governments do, and the effectiveness of their activities derives from the resources they command because those will define their relative bargaining power vis à vis the societal actors.

This concept was prominent in the "Steuerungsdebatte" of the

60s and 70s. It changed when research began to focus on the "implementation deficit". A different analytical perspective slowly emerged: The problems of "governability" were no longer perceived in terms of "insufficient intelligence of the bureaucracy, in the lack of the government's ability to make decisions or in a choice of wrong instruments, but in the particular character of the objects of governing attempts" (Mayntz, 1993a: 14). These "objects of governing" were now conceived of as complex "societal subsystems". They have their own internal dynamics that make them "impenetrable for outsiders in a double sense, both cognitively as well as in terms of the possibility to be purposefully influenced." (Ibid.).

Policy analysis provided additional empirical evidence that governing has little to do with the popular notion of centralized direction within an encompassing organization. It rather reproduced the picture of networks of highly interdependent but autonomous actors willing to join in corporate actions agreed upon in negotiations rather as in response to authoritative decree.

Therefore, consecutive research centered on the question of how to conceptualize the "problematique" of governance as it became obvious that political guidance through command and control over "target-group behaviour" cannot be achieved. Interestingly enough, this new perception of the problems of governing was shared by economists who started to ponder about the declining efficiency of hierarchical patterns of regulation.

Different schools of thought have tried to come to grips with the "new economic landscape" brought about by structural change in the advanced economies in the last decade. "Flexible specialization" is one of the key words (Piore/Sabel, 1984; Sabel, 1989) to characterize the strategic reaction of industry to the challenges of market fragmentation and volatility, to the dynamic and extensive deployment of new technologies, and the dramatic reductions in the life cycles of products. The enthusiasm that by dividing tasks and transferring responsibilities to loosely inter-connected units will make sure that production and distribution will be best geared to "ever-changing markets" (Amin/Dietrich, 1991:5f) has given way to a more sober and differentiated evaluation. Nevertheless, there is agreement that adaption can only be brought about by institutional change. A recurrent theme of recent years in economics as well as in political science has been the effective organization of social-political and economic relations between "markets and hierarchies" (Williamson, 1975). As exchange has become one of the central concepts, the reduction of "transaction costs" has been one of the main foci in economic as well as in political science analysis. Research about industrial structures, business relationship and industrial marketing, in particular, has in recent years devoted much attention to the social "embeddedness" (Grabher, 1993) of exchange relations but also looked at the industrial functions of business networks.[22]

In international relations, a parallel debate evolved relating to problems of international interdependence and the globalization of problems like in the environment. Analysing the chances of cooperation between independent actors in order to avoid sub-optimal outcome of autonomous action stimulated the discussion on international governance. The broad discussion about the management of interdependence, international regimes and the purposeful organization of international order went along with deliberations about "governing beyond the state", which by defi-nition was about "governance without government" (Rosenau/ Czempiel, 1992; Kohler-Koch, 1993).

In all these writings there is a common understanding that governance is about coordinating multiple players in a complex setting of mutual dependence. "Governing" then is not just what governments do by themselves but "... all those activities of social, political and administrative actors that can be seen as purposeful efforts to guide, steer, control or manage (sectors or facets of) societies ... Social-political forms of governing are forms in which public or private actors do not act separately but in conjunction, together, in combination, that is to say in co-arrangements ... 'governance' (is) the patterns that emerge from governing activi-ties ..." (Kooiman, 1993:2).

The proliferation of networks is a condition as well as a con-sequence of the growing differentiation of functional subsystems, the political emancipation of big corporate actors able to take strategic actions by themselves, and the increasing complexity of interdependence (Mayntz, 1993b:43). At the same time it is an expression of the progressing recognition on the part of social and political actors that a new mode of governance has to develop that rests on the continuous process of interaction. In business relations, too, network structures are by now not only considered to be a passing phenomen in times of "market failure" but a persistent trait of exchange relations. They thrive thanks to their productive features. Taking the assumption that resources and products exchanged between economic actors are not homogeneous and given but have different values depending on how they are combined with other resources, then the exchange of this knowledge and its further development through cooperation becomes most important: "... collective learning is identified as a key issue in dealing with heterogeneous resources on the firm level" (Håkansson, 1993: 209).

There is not yet an established "conceptual hegemony", but it looks as if some kind of "epistemic community" (P. Haas, 1992) had developed around the notion of a new mode of governance. The central message is that governing has to take into account the specific rationality of highly organized social subsystems, and that it can only unleash the productive forces within its constituency if it succeeds to mobilize "indigenous resources". This has a lot to do with setting free innovative capabilities and the willingness to get engaged which will hardly be brought about by authoritative regulation. From a political system's point of view governing has to be organized in a way "to enhance the independent adaptive, reactive, and problem-solving capacities of societal actors, which means to motivate and to enable them to react purposefully at any moment to changing conditions." (Mayntz, 1993a:15) In industrial relations network structures are identified as the most promising "governance form" because they ensure in a relationsship the necessary stability and variety in a relationship which is a prerequisite for productive learning (Håkansson, 1993; 1994). "Joint learning" is considered to be most productive as it is based on the knowledge and experience of more than one actor and results in a double — or mutual — specialization. To make joint learning possible it is necessary to develop stable relationships with a variety of suppliers and customers of resources (Håkansson, 1993:215).

This new notion of governance respects the autonomy of societal actors and contrary to conventional thinking does not consider the successful reduction of complexity a prerequisite to effective government. "Difficult complex relations and strategic drastic changes are no longer considered as problems and difficulties which have to be mastered, but rather as sources of innovation ... Management of complex networks is then not the maintenance of sensitive intricate balances, but the deliberate use of imbalances for the sake of renewal." (Kickert, 1993:202) "Good governing" then would contribute to a "decrease in the unilateral steering by government, and hence an increase in the self-governance of the networks."(Ibid: 204).

March and Olsen have expressed this change in governance by saying that "governance becomes less a matter of engineering than of gardening" (March/Olsen, 1983:292). This change entails a transformation in four respects: namely in the *role of the state*, the *rules of behaviour*, the *patterns of interaction* and the *level of action*.

The state is no longer an actor in its own rights. Its *role* has changed from authoritative allocation and regulation into the role of partner and mediator. It has abandoned its ambition to direct the economy and to steer research and technology into the right direction. Instead, the state executive transmuted into a broker bringing together the relevant actors of society. Networking is the main task, which means to offer the institutional framework within which transaction costs can be reduced and successful self-regulation can be supported. Instead of providing economic incentives through the transfer of own resources, state agencies act as consultants enabling societal actors to find the right access to external funds like those of the EC. This change "from actor to arena" takes different forms. That it reflects diverging policy styles varying between and even within individual countries should be less surprising than the rapid spread of this new phenomenon.

"Partners" will behave in a different manner than "rulers" and "subjects" did. *Rules of behaviour* and the norms prevailing within a "negotiating state" (Scharpf) will differ from those prevalent in a hierarchical state or those in an anarchical "self-help system". Actors are still profit oriented, but bargaining is more about the distribution of benefits in joint problem-solving rather than enhancing one's own position in relation to others. The upgrading of common interests, the committment to a collective good is as well part of the game as the pursuit of particular interests.

Distinct *patterns of interaction* evolve. Hierarchy and subordination give way to an interchange on a more equal footing. The formerly clear cut borderlines between the private and the public become blurred. Multiple, overlapping negotiating arenas emerge. The state is divided into functionally differentiated substructures, each of which is part of particular "policy communities" that depending on the problems to be solved, will engage in specific "issue networks".[23]

Accordingly, the *level of political action* is brought down to those that are effected by the policy and whose active support is needed for implementation. Network relations that are based on mutual trust necessitates that partners will have to meet in face-to-face contact; joint problem-solving will be functionally more specific and will therefore take place in smaller units. "Authoritative allocation" could be executed at higher levels, and would even function in a mass society spread over a vast territory. It responds to the demands aggregated and articulated by intermediary organizations representing existing preference structures and cleavages. Support depends on performance and may be gained by efficient andministration. Not so a policy that is geared to the "mobilization of indigenous resources" and "joint learning". This has to be decentralized and carried out at lower levels.

The transformation of governance — a European "leading idea"

The emergence of this new type of governance[24] is in general related to changes taking place in the "real world"; the evolution of our societies, the globalization of the economy, the dynamic progress of science and technology. And there is a growing body of literature that finds elements of this new mode of governance nearly everywhere and relates it to the transformation in the empirical environment. I will not deny the importance in material changes.[25] The point I want to make is that actor strategies and changes in the general perception are about as important as changes in the material world. The same holds true for the relation between actual practise and the interpretation of that practise. The assertion I want to prove is that the proliferation of the concept is as relevant as are the actual changes in roles, structures and procedures. Change is brought about not so much by what political actors and their social and economic counterparts do, but by the common understanding that what they are doing constitutes a "new mode of governance". I should like to contest the familiar argument that "... the growing complexity, dynamics and diversity of our societies, as 'caused by social, technological and scientific developments', puts governing systems under such new challenges that new conceptions of governance are needed" (Kooiman, 1993: 6). Structural conditions do not bring about new patterns of behaviour by the sheer force of necessity. Even "the growing recognition on the part of social and political actors of the complexity, dynamics and diversity of social-political systems" (ibid) will not be sufficient. There has to be a leading idea, a concept that gives a clear image of the logic of one's own dealings.[26] A new "belief system" in the sense of providing shared assumptions about causal facts and legitimate reasons has to be produced in order to orient collective action. "Framing" (Rein, 1991) is a necessary prerequisite for collective agreements upon the setting of a problem and the adequate way of dealing with it.

My hypothesis is that European integration is closely linked with the dissemination of that concept of a new mode of governance. The reasons for this are threefold; 1) the Community brings together actors that take the greatest interest in and are open to the idea of a change of governance, 2) it is most active in those policy areas in which governing by coordination seems most plausible, 3) It follows a strategy that allows to minimize opposition.

European research and technology policy as well as European regional policy can be taken as good reference points to illustrate the mechanisms at work. Research and technology is the policy area which already at the national level was an early testing ground for "public-private partnership". It thrived on the mutually shared assumption that the problem structure was such that only by close cooperation promising strategies could be developed. Uncertainty and risk, long turnout effects, extensive resources needed made it — at least from an actor's perspective — imperative to work together in order to come to a common understanding of ways and means to tackle the problem.[27]

The history of the EC-research and technology programmes, especially in the field of information technology gives ample evidence that those actors joined that hoped to profit most from a concerted action. The story of the "Round Table" is often told in a way that implies that is was the coalition of big business that brought about the first spectacular programmes in information technology (Sharp, 1991). Others point to the fact that it was the Commission that forged that coalition together and used it for its own pupose, namely to gain the Council's unanimous vote for its proposal (Grande, 1996). In my reading it was less a case of instrumentalizing one partner by the other, but an exercise in joint cooperative governance. The Round Table was a success story because a technocratic consensus supported the legitimacy of business and the Commission acting together. It is well established conventional wisdom in Western Europe that the Community is about competitiveness: The ensuing argument is that competiveness depends on the capability for technical innovation, and that scientific knowledge and insight into the requirements of the economy is what is most needed in order to design a good policy. Furthermore, it was a new policy and fixed patterns for choosing policy options were yet not set. This made it easy to form a transnational/supranational coalition based on a common understanding of the nature of the problem. To interpret it in terms of an transnational "advocacy coalition" that just influenced the decision-making of the Council would miss the point. All relevant actors became part of the policy network and joined in to come to a common understanding of the nature of the problem, the options and measures to be taken.

Regional policy is another case which gives even better proof of the argument. The story in conventional terms is generally told along the following lines.[28] The increase in structural funds, the reforms in objectives and procedures of EC-regional policy at the end of the 80s, the informal and formal[29] channels of regional representation all have contributed to an upgrading of the European regions. It is a highly disputed issue in the meantime whether and to what extent this has increased their political weight to the detriment of the states.

From my point of view neither comparative studies on the influence that regional representatives have on the process of policy formulation and implementation nor a thorough investigation of the role of the Committee of the Regions will provide a satisfactory answer. The regional policy of the EC supports a change in governance to the extent that it offers a new concept of governing and provides procedures and resources that induce actors at the sub-national level to become part of the new game. The EC does not try to impose or a concept. Instead, it opens a "window of opportunity" for regional actors to use the resources offered. These are threefold: funds, strategic concepts and legitimacy.

Financial assistance is attractive and regional actors have employed different strategies to get hold of it. The Community does not only offer money, but also a philosophy about the right use and the overarching objective of regional structural policy. The idea centres around the principle of "partnership". But apart from this principle, the whole "framing" sells the message of cooperative governing. It is remarkable to see to what extent this philosophy is shared by regional actors. They have started talking about the new role of the "regional state": "It should moderate and organize the ongoing dialogue between employers and employees, between the world of science and of business. Without such a bringing together and networking of regional forces the structural problems will not be solved and the development potential of the region will not be used" (Lafontaine, 1994:10).[30] Ministers talk about a "new model of governance"[31] (Spöri, 1994: 66), the necessity to organize a "dialogorientierte Wirtschaftspolitik" (dialogue oriented economic policy), and have institutionalized cooperation in collective bodies like the "Gemeinschaftsinitiative Wirtschaft und Politik", an expert-based body for joint problem-solving. Municipalities have jumped on the band-waggon (Hennerkes, 1994).

In addition, the Community programmes in regional affairs, especially the "Community initiatives" provide a full-fledged regime for cooperative governing. It entails principles, devises norms, rules and procedures that support or even bring about the institutionalization of networks. Regional and sub-regional actors quite often consider the implementation of this regime to be time-consuming, expensive and not particularly efficient.[32] Nevertheless, the same actors may well be in favour of that principle and its application in regional development programmes. They expect that it is bound to strengthen their own position perhaps less with regard to that specific programme than in general terms.

Governing in networks

The most fascinating result of empirical research on the effects of Europeanization of regions is the growing importance of network building. Most authors tend to discard this aspect as being of secondary importance. They are looking for "decisive institutional shifts" or at least hard evidence for a more influential role of regions as compared to municipalities, nations and the EC (Hooghe, 1995). When looking for more "subtle changes", rescue is taken to causal explanations such as "rising expectations", "a mobilization of demands" or "concerted attempts" (Marks, 1996). Instead of recalling the metaphors of the "Third World" discourse, one should rather take a closer look at the effects the emergence of sub-national networks brings about.

Although there are great variations in all different aspects of network characteristics (Conzelmann, 1995), they have some particular properties in common. They are built on voluntary participation and on acknowledged mutual self-interest. Trust, so central to their functioning, is supposed to be based on close personal relations. But trust does not only arise from interaction. It is supported by a "common understanding". Networks as "patterned relations" are embedded in overarching institutions, in sets of principles, norms and rules of a higher order which are internalized by actors in common beliefs systems.

From a "reflective institutionalist" approach the concept of "cooperative governing" is about to become such a point of reference.

If one agrees with the notion that "... action is taken on the basis of a logic of appropriateness associated with roles, routines, rights, obligations, standard operating procedures and practices" (March/ Olsen, 1994:5), the active propagation of the network-model of governing is of the highest relevance. There are good reasons to believe that the European Commission and regional public actors will join to do so. Regions have a comparative advantage in building networks that rest on proximity, mutual experience and sometimes even a feeling of political community. The Commission looks for procedures and partners which will help to improve its performance and bring it closer to the citizens. Governing through network coordination has its in-built limits. But in a situation where regional public actors have little options to govern their environment by other means, the positive effects of network-governingscore high. From this point of view, the evidence that "policy networks are more likely to emerge and play a significant role in a unitary state such as the UK than in more federal or de-centralised countries ..." is not a "paradox" (Burton/ Smith, 1994: 47) but rather supports the logic of the argument.

The functional advantage of networks is that they can com-pensate for the rigidities of institutions. There is evidence abound that networks emerge in a situation when existing institutions due to their immobility can no longer cope with a situation and despite their inefficiency resist institutional adaptation. Networks can bring together different actors in a rather flexible manner and bridge the gap between institutions. Because they are built on voluntary participation, they have a higher elasticity with respect to changing demands. Their effectiveness, however, is limited just because the exit-option is always open. This explains the obvious tendencies of many networks to become institutionalized. They are in constant danger to lose their most attractive property — voluntary commitment to joint problem-solving in shifting alliances — because they have the tendency to get institutionalized in order to become more effective and on the other hand they are constantly threatened to get subdued by existing institutions that strive for control (Benz, 1994; Fürst, 1993).

Wherever more encompassing issue networks like in EC regional policy produce narrower "subnetworks", those tend to develop a high stability despite a low degree of institutionalization (Staeck, 1994:50). The main reasons are the limited number of participants, the longterm perspective of cooperation spreading the "shadow of the future", and the reflex of higher institutions.

So far, European integration has not contributed to endow regions with stronger constitutional prerequisites or political power. The "sandwich model", which projects that in the coming future the state will be squeezed between two dominant political actors — the Community and the regions — lacks descriptive accuracy and explanatory power. Changes in the role of the nation-state will come about through the transformation of governance.

At first sight, the role of the "state" will be less dominant. It is weak in terms of being reduced to a partner and broker. It has lost its capacity to regulate by decree and orient the action of societal actors by coercive measures. Apart from the intricate question, whether this perception of the state was ever close to reality, public administration gains strength from its weakness. The mushrooming of "joint initiatives" and similar network activities has enabled the executive — in particular at sub-national level — to penetrate society even more. The "centrality" (Benz, 1992) of state actors is even more important. It is not by chance that thus far they have played the role of "political entrepreneurs". They decide to whom they want to become partners, on what issue it is worthwhile to engage in cooperative effort. Above all, they are close to politics. It is in the context of the political process that new governing concepts are validated.

Notes

* For critical remarks I want to thank my collaborators in the Mannheim team: Thomas Conzelmann, Rainer Eising, Markus Jachtenfuchs, Thomas Schaber, Martin Schmidberger and Cornelia Ulbert.

1. Hallstein was the first and long-term president of the EEC-Commission who published his work on the Community under the title "Der unvollendete Bundesstaat".

2. For the distinction between "positive" and "negative" integration see Tinbergen 1965. Economic exchange and interdependence grew considerably with reference to the previous years. If, however, the level of interdependence was any higher than 100 years ago, is highly disputed.

3. A thorough political science analysis of Euro-Barometer Data is presented in Niedermayer/Sinnott 1995.

4. Recent contributions to the state of the debate see Keohane/Hoffmann 1990; Weiler 1991; Sbragia 1992; Bogdandy 1993a, 1993b.

5. In the case of "directives" which are only framework regulations, the national legislature will vote on the more detailed legal provisions; nevertheless, the directive itself is binding law irrespective of any national legislative decision. In addition, experience shows that Community law is implemented about as effectively as national law. (Siedentopf/Ziller 1988)

6. According to Art. 3b "the Community shall take action, in accordance with the principle of subsidiarity, only if and in so far as the objectives of the proposed action cannot be sufficiently achieved by the Member States and can therefore, by reason of the scale or effects of the proposed action, be better achieved by the Community".

7. The Commission called for the development of an institutional structure that, taking into account the acceptability of the public and the Member States should serve the "gemeinsame Ausübung der geteilten Souveränität". (Kommission 1990:3)

8. The Council, however, can override the EP by unanimity when a policy is based on Art. 189c, which gives the European Parliament the right of cooperation or concerning amendments made by the Parliament based on Art. 189b when the EP is given the right of co-determination. In the latter case the Council has no power to redress a negative vote of the Parliament.

9. In many instances, however, trans-institutional advocacy coalitions were inhibited by inter-institutional conflicts about legal prerogatives and procedural matters. (Miller 1995)

10. Though already in 1977 the European Court ruled that, just as national state aids, state aids by local and regional authorities are subject to Commission review under the scope of art. 92 of the EEC-Treaty, a growing portion of such state aid was accorded to the regional and even sub-regional level. By law such aids had to be notified to the Commission in the same way as national subsidies, in practice, however, the operation of subnational state aids was beyond the Commission's control. The Commission was overburdened with such a task and unable de facto to fulfill its role of supervisor in face of an increased fragmentation of state aid policies. (Kohler-Koch 1994b)

11. For a detailed description of the German case see Bruder 1986.

12. For a more detailed account see Corbey 1993.

13. Corbey 1993 compared the economic policies of five member-states. Comparative research on social policies, Leibfried/Pierson 1995, and environmental policies, Héritier et al. 1994, supports these findings.

14. She, however, points out that the policy elite of Belgium and the Netherlands — the two countries she has been investigating — do not contemplate policies that are at odds with the Community's preferences. (Ibid)

15. Anderson 1995 presents some interesting cases for Germany.

16. Contrary to neo-functional reasoning private interest organizations did not take the lead but rather followed political initiatives. (Kohler-Koch 1992)

17. For a more detailed account in relation with the effects on interest intermediation in the EC see Eising/Kohler-Koch 1994.

18. An empirical insight into the intensity of cooperation in quantitative terms is presented by Wessels 1996 on the basis of the number of committee meetings attended by national experts from the member-governments and Commission representatives.

19. A very telling empirical study on UNICE, the European federation of industry and employers and ETU, the European Trade Union Federation is presented by Sadowski/Timmesfeld 1994.

20. That these mechanisms are at work in national federal systems as well has been documented in a thorough investigation of policy coordination between German Länder. (Benz et al. 1992)

21. For a more detailed presentation of the argument see Kohler-Koch 1994c

22. I want to thank Håkan Håkansson for drawing my attention to this rich and for a political scientist very stimulating research on Industrial Networks. (1993)

23. The terminology follows Marsh/Rhodes 1992.

24. It comes close to what Jørgensen 1993 has called the "responsive state".

25. A cynical interpretation would be that the social sciences are just about to catch up with the complex pattern of reality, and that the reality never conformed to the ideal type of the state and of governance as presented in our textbooks. (Beyme 1991) In the context of my argument, however, it is not particularly relevant whether social life and academic reasoning are finally brought into line or if we are confronted with a new phenomenon.

26. There is a growing interest in the role of ideas in social and political life in international relations as well as in policy analysis. For a recent summary see Jachtenfuchs 1995.

27. Hofmann 1993 gives a very instructive account of the change in philosophy of governance in technology, particularly with respect to regional technology policy.

28. The literature on European regional policy and the role of regions in the EC politics has expanded dramatically in recent years. A condensed account is presented by Benz 1993.

29. In particular through the establishment of the Committee of the Regions.

30. The German original reads as follows: "Der Staat kann nicht alles ... Er kann den kontinuierlichen Dialog von Unternehmern und Arbeitnehmern, von Wissenschaft und Verbänden moderieren und organisieren. Ohne eine solche Bündelung und Vernetzung der regionalen Kräfte können die strukturellen Probleme nicht gelöst und das Entwicklungspotential nicht ausgeschöpft werden." Lafontaine is Prime Minister of the Saarland.

31. In German: "ein neues Politikmodell"; Spöri is Minister of Economics and Deputy Prime Minister of Baden-Württemberg.

32. These are the preliminary results of a comparative empirical study on the role of regions as political actors in EC politics I am engaged in at present.

References

Amin, A. / Dietrich, M. (1991), "Deciphering the Terrain of Change in Europe", in: Amin / Dietrich (eds.), *Towards a New Europe? Structural Change in the European Economy*, Aldershot: Edward Elgar, 3–17.

Anderson, B. (1991), *Imagined Communities. Reflections on the Origin and Spread of Nationalism*, London et al.: Verso.

Anderson, J. (1995), *A United Germany in Europe: Regulative Politics and the Reciprocal Exercise of Power*. Paper presented at the Conference on "The Influence of Germany and the European Community on the Smaller European States", Budapest, Hungary, May 31 to June 3, 1995, Budapest.

Benko, G. B. / Amin, A. eds., (1992), *Les régions qui gagnent. Districts et réseaux: les nouveaux paradigmes de la géographie économique*, Paris: Université de France.

Benz, A. (1994), *Netzwerke und Institutionen: Zur paradoxen Struktur interorganisatorischer Politik*, University of Konstanz (unpublished manuscript).

Benz, A. (1993), "Regionen als Machtfaktor in Europa", in: *Verwaltungsarchiv*, 84, 328–348.

Benz, A. / Scharpf, F.W. / Zintl, R. (1992), *Horizontale Politikverflechtung. Zur Theorie von Verhandlungssystemen*, Frankfurt/M.: Campus.

Beyme, K. von (1991), *Die Theorie der Politik im 20. Jahrhundert. Von der Moderne zur Postmoderne*, Frankfurt/M.: Suhrkamp.

Bogdandy, A. von (1993a), "Die Verfassung der europäischen Integrationsgemeinschaft als supranationale Union", in: Bogdandy, A. von (ed.), *Die europäische Option. Eine interdisziplinäre Analyse über Herkunft, Stand und Perspektiven der europäischen Integration*, Baden-Baden: Nomos.

Bogdandy, A. von (1993b), "Supranationale Union als neuer Herrschaftstypus: Entstaatlichung und Vergemeinschaftung in staatstheoretischer Perspektive", in: *Integration*, 16, 4, 210–225.

Bruder, W. (ed.), (1986), *Forschungs- und Technologiepolitik in der Bundesrepublik Deutschland*, Opladen: Westdeutscher Verlag.

Bull, H. (1977), *The Anarchical Society. A Study of Order in World Politics*, London: Columbia University Press.

Bulmer, S.J. (1994), "The Governance of the European Union: A New Institutionalist Approach", in: *Journal of Public Policy*, 13, 4, 351–380.

Burton, P. / Smith, R. (1994), *Policy Networks and the European Structural Funds: Great Britain — the case of a unitary state in the developed north*, paper presented to the conference "Policy Networks and Regional Policy in EU Member States", Hannover, 25–26 November 1994.

Conzelmann, T. (1995), "Networking and the Politics of EU Regional Policy. Lessons from North Rhine-Westphalia, Nord-Pas de Calais and North West England", in: *Journal of Regional and Federal Studies* (forthcoming).

Corbey, D. (1993), *Stilstand is vooruitgang. De dialectiek van het Europese integratieproces*, PhD.-Thesis, Leiden: Rijksuniversitaet.

Czempiel, E-O. (1981), *Internationale Politik. Ein Konfliktmodell*, Paderborn: Schöningh.

Dehousse, R. (1994), "Community Competences: Are there limits to growth", in: Dehousse, R. (ed.), *Europe after Maastricht: an ever closer Union?*, München: Beck.

Dehousse, R. (1992), "Integration vs. Regulation? On the Dynamics of Regulation in the European Community", in: *Journal of Common Market Studies*, 30, 4, 383–402.

Eichener, V. (1996), "Die Rückwirkungen der europäischen Integration auf nationale Politikmuster", in: Jachtenfuchs / Kohler-Koch, (eds.) 249–280.

Eising, R. / Kohler-Koch, B. (1994), "Inflation und Zerfaserung. Trends der Interessenvermittlung in der Europäischen Gemeinschaft", in: Streeck, W. (ed.), *Staat und Verbände* (PVS-Sonderheft 25), Opladen: Westdeutscher Verlag, 175–206.

Ellwein, T. (1992), "Staatlichkeit im Wandel. Das Staatsmodell des 19. Jahrhunderts als Verständnisbarriere", in: Kohler-Koch, B. (ed.), *Staat und Demokratie in Europa*, Opladen: Leske + Budrich, 73–82.

Everling, U. (1993), "Die Stellung der Judikative im Verfassungssystem der Europäischen Gemeinschaft", in: *Zeitschrift für Schweizerisches Recht*, 112, 337–348.

Fürst, D. (1993), "Regionalkonferenzen zwischen offenen Netzwerken und fester Institutionalisierung", in: *Raumforschung und Raumordnung*, 3, 184–192

Garofoli, G. (1992), "Les systèmes de petites entreprises: un cas paradigmatique de développement endogène", in: Benko / Amin, (eds.), 57–80.

Grabher, G. (ed.), (1993), *The Embedded Firm. On the Socioeconomics of Industrial Networks*, London: Routledge.

Grande, E, (1994), *Vom Nationalstaat zur europäischen Politikverflechtung. Expansion und Transformation moderner Staatlichkeit — untersucht am Beispiel der Forschungs- und Technologiepolitik*, Habilitationsschrift, Konstanz: University of Konstanz.

Grande, E. (1996), "Forschungspolitik und die Einflußlogik europäischer Politikverflechtung", in: Jachtenfuchs / Kohler-Koch, (eds.), 373–399.

Haas, E. B. (1958), *The Uniting of Europe: Political, Social, and Eco-*

nomic Forces, Stanford, CA: Stanford University Press.

Haas, P. M., (ed.), (1992), "Knowledge, Power, and International Policy Coordination", special issue of *International Organization*, 46, 1.

Håkansson, H. (1994), "Economics of Technological Relationships", in: Granstrand, O. (ed.), *Economics of Technology*, Amsterdam: Elsevier, 253–270.

Håkansson, H. (1993), "Networks as Mechanism to Develop Resources", in: Beije, P. R., et al., (eds.), *Networking in Dutch Industries*, Leven-Apeldorn: Garant, 207–223.

Håkansson, H. / Johanson, J. (1993), "Industrial Functions of Business Relationships", in: *Industrial Networks* (Advances in International Marketing, Vol. 5), Greenwich, CT: JAI Press, 13–29.

Hallstein, W. (1969), *Der unvollendete Bundesstaat. Europäische Erfahrungen und Erkenntnisse*, Düsseldorf: Econ.

Hennerkes, J. (1994), "Funktion und Reorganisation kommunaler Verwaltungen im Strukturwandel", in: Klepsch / Legrand / Sanne, (eds.), 113–124.

Héritier, A. et al., (1994), *Die Veränderung von Staatlichkeit in Europa. Ein regulativer Wettbewerb: Deutschland, Großbritannien und Frankreich in der Europäischen Union*, Opladen: Leske + Budrich.

Héritier, A. (ed.), (1993), *Policy-Analyse. Kritik und Neuorientierung* (PVS-Sonderheft 24), Opladen: Westdeutscher Verlag.

Héritier, A. (1993), "Policy-Netzwerkanalyse als Untersuchungsinstrument im europäischen Kontext: Folgerungen aus einer empirischen Studie regulativer Politik", in: Hèritier, ed., 432–447.

Hoffmann, S. (1966), "Obstinate or Obsolete? The Fate of the Nation-State and the Case of Western Europe", in: *Daedelus*, 95, 862–915.

Hofmann, J. (1993), *Implizite Theorien in der Politik. Interpretationsprobleme regionaler Technologiepolitik*, Opladen: Westdeutscher Verlag.

Hooghe, L. (1995), "Building a Europe with the Regions: The Politics of the Commission Bureaucracy under the Structural Funds", in: Hooghe, L. (ed.), *Cohesion Policy. European Community and Sub-*

national Government, Oxford: Oxford University Press, (in print).

Jachtenfuchs, M./ Kohler-Koch, B. (eds.), (1996), *Europäische Integration*, Opladen: Leske + Budrich.

Jachtenfuchs, M. (1995), "Ideen und internationale Beziehungen", in: *Zeitschrift für internationale Beziehungen*, 2 (forthcoming).

Jansen, D. / Schubert, K. (eds.), (1995), *Netzwerke und Politikproduktion. Konzepte, Methoden, Perspektiven*, Marburg: Schüren

Joerges, C. (1996), "Das Recht im Prozeß der europäischen Integration. Ein Plädoyer für die Beachtung des Rechts durch die Politikwissenschaft", in: Jachtenfuchs / Kohler-Koch, eds. 73–108.

Joerges, C., (1993), "Wirtschaftsrecht, Nationalstaat und der Vertrag von Maastricht", in: *Leviathan*, 21, 4, 493–516.

Jørgensen, Torben Beck, 1993: "Modes of Governance and Administrative Change", in: Kooiman, ed., 219–232.

Keohane, R. O. / Hoffmann, S. (1991), "Institutional Change in Europe in the 1980s", in: Keohane / Hoffmann, (eds.), *The New European Community. Decisionmaking and Institutional Change*, Boulder, CO, et al.: Westview, 1–39.

Keohane, Robert O. / Hoffmann, Stanley, 1990: "Conclusions: Community Politics and Institutional Change", in: Wallace, W. (ed.), *The Dynamics of European Integration*, London et al.: Pinter Publishers, 276–300.

Kickert, W. (1993), "Complexity, Governance and Dynamics: Conceptual Explorations of Public Network management", in: Kooiman, (ed.), 191–204.

Klepsch, T./ Legrand, H-J. / Sanne, A. (eds.), (1994), *Integrierte Strukturpolitik. Eine Herausforderung für Politik, Wirtschaft und Kommunen*, Bonn: Bund-Verlag.

Kohler-Koch, B. (1994a), "Patterns of Interest Intermediaton in the European Union", in: *Government and Opposition*, 29, 2, 166–180.

Kohler-Koch, B. (1994b), *Regions as Political Actors in the Process of European Integration* (MZES-Arbeitspapier), Mannheim.

Kohler-Koch, B. (1994c), *The Evolution of Organized Interests in the EC Driving Forces, Co-Evolution or New Type of Governance?* Paper prepared for presentation at the XVIth World Congress of the International Political Science Association, August 21–25, 1994, Berlin.

Kohler-Koch, B. (1993), "Die Welt regieren ohne Weltregierung", in: Böhret, C. / Wewer, G. (eds.), *Regieren im 21. Jahrhundert — zwischen Globalisierung und Regionalisierung*, Opladen: Leske + Budrich, 109–141.

Kohler-Koch, B. (1992), "Interessen und Integration. Die Rolle organisierter Interessen im westeuropäischen Integrationsprozeß", in: Kreile, M. (ed.), *Die Integration Europas* (PVS-Sonderheft 23), Opladen: Westdeutscher Verlag.

Kommission der Europäischen Gemeinschaften, (1990), Stellungnahme der Kommission vom 21. Oktober 1990 zu dem Entwurf zur Änderung des Vertrags zur Gründung der Europäischen Wirtschaftsgemeinschaft im Zusammenhang mit der Politischen Union, Luxemburg: Amt für Veröffentlichungen der Europäischen Gemeinschaften.

Kommission der Europäischen Gemeinschaften, (1985), Vollendung des Binnenmarkts. Weißbuch der Kommission an den Europäischen Rat, Luxemburg: Amt für Veröffentlichungen der Europäischen Gemeinschaften.

Kooiman, J. (ed.), (1993), *Modern Governance. New Government-Society Interactions*, London: Sage.

Kooiman, J. (1993), "Social-Political Governance: Introduction", in: Kooiman, (ed.), 1–9.

Kurzer, P. (1995), "Money, Welfare, and Policing: The Low Countries and the Federal Republic of Germany in the EU", (manuscript to be published in: Katzenstein, P.J. ed., *The Influence of Germany and the European Community on the Smaller European States*).

Lafontaine, O. (1994), "Geleitwort", in: Klepsch / Legrand / Sanne, (eds.): 7–10.

Leibfried, S. (1996), "Wohlfahrtsstaatliche Perspektiven der Europäischen Union: Auf dem Wege zu positiver Souveränitätsverflechtung?", in: Jachtenfuchs /Kohler-Koch, (eds.) 455–477.

Leibfried, S. / Pierson, P. (1995), "Semi-Sovereign Welfare States:

Social Policy in a multi-tiered Europe", in: Leibfried, S. / Pierson, P. (eds.), *Fragmented Social Policy: The European Union's Social Dimension in Comparative Perspective*, Washington, DC: The Bookings Institution (in print).

March, J.G. / Olsen, J- P. (1983), "Organizing Political Life: What Administrative Reorganization Tells Us about Government", in: *American Political Science Review*, 77, 281–296.

March, J. G. / Olsen, J- P. (1994), *Institutional Perspectives on Political Institutions*, Arena Working Paper No. 2, Oslo.

Marks, G. (1996), "Decision Making in Structural Policy: Exploring and Explaining Variations", in: Jachtenfuchs / Kohler-Koch, (eds.) 313–343.

Marks, G. (1993), "Structural Policy and Multilevel Governance in the European Community", in: Cafruny, A.W. / Rosenthal, Glenda G. (eds.), *The State of the European Community. The Maastricht Debates and Beyond*, Harlow / Boulder, CO: Longman / Lynne Rienner, 391–410.

Marsh, D. / Rhodes, R.A.W. (1992), "Policy Communities and Issue Networks", in: Marsh, D. / Rhodes, R.A.W. (eds.), *Policy Networks in British Government*, Oxford: Oxford University Press.

Mayntz, R. (1993a), "Governing Failures and the Problem of Governability: Some Comments on a Theoretical Paradigm", in: Kooiman, (ed.), 9–21 (german original, 1987: Politische Steuerung und gesellschaftliche Steuerungsprobleme — Anmerkungen zu einem theoretischen Paradigma, in *Jahrbuch zur Staats- und Verwaltungswissenschaft*, 1, 89–110).

Mayntz, R. (1993b), "Policy-Netzwerke und die Logik von Verhand-lungssystemen", in: Héritier, ed., 39–56.

Miller, G. (1995), *Post-Maastricht Legislative Procedures: is the Council "institutionally challengend"?* Paper presented to the 4th Biennial International Conference of ECSA, Charleston, South Carolina, 11–14 May 1995, Charleston, SC.

Milward, A. S. (1992), *The European Rescue of the Nation-State*, London: Routledge.

Mitrany, D. (1943), *A Working Peace System*, London: Oxford

University Press.

Moravcsik, A. (1991), "Negotiating the Single European Act. National Interests and Conventional Statecraft in the European Community", in: *International Organization*, 45, 3, 660–696.

Moravcsik, A. (1994), *Why the European Community Strengthens the State: Domestic Politics and International Cooperation*, Working Paper # 52, Harvard University, Center for European Studies.

Niedermayer, O. / Sinnott, R. (eds.), (1995), *European Publics and International Governance*, Oxford: Oxford University Press (to be published).

Niedermayer, O. (1994), "Maastricht und die Entwicklung der öffentlichen Meinung zu Europa", in: Glaeßner, G-J. / Sühl, K. (eds.), *Auf dem Weg nach Europa. Europäische Perspektiven nach dem Ende des Kommunismus*, Opladen: Westdeutscher Verlag, 57–73.

Piore, / Sabel, C. (eds.), (1984), *The Second Industrial Divide. Possibilities for Prosperity*, New York: Basic Books.

Putnam, R.D. (1988), "Diplomacy and Domestic Politics: The Logic of Two-Level Games", *International Organization*, 42, 427–460.

Pyke, F. et al., (eds.), (1990), "Industrial Districts and Inter-Firm Cooperation in Italy", Geneva: *International Institute for Labor Studies*.

Rein, M. (1991), "Frame-Reflective Policy-Discourse", in: Österreichische Zeitschrift für Soziologie, 12, 27–45.

Rosenau, J. N. / Czempiel, E-O. (eds.), (1992), *Governance Without Government. Order and Change in World Politics*, Cambridge et al.: Cambridge University Press.

Sabatier, P. / Jenkins-Smith, H. (eds.), (1993), *Policy Change and Learning. An Advocacy Coalition Approach, Boulder*, CO: Westview Press.

Sabatier, P.A. / Pelkey, N. (1987), "Incorporating Multiple Actors and Guidance Instruments into Models of Regulatory Policymaking. An Advocacy Coalition Framework", in: *Administration & Society*, 19, 2, 236–263.

Sabel, C. F. (1989), "Flexible Specialization and the Re-emergence of Regional Economies", in: Hirst, P. Q. (ed.), *Reversing Industrial Decline? Industrial Structure and Policy in Britain and Her Competitors*, Oxford / New York: Berg, 17–70.

Sadowski, D. / Timmesfeld, A. (1994), "Sozialer Dialog. Die Chancen zur Selbstregulierung der europäischen Sozialparteien", in: Eichener, V. / Voelzkow, H. (eds.), *Europäische Integration und verbandliche Interessenvermittlung*, Marburg: Metropolis-Verlag.

Sandholtz, W. / Zysman, J. (1989), 1992: "Recasting the European Bargain", in: *World Politics*, 42, 1, 95–128.

Sbragia, A. (1992), "Thinking about the European Future. The Uses of Comparison", in: Sbragia, A. (ed.), *Euro-Politics. Institutions and Policymaking in the "New" European Community*, Washington, DC: The Brookings Institution, 275–291.

Scharpf, F. W. (ed.), (1993), *Games in Hierarchies and Networks. Analytical and Empirical Approaches to the Study of Governance Institutions*, Frankfurt/M.: Campus.

Scharpf, F.W. (1985), "Die Politikverflechtungs-Falle. Europäische Integration und deutscher Föderalismus im Vergleich", in: *Politische Vierteljahresschrift*, 26, 4, 323–356 (english version, 1988: "The Joint-Decision Trap: Lessons from German Federalism and European Integration", in: *Public Administration*, 66, 3, 239–278.

Sharp, M. (1991), "The Single Market and European Technology Policies", in: Christopher Freeman et al., eds., *Technology and the Future of Europe. Competition and the Global Environment in the 1990s*, London: Pinter, 59–78.

Siedentopf, H. / Ziller, J. (eds.), (1988), *Making European Politics Work. The Implementation of Community Legislation in the Member States*. Vol. 1–2, London: Sage.

Spöri, D. (1994), "Neue Wege in der marktwirtschaftlichen Industrie- und Strukturpolitik", in: Klepsch / Legrand / Sanne, eds.: 65–77.

Staeck, N. (1994), *Die europäische Strukturfondsförderung in einem föderalen Staat am Beispiel des deutschen Bundeslandes Niedersachsen*, paper presented to the conference "Politiknetzwerke der Regionalpolitik in EU-Staaten", Hannover, 26–27 November 1994.

Tiedemann, R. (1994), *Aufstieg oder Niedergang von Interessen-verbänden? Rent-seeking und europäische Integration*, Baden-Baden: Nomos.

Tinbergen, J. (1965), *International Economic Integration*, Amsterdam: Elsevier.

Walker, R.B.J. / Mendlovitz, S. (eds.), (1990), *Contending Sovereignties. Rethinking Political Community*, Boulder, CO: Lynne Rienner.

Wallace, W. (1994), *Regional Integration: The West European Experience*, Washington, D.C.: The Brookings Institution.

Weiler, J. H. H. (1991), "The Transformation of Europe", in: *Yale Law Journal*, 100, 8, 2403–2483.

Wessels, W. (1996), "Verwaltung im EG-Mehrebenensystem: Auf dem Weg zur Megabürokratie?", in: Jachtenfuchs / Kohler-Koch, (eds.) 165–192.

Wildenmann, R. (ed.), (1991), *Staatswerdung Europas? Optionen für eine Europäische Union*, Baden-Baden: Nomos.

Wilks, S. / Wright, M. (ed.), (1987), *Comparative Government — Industry Relations*, Oxford: Clarendon Press.

Williamson, O.E. (1975), *Markets and Hierarchies. Analysis and Antitrust Implications. A Study in the Economics of Internal Organization*, New York, NY: Free Press.

Zuleeg, M. (1994), "Die Rolle der rechtsprechenden Gewalt in der europäischen Integration", in: *Juristenzeitung*, 49, 1994, 1–8.

by Philippe C. Schmitter,
Stanford University

If the Nation-State Were to Wither Away in Europe, What Might Replace It?

Introduction

The demise of the nation-state has been predicted many times and on many grounds — and yet the announcement of its death has (so far) been premature. Despite its manifest policy incompetence, its multiple institutional entanglements, its burgeoning economic interdependence, its increasingly challenged status, its diminished capacity for unitary action, its ineffectual claims to sovereignty and even its demonstrable irrelevance in solving many of the problems that preoccupy its citizen/subjects, the state malingers on. It still spends much more money, inflicts vastly greater damage, rewards a larger number of persons and attracts considerably more attention and loyalty than any other type of political unit.[1]

Nevertheless, it is in deep trouble and nowhere more so than in its *pays d'origine*, namely, Western Europe. When speculation arises about the withering away of the state, it almost never starts in Asia where its prominence seems to have been reinforced rather than undermined by the accelerated pace of technological change and the successful integration of Japan and the Four Tigers into an increasingly interdependent global economy.[2] In Latin America, the issue of "downsizing" the domestic role of the state and even of escaping from excessively "state matrixed" social relations was certainly arisen, but no one has carried this speculation so far as to suggest that it might be replaced by some other type of political organization.[3] Some countries in Sub-Saharan Africa: Zaire, Somalia, Angola, Ethiopia. Sierra Leone, Liberia, Rwanda are haunted by the specter of "the Stateless State", i.e. not a gradual and consensual withering away of the institution that previously held "a legitimate monopoly of organized violence within a given territory," but a dramatic and complete collapse of all legitimate forms of authority and their replacement by a Hobbesian "war of all against all".[4]

So, with the caveat in mind that whatever the trend may be, it is hardly uniform across the globe or even across continents, I blatantly propose to "sample on the dependent variable" and concentrate on that geo-cultural segment of contemporary reality where we are most likely to find some evidence of the state's withering away (which also happens to be the area of my own expertise). As consolation, I offer the possibility that these developments in the Western tip of Europe will have a major influence on those polities on its Eastern steppe that are currently undergoing momentous changes in their national political and economic institutions. And who knows? If Europe can manage to escape from the interstate system that produced so much human misery and armed conflict, maybe its example will be imitated by others!

Two common assumptions

Before examining what, if anything, may be replacing the tired old Sovereign-Nation-State (henceforth, SNS) and its even more exhausted god-father and step-child, the Inter-State System (ISS) in Western Europe, let us focus on two common assumptions, both of which are likely to influence how we explore this *terra incognita.*

The first is teleological and I would call it, the *"Law of Conservation of Political Energy"*. It postulates that nothing ever disappears in political life until its replacement has already been discovered and is functioning effectively. A sub-corollary of the *natura non facit salta* maxim that all of history tends to be gradual and continuous, this law would inhibit actors from simply jumping into the unknown and willingly abandoning any practice, unless they were very sure that a replacement were available. Sub-optimality or even extreme disfunctionality is not enough to bring about the demise of an existing institution — least of all one as materially and symbolically important as the SNS. Perhaps minor political arrangements can just expire without a fuss, but major ones require the prior reassurance that there is another way — another regime, if you will — that can fill the vacuum and produce at least as good, if not better, collective outcomes. This law would even apply to revolutionary situations in which the *salta* to a new order is "facilitated" by violence and rapid innovation. The revolutionaries, no matter how enraged with the *ancien régime* and impatient to install a new one, must have initially had some alternative set of viable practices in mind, no matter how ideologically misguided they were and subsequently disillusioned they become.

For our speculations, the implication of this law should be clear: whatever is going to replace the SNS in Europe must already exist, even if it is not yet been acknowledged as such or has yet to reach the magnitude to make it a viable substitute. Unless and until a sufficient number of actors recognize that there exist alternatives, as we shall see, beneath and beyond the existing SNS and ISS, it is highly likely that both will survive no matter how badly they perform.

If this law of the conservation of political energy were not valid, we would might well be facing what Marx and Engels once referred to as a "catastrophic balance". This, supposedly rare, moment in history emerges when the forces behind the previous structure of power are exhausted or incapable of reforming their practices, but the new forces that might replace them do not yet exist in sufficient numbers or with sufficient conviction. As Marxs and Engels put it when speaking of Napoléon III and the Second French Empire, the bourgeoisie of France in 1848–52 was no longer capable of ruling and its proletariat was not yet capable of doing so. Into this stalemate rides the man-on-horseback, the providential leader who is firmly attached to neither side but convinced that he or she knows what to do and is prepared to impose that course of action upon others by authoritarian means. In short, the political replacement may not always be available and its absence combined with the demise of the *ancien régime* can lead to a period of alienation, uncertainty and demagoguery which, in turn, may trigger the intervention of "outside" forces and persons that would normally not have a chance at winning.[5]

In the contemporary IR literature, the functional equivalence of bonaparatism is the specter of "the new world disorder" — a scenario in which the Cold War is lost by the Soviets, but not won by their Western opponents. Instead of a triumphant, hegemonic United States capable and ready to intervene by replacing bipolar stalemate with a unipolar order of its own creation, "the system" drifts towards a catastrophic balance — a multipolar clash of civilizations in its most overdramatized version — and awaits its providential leader.

The second law, I would call: the *"Law of Increasing Political Returns to Scale."* It is more empirical in nature (and, hence, more easily subject to falsification) and down-to-earth in its implications: if some set of practices or institutions is removed or falls into disuse, it must be replaced by another set which is more efficient and effective and for this to occur the previous ones must be replaced by practices and institutions that operate on a larger scale of production, distribution or authority. The rationale behind this supposition depends on the (alleged) existence of substantial positive economies of scale which are underexploited within existing SNS. Hence, if these were to wither away and be replaced by some other political arrangement, that arrangement would have to be appreciably larger, more encompassing and more complex than its fragmented, insulated and (allegedly) sovereign predecessors.

Two distinguished observers of recent social trends have unqualifiedly endorsed this proposition:

> "One of the obvious features of the modern world is the increase in the scale of social political units"
>
> (Gellner 1978:133)

"Under the pressures of economics, science and technology, mankind is moving steadily toward large-scale cooperation. Despite periodic reverses, all human history clearly indicates progress in this direction."

(Brzezinski 1970:296)

At its most naive, this might just be a product of the *hubris* of scholars from the United States or other large countries (although ironically both of the above testimonials come from exiled East Europeans) who imagine that only units of that dimension could be expected to make "real" choices and realize "real" economies. For example, Barrington Moore Jr. has argued that small countries are so dependent on what happens in large ones that they are not even worth studying, much less considering as possible alternatives for the future (Moore 1966:xiii). But the most common assumption behind this "law" is that the underlying factor is technology: the enlarged size of the market makes possible an increase in the division of labor and the longer production runs and more standardized products will lower unit costs. Presumably, the same economies can be reaped in the political realm.

But the recent experience of Western Europe suggests that this *telos* may not be so strong and may even be running in the reverse direction. Small countries are not doing worse than large ones; nor do they seem to be condemned to repeating the policies of their "superiors". Indeed, some micro-states like Andorra, Liechtenstein, Luxembourg, Monaco and San Marino have been remarkably successful at experimenting with novel political arrangements and filling quite specialized *niches* in an otherwise enlarged market space.[6]

Which is not to intone the fashionable slogan: "Small is Beautiful" (Kohr 1957; Schumacher 1973; Sale 1980). Technology — or, more specifically, the capability of networks of computers to disperse information with great speed and low cost to the most minute and remote of locations and the power of micro-processors to program machines to make highly customized products from sub-components produced at very dispersed sites — may be opening up new possibilities for a downward shift in scale, but that is manifestly insufficient to explain the complex and contrary changes that have been occurring in contemporary Europe.[7] For there has been movement in contradictory directions. Some firms, cultures and polities have continued to enlarge themselves and to concentrate their share of the benefits, but within them subgroups and segments are acting more affirmatively and autonomously. In other fields, small units are combining in novel ways to produce larger and larger effects. Neither technologies nor markets seem to be pushing inexorably in one or the other direction; therefore, it is futile to presume that there must be an 'optimal' unit for production, identity or authority, much less that this optimality will suffice to make it the 'natural' replacement for the SNS. Even if one could establish some abstract rationale for a given scale of organization, the 'turbulence' that characterizes the contemporary environment would soon eliminate whatever advantages it had. While there is no *a priori* reason why the largest scale solution should always be the most productive, appealing or governable, there is likewise no grounds for assuming that the smallest units will always do much better. What seems to work best is *a mixture of units at different scales* — small units set within a range of larger ones; large ones composed of multiple, relatively autonomous subunits; medium-sized — "regional" or "provincial" — ones interjected between the smaller, "municipal", and larger, "national", levels.[8] It is the interaction among them, each with its differing capacity for control, tolerance, innovation, cooperation, flexibility, sustained effort and symbolic identification, that seems to be the best guarantor of success.

And nowhere is this lesson more apposite that in Western Europe, since one of its unique historical features has been the extraordinary variety in the size, intensity and scope of its component units. Not only have they never been subordinated for any long period of time to a singular economic, cultural or political order, but unique mechanisms of interdependence, competition and equilibration have served to preserve that variety down to the present. Without the preservation of this variety, (and, let us admit it, the consequent free-riding of the smaller nation-states on public goods produced and paid for by the medium and large ones), Europe would have long since lost its most peculiar comparative advantage.[9]

One contestable observation

The nation-state is a rather peculiar unit upon which to base a system of political order. It is of relatively recent vintage — ca. 500 years at the most — and only emerged under very unique historical circumstances on a small and obscure peninsula of the vast Asian continent. Had Europe not been so spectacularly successful in expanding itself *via* trade, investment, colonization and imperialism, its nation-states would have had a difficult time competing with the bureaucratic empires, tribal hordes, royal dynasties, tribute systems (suzerainties), theocratic movements and charismatic followings that characterized the rest of the world. However, it was precisely the comparative advantage of this peculiar type of socio-political unit and, especially, the intense competition between these units that account for that success and for the subsequent diffusion of it as a model for organizing all of the planet's political life.

And it is not over yet! Units that call themselves nation-states are still emerging, struggling to secede from existing ones, and demanding certification from their peers in the United Nations. Over the last three years, twenty-five new nation-states have been admitted to the club — including one, the FYROM, which does not even have a recognized name! From the present 184 UN members, the number could well top 300 during the next century.

Obviously, not all of the 184 "deserve" the prestigious label: "nation-state." Cynically, it has been suggested that any human group with a headquarters, a flag and an army can acquire it. For analytical purposes, the central feature of the nation-state as a distinctive form of political organization consists of the *spatial-temporal coincidence* of three properties:

(1) a unique (and usually contiguous) spatial location (territory);

(2) an autonomous set of functional tasks (compétences);

(3) a distinctive and shared set of symbols (identity).

Where and when these coincide historically and are, therefore, organized into a single polity, there exists a nation-state *strictu sensu.* In this ideal modular unit of the ISS, the exercise of public authority in different functional domains is coincident with a specific territory and a distinctive identity based on a common language, culture or descent group (*éthnie*). When one arrives at its physical borders, the legitimate exercise of coercion in all these domains ends, as does the feeling of a shared "community of fate" (*Schicksalsgemeinschaft*). The polity on the other side of that boundary should have no right to command obedience in any domain on one's own side or to expect solidarity in time of necessity — and there presumably exists no superordinate entity capable of exercising authority and redistributing benefits over both sides.

Needless to say, most so-called SNS have always been imperfect approximations of this model. Even in the European *pays d'origine*, many of them had undefined or indefensible boundaries, were incapable of performing many of the functional tasks of governance (including that of maintaining an effective monopoly over organized violence), were compelled to allow persons with other identities to live within their boundaries, depended upon non-nationals for key resources (even their very survival), consented to alien powers exercising authority over specific issues and/or subordinated their own exercise of authority to international norms. Originally, a small number of units managed to combine the first two qualities, territory and functional *compétences*, into a state and were subsequently able to exploit this newly acquired monopoly power to forge a singular common identity, i.e. to become a nation. Latecomers in Europe and elsewhere usually proceeded in the inverse direction, using the shared symbols of a putatively national language and culture as a basis for laying claim to a particular turf and independent capacity for self-rule.

All of which means that this "coincidence" or "congruence" of territory, functional authority and identity has always been approximate and subject to contestation. *What characterizes the present epoch in Europe, however, is a remarkable and, I believe, irrevocable increase in the dissociation of these three properties.*[10]

This, in turn, has triggered a multifarious effort by a wide variety of actors to experiment with the scale of their territorial constituencies, functional interest categories and collective identities. The SNS is being undermined, all right, and at an unprecedented pace, but it is not being replaced by a single institution or arrangement. Instead, what we witness is a proliferation of "experiments in the scale of governance, production and identity", some of which reach *beyond* the existing nation-states and others which burrow *beneath* them.[11]

Consider the following *Gedankenbild:* Try to imagine a stable political arrangement that did *not* have the following:

(1) a locus of clearly defined, unchallengeable supreme authority;

(2) an established, central hierarchy of public offices;

(3) a pre-defined and distinctive sphere of competence within which it can make decisions binding on all;

(4) a fixed and contiguous territory over which it exercised authority;

(5) an exclusive recognition by other polities, right to membership in international organizations and capacity to conclude international treaties;

(6) an overarching identity and symbolic presence for its subjects/citizens;

(7) an established and effective monopoly over the legitimate means of coercion;

(8) a unique capacity for the direct implementation of its decisions upon intended individuals and groups; and (9) an exclusive capacity for controlling the movement of goods, services, capital and persons within its borders —

but *did* have the capability to take decisions, resolve conflicts, produce public goods, coordinate private behavior, regulate markets, hold elections, respond to interest pressures, generate revenue, allocate expenditures, engage in binding negotiations with external powers, and perhaps even declare and wage war! If you can do this, you will have succeeded in at least mentally superseding the limits imposed by the nation-state upon our habitual ways of thinking about politics, although it may still be difficult to imagine how such a "post-sovereign", "post-nationalist", "poly-centric", "neo-medieval," "multi-layered" arrangement could possibly be stable in the longer run, much less effective and efficient in the authoritative allocation of values.

Some novel terminology

So, what if the territorial, functional and symbolic domains were less and less congruent with the same national system of production or authority? What if there were a plurality of polities at multiple levels of aggregation — national, sub-national and supranational — that overlapped in a wide range of policy areas? Moreover, what if these authorities did not have well-established layers of hierarchical relations, but negotiated with each other in some continuous way to perform common tasks and resolve common problems? What, in other words, if there were no sovereignty, no definitive center for the resolution of conflicts or for the allocation of public goods — just a process? And what if the participants in this process were not just a fixed number of national states, but an enormous variety of sub-national units and networks, supranational associations and movements and transnational firms and parties?

For one thing, our language for talking about politics — especially stable, iterative, "normal" politics — would have to change considerably. Virtually all the terms we have are indelibly impregnated with "statist" assumptions. Whenever we refer to the number, location, authority, status, membership, capacity, identity, type or significance of political units, we employ concepts that implicitly or explicitly refer to a universe dominated by SNS and "their" surrounding national societies. It seems self-evident to us that this particular form of organizing political life will continue to dominate all others, spend most publicly generated funds, authoritatively allocate most resources, enjoy a unique source of legitimacy and furnish most people with a distinctive identity. But what if the issue were *not* the outright demise of its peculiar brand of "high politics" and replacement by the "higher politics" of a new sovereign authority, i.e. a supra-national state? What if something qualitatively different were evolving that would blur the distinction between "high" and "low politics" and eventually produce a new form of multi-layered governance without clear lines of demarcated jurisdiction and identity? How could we identify these emergent properties, and what would we call them?

One possible source of conceptual inspiration already exists in the form of "Euro-speak", the *Volapuk integré* that is constantly being invented to describe *ad hoc* or *de jure* solutions to EC/EU problems. Originally, these expressions had a distinctively neo-functionalist cast, e.g. *l'engrenage, le "spill-over", la méthode communautaire, l'acquis communautaire* and *la supranationalité*, but recently they have increased greatly in number and seem to be emanating more and more from European jurisprudence or treaty provisions, e.g. *subsidiarity, proportionality, additivity, complementarity, transparence, compétences, direct effect, unanimity, qualified majority voting, co-responsibility, transposition, géométrie variable, juste retour, mutual recognition, home country control, co-decision, pooled sovereignty, opting-out, opting-in, economic and social cohesion, sustainable convergence, euro-compatibility, balanced support,* and so forth.[12] There are even a few terms that seek to describe the process of integration as a whole and/or its eventual outcome, e.g. "*Comitologie*", the way in which Commission drafts are subjected to an extensive exchange of views among national administrators, interest representatives and Eurocrats until a consensus position is reached and a policy proposal put forth; "*Troika*", the system of collective executive power through which the President of the Council of Ministers during the six-month term in office of his/her country is associated with the preceding and succeeding presidents; "*Concentric circles*", the assumption that all institutional development within the EC/EU revolves around a single administrative core, i.e. the Commission, and eventually leads to accretions of its *compétences*.

Four ideal types

These discrete expressions may provide a better glimpse of emerging properties than terms drawn from the existing vocabularies of national politics, but they can hardly be expected to capture the general configuration of territoriality/ authority /identity that is emerging in Europe at the supra-national level. Heretofore, the *porte-manteau* term for such a multi-layered configuration has been *federation.* Not only does this common label disguise a fairly wide range of institutional formats, but it strongly implies the existence of an orthodox sovereign national state at its core — regardless of how political authority and identity may be shared among its sub-national territorial constituencies or functional domains.[13] Or, it is precisely the possibility that this core may never emerge to resolve the growing incongruence within Europe that is my major (and admittedly speculative) hunch.

Fig. 1 Territorial and functional elements in the formation of politics

TERRITORIAL CONSTITUENCIES

FUNCTIONAL CONSTITUENCIES:	variable tangential egalitarian differentiated reversible	fixed contiguous hierarchical identical irreversible
variable dispersed shared overlapping	CONDOMINIO	CONSORTIO
fixed cumulative separate coincident	CONFEDERATIO	STATO/ FEDERATIO

Elsewhere, I have tried to provoke a discussion of what might be emerging at the supra-level by resorting to the deduction of ideal types with Neo-Latin appellations — better to remind the reader of the novel arrangements they represent.[14]

The main assumption behind Figure One is that modern politics is rooted in different forms of representation. Where the units of authority have grown larger in area and population, and more heterogenous in social and economic interests, rulers and ruled have relied increasingly on regularized mechanisms of indirect participation to communicate with each other.[15] *Grosso modo*, these linkages conform to two different principles of aggregation: the *territorial* and the *functional.* Various intermediaries — parties, associations, movements, clienteles, notables — identify with the constituencies formed by these principles and *re*-present their interests vis-a-vis authorities. It is this mix of territorial constituencies and functional domains, along with their corresponding internal relations of authority and accountability that defines the type of polity.

And the emerging Euro-polity is no different. It began with a dual bias:

(1) toward channeling the representation of territorial interests exclusively through the national governments of member states; and

(2) toward privileging the development of functional representation through trans-national, European-level interest associations.

The deliberate neo-functionalist strategy of Jean Monnet *et Cie.* was to concede the former as an inescapable (if eventually mutable) feature of the international system and to build gradually and surreptitiously upon the latter. After some initial successes, this failed for a variety of reasons and the ensuing period of "intergovernmentalism" from the mid-1960s to the mid-1980s saw even the functional interests being transmitted largely through national territorial channels.[16] Since then, the mix of functional domains and territorial constituencies at various levels has shifted significantly, giving rise to the present uncertainty about the eventual outcome.

(Whether this Euro-polity is going to be "national" or not depends on the third dimension that we have discussed above, namely, the acceptance by its members of a common identity and community of fate. So far, the data consistently gathered by *Eurobaromètre* on public opinion in the member states clearly demonstrates that this dimension is the slowest to change and the most difficult to manipulate. Very few people have come to identify themselves with any frequence as "European" and the proportion has tended to decline, rather than rise, since the mid-1980s when the pace of economic integration accelerated.[17] Hence, it is my assumption that the effective choices for the present involve territorial constituencies and functional domains, and that symbolic adherence will only emerge, if at all, much later *pace* Karl Deutsch and the social communications approach to international integration.[18] Put more colloquially, the problem of moving beyond the SNS and the ISS in Europe necessarily involves "making a Euro-polity without first making Europeans."

There is no need to discuss the bottom two ideal types in Figure One since they correspond to the alternative outcomes that students of European integration have long discussed — and disputed:

(1) the confederatio or intergovernmental organization that would be limited to the collective pursuit of those tasks which protect and enhance the sovereign autonomy of its member states;

(2) the stato/federatio or supra-national state that would inherit most of the tasks currently performed by its member states which will have transferred their sovereignty to this new set of authoritative institutions.

Other outcomes have proven difficult even to imagine, much less to conceptualize accurately. For one thing, as I noted above, our political vocabulary lacks the proper terminology. We are familiar with the properties of states and intergovernmental organizations — even if we recognize that they come in various sizes and shapes — but we would have to go far back in European history to recapture a more diverse language about political units.[19] And, even if we could recover ancient labels or invent new ones to describe other political forms, we might still find it difficult to accept them as stable solutions to the problem of political order. There is an almost inevitable temptation to assume that such things as *confederacies, covenants, compacts, leagues, co-principalities, confraternities, commonwealths, Bündnisse, Ämter, Eidgenossenschaften, Stammesherzogtümer, Städtebünde, Reich, consortii, communae, regnae, conjuratii, parléments, confrèries, leghe, repubbliche,* etc. are only passing phenomena, destined eventually to be molded into more coherent states, even nation-states.

Moreover, it is abundantly clear that the contemporary promoters of the integration process do not themselves have a consistent "model" of where they are headed politically — least of all, one that has an obvious historical referent.[20] The closest approximation used to be the notion of the "United States of Europe", but virtually no one today seems to believe that the United States of America offers an attractive *Vorbild* to Europeans. As I mentioned above, *federation* is probably the concept that best expresses where most of them think they are headed, but even that is subject to diverse interpretation, not to say, "essential contestation".[21]

If my hunch is correct, the "experiments with scale" that are occurring simultaneously throughout Europe in production, culture and governance are producing a type of polity that will resemble neither the inter-governmental *confederatio* nor the supra-national *stato* or *federatio*. In a tentative effort to describe this potentially novel form of political order, I derived two ideal types in the upper cells of Figure One.

The *consortio* is a form of collective action practiced more by consenting firms than consenting polities. In it, national authorities of fixed number and identity agree to cooperate in the performance of functional tasks that are variable, dispersed and overlapping. They retain their respective territorially-based identities, form a relatively contiguous spatial bloc and accept positions within a common hierarchy of authority, but pool their capacities to act autonomously in domains that they can no longer control at their own level of aggregation. There seem to have been relatively few salient historic examples of this type given its implications for national sovereignty, but one suspects that a detailed investigation of the bilateral relations between any two contiguous states would reveal a large number of "regional" commissions and task forces designed to cope with specific problems without endangering the international status of their participants. Once these proliferate enough to interact and stimulate each other, then, it may be accurate to speak of a *consortio* having replaced strictly state-like relations, say, between the United States and Canada or Norway and Sweden.

The *condominio* would be the most unprecedented, even unimaginable, outcome of all since it would be based on variation in both territorial constituencies and functional domains. Precisely what the state system had taken so long to fix into a coincident interrelation would be sundered and allowed to vary in unpredictable ways. Instead of one Europe with recognized and contiguous boundaries and, hence, a singular and definite population, there would be many Europes. Instead of a Eurocracy accumulating organizationally distinct but politically coordinated tasks around a single center, there would be multiple regional institutions acting with relative autonomy to solve common problems and produce different public goods. Moreover, their dispersed and overlapping domains — not to mention their incongruent memberships — could result in competitive, even conflictual, situations that would certainly seem inefficient when compared with the clear demarcations of competence and hierarchy of authority that (supposedly) characterize existing national states. While it seems unlikely that anyone would set out deliberately to create a *condominio* — and no long-lasting historical precedents come to mind — one can imagine a scenario of divergent interests, distracted actors, improvised measures and compromised solutions in which it just emerges *faute de mieux* and rapidly institutionalizes itself as the least threatening outcome.

None of the prevailing theories of international integration can predict which (if any) of the above four ideal types will be closest to the Euro-polity that is emerging. All focus on process not outcome. All presume that integration will eventually lead to some kind of stable institutionalized equilibrium, but fail to specify how and when this can be expected to occur.

Which of these abstract models the actual EC/EU will resemble depends on at least four intervening conditions whose discrete impact and compound effects cannot presently be foreseen:

(1) the heavy reliance on indirect policy implementation by the member states and their local units will make the effective and uniform realization of new EC/EU responsibilities more difficult;

(2) the growing skepticism in public discourse and the unprecedented politicization that was triggered by the process of ratifying the Maastricht Treaty will constrain the freedom of action of those proposing "Eurocratic" solutions;

(3) the incorporation of new members, especially the post- communist ones in Eastern Europe and the former Soviet Union, is bound to put more stress on existing arrangements for representation and decision-making; and

(4) the increasing attention that will have to be paid to issues of external insecurity and foreign threats may force some dramatic revisions in Europe's collective capacity for problem-solving.[22]

These intervening factors: implementation, enlargement, politicization and insecurity are pushing the future Euro-polity in different directions. Some toward the acquisition of greater qualities of stateness; others toward confederal solutions; and still others toward the novel hybrids of consortio and condominio. The only thing that it seems safe to presume is that the problems of reaching a compromise on Community/Union institutions will intensify rather than diminish as the member states move toward their 1996 *rendez-vous* with institutional reform.

One shift in level

Up to this point we have been committing an elementary fallacy, all too common among students of European regional integration in particular, and international cooperation in general. We have concentrated exclusively on the formal interaction between established nation-states and emerging supra-national organizations. Not only have we barely mentioned the possibility that the autonomy of these SNS might be increasingly constrained, even defined, by powerful domestic and international forces, but we have not even entertained the thought that sub-national actors might be capable of establishing independent relations of influence and even of authority with the supra-national ones.

As long as the Law of Increasing Political Returns to Scale was a reliable guide, there was no need to descend to lower, i.e. municipal, provincial, sectoral or branch, levels of aggregation. By definition, the SNS was supposed to be sufficiently unitary in its capability to act, autonomous in the way that it defined its so-called "national interests" and monopolistic in its control over all political transactions with external actors. The only possible threat to its preeminence had to come from above — from its replacement by a higher and equally sovereign entity.

However, as suggested above, the experiments in scale that have been occurring in Europe have not been confined to the supra-national level. Not only have there been more articulate and insistent demands on behalf of smaller territorial constituencies and more specialized functional domains, but even in the area where the SNS seemed most secure, that of collective symbols, sub-national units have advanced strong competing claims on individual identities. If this were not troubling enough, there is growing evidence of trans-national alliances forming between these sub-national groups, either in the form of functionally-based interest associations, cartels, multi-national enterprises, semi-public self-regulatory schemes — not to mention the burgeoning network of strategic alliances and joint ventures between firms from different countries — or territorially-based arrangements between provinces, cantons, communes and even municipalities across national borders. In short, instead of focusing so exclusively on a Euro-Polity in our search for a replacement for the withering nation-state, we should have also been looking for the prospective emergence of a Euro-society.

Jean Monnet's famous neo-functionalist method of integration, initiated with the European Coal and Steel Community in the early 1950s and subsequently extended with EURATOM and the European Economic Community, was rooted precisely in the gradual and inexorable formation of just such a "*European Civil Society*". It assumed that with the shift of limited functions to a supra-national secretariat and its active encouragement of a surrounding set of interest associations the basis was set for an eventual transformation of the SNS. If and when these functions "spilled-over" into other policy areas, other functional interests organized at the level of the Community as a whole would follow suit. The subsequent pace of European integration may have been slower than the neo-functionalists presumed; the extent of spill-over a good deal more uneven and contentious.[23] Nevertheless, something like a novel system of organized interests did grow up around the Bruxelles-Luxembourg-Strasbourg nexus, and in recent years it has been extended to include an impressive range of transnational social movements. There is no question that Western Europe has acquired by far the densest regional network of NGOs in the world. Students of this phenomenon may agree that its coverage is considerably more specialized in scope and skewed in favor of business interests than the national systems of member states, but — when combined with the much more intensive trans-national exchanges between firms and agencies — it still consti-tutes a major (and accelerating) shift in the scale of political rela-tions.[24]

Seen from this sub-national perspective, the link between liberalization of regional economic markets and eventual political integration depends *less* upon the highly visible and formalized processes of intergovernmental bargaining, regional treaty-making or the drafting of an EC/EU constitution and *more* upon the in-visible and dispersed processes of forging class, sectoral and pro-fessional relations across national boundaries and their trans-formation into informal practices within private associations, parties, movements, even individual enterprises and firms. The European SNS would be displaced by gradual and almost surrepti-tious private process, rather than by a dramatic and highly public event.[25]

A novel (and quite unexpected) element has been added to this scenario in the late 1980s by a radical change in the ISS. With the collapse of the Cold War, many of the territorial units that had been frozen into place by polarized security calculations found themselves in a position to pursue more independent foreign policies. In Europe, sub- and trans-national identities were suddenly free to experiment with different boundaries, alliances and strategies. The very process of regional integration had shifted policy-making to a more remote site and comprehensive level, thereby, making individuals and groups more conscious of their local and provincial peculiarities. Moreover, previous economies of scale for producers in large countries had largely disappeared with the existence of a well-established, overarching institution that guarantees market access, property rights, legal protection, product standardization, exchange rates (for some) and civic freedoms and democratic processes to even the smallest of its component units. Under the umbrella of EC/EU jurisdiction, it is now possible to demand much greater political autonomy without fearing the wrath and retribution of central national authorities and without paying the costs of limited market size. It is increasingly possible "to have one's cake and eat it too", i.e. to enjoy the benefits of small and large scale governance. As a result, the original emphasis on functionally-defined lines of interest has now been enlivened and made more complex by the superimposition of newly emergent, culturally-defined forms of sub-national identity.[26]

This, in turn, has introduced a whole new dimension to the territorial question in Europe, namely, *subsidiarity* or what level of aggregation should be relevant in deciding and implementing which policies. Until recently, everyone took it for granted that the natural and irreducible spatial constituencies were defined by SNS — in their existing and highly unequal configuration.[27] This is how voting quotas, financial contributions, nominations for European Commissioners and Judges, seats on the Council of Ministers, and so forth are distributed. Indeed, the orthodox assumption has long held that the creation of the EC actually served to strengthen the role of national states over lesser political units.[28]

Subsequent changes from below in the territorial distribution of authority within these states[29] and from within in the magnitude and distribution of Community regional funds[30] have resulted in a veritable explosion of attention by sub-national political units to the integration process. Regions, provinces, municipalities, and even whole "unrepresented nations" (e.g. Catalans, Welsh, Basques and Bretons) have opened up quasi-embassies in Brussels and sought to establish direct contact with EC officials to influence the distribution of structural funds and the direction of sectoral policies. They have been forming associations, alliances and commissions across national borders and pressing for the special status of *Euro-regiones* that group adjacent units from different countries.[31] It would obviously be premature to suppose that this flurry of activity and the creation of informal channels of sub-national representation will succeed in "outflanking" the heretofore dominant position of national member states within the formal institutions of the EC/EU, and eventually drive the outcome toward a *condominio* in which varying and overlapping scales of territorial aggregation would interact with varying and overlapping domains of functional competence. The recent insertion in the Maastricht Treaty of a "Committee of Regions" does, however, marginally enhance that probability.[32]

One possibel conclusion

With the impending Intergovernmental Conference of 1996 we should have a much better idea about what type of supra-national polity the EC/EU will become and whether it will strengthen or weaken existing SNS. We should also have a better grasp on how successful the territorial and functional sub-national units are going to be in circumventing the unitary control of their respective SNS and establishing working relationships among themselves and directly with the EC/EU.

To this author both processes look irreversible — even if the end-state is still far from obvious. Too many entanglements and commitments have already been accepted. Too many expectations have been lodged in these exchanges. Too many problems no longer seem manageable within national states. Indeed, there is even a danger that the supra-level will be called upon to bear a excessive burden. National politicians have increasingly looked to the Community to provide the only way out of the political stalemates and sub-optimal equilibria in which they are entrapped. Sending intractable issues to Brussels and blaming it for the need to implement unpopular policies at home has become a standard feature of European national politics. *The great irony of this moment in the integration process is that it is the national executives of the member states, i.e. those who are presumably most entrusted with defending the SNS, who have been most inclined to devolve new compétences and territoires upon the institutions of supra-national governance.*[33] *And it has been large segments of the national citizenries of these same countries, presumably more concerned with material than symbolic concerns, who have opposed these initiatives. Whether these two forces beyond and beneath existing national states can compromise upon some innovative form of multi-level governance with overlapping arenas of policy and multiple layers of identity may well determine the future of this unprecedented effort at peaceful and consensual integration — and might even set a precedent that will determine the future of the sovereign national state.*[34]

Notes

1. For a particularly eloquent (but, in my view, misleading) defense of its "limited but real powers", see Hoffmann (1982).

2. See, for example Amsden (1985) and Wade (1988). Chalmers Johnson's discussion (1982) of a distinctive Asian "developmental state" in his *MITI and the Japanese Miracle: The Growth of Industrial Policy* was an early exploration of this theme.

3. Marcelo Cavarrozi (1982) has stressed this in his "Beyond Transitions to Democracy in Latin America"; also O'Donnell (1993).

4. See, for example, Darnton (1994) "Stateless State: a New Specter Stalking Africa". Or as another author put it, "From the perspective of loyalty and legitimacy, there is simply not much 'there there' in two-thirds of the entities masquerading as nation-states ... (and) this lack of political cohesion in ex-colonial and non-Western territories has become more glaring as Cold War politics disappears: *sans* the Great Game with the Soviets, the rich Western world now has fewer reasons to care", (Clad 1994:671).

5. Antonio Gramsci had a slightly different way of making the same point: "The old is dying and the new cannot be born ... in this interregnum a great variety of morbid symptoms appear".

6. *The Economist* (27 August 1988) refers to these countries as the "Five Tiny Secrets of Success" and "Europe's High-Fliers" in the 1980s. "Once, with the exception of the Vatican, the common denominators were size and poverty", but this has dramatically changed — again, except for the Vatican, which has fallen on hard times. The article warns, however, that they will need all the ingenuity that made them Europe's "great survivors" to succeed after 1992.

7. For such a simplistic (and popular) interpretation, see Naisbitt (1994) where the pithy aphorism is offered that "the bigger the world economy, the more powerful its smallest players" (p. 5).

8. This notion that a "mixture of scales" provides the optimal combination seem to be catching on in the literature on business ad-

ministration, although it has been associated there more with Japan than with Europe. See, for example, the article in *The Financial Times* (14 July 1989) entitled: "Where Large and Small Work Together in Perfect Harmony". It recounts the "change in industrial culture" brought to Northeast England by the implantation of a Japanese firm, Nissan. This company deliberately fostered "a complicated network of industrial interdependence ... between large and small. ... They started out with fairly lengthy supply lines but they have gradually drawn many of them in and are going more and more for really local content. ... The Japanese need local content for their products to be classed as European; the suppliers need investment and tuition to achieve and maintain the necessary quality."

9. These issues I have discussed more extensively in "Experimenting with the Scale of Production, Culture and Governance in Western Europe" to be published in P. C. Schmitter (ed.), *Experimenting with Scale in Western Europe* (forthcoming, Cambridge University Press).

10. For a rather similar perception, see Brown (1995), where this is referred to as "the problem of incongruence".

11. In addition to the essay cited in FN. , see my conclusion to the same volume: "Afterthoughts and Forebodings about Experimenting with Scale" where I discuss the contributions to this theme by Arnaldo Bagnasco, Victoria de Grazia, Gudmund Hernes, Victor Pérez-Diaz, Charles Maier, Charles Sabel, Fritz Scharpf and L. J. Sharpe.

12. Perhaps it is also significant that many of the new items of Euro-speak seem to be emerging in English, rather than French which was the language initially dominant within the Eurocracy. When using these expressions in this article, I have placed the neo-functionalist ones in *italics* print and those in Euro-speak in <u>underlined</u> *italics* for the convenience of the reader.

The Economist recently asked its readers: "Sprechen Sie Maastricht?" To the concepts of *cohesion, convergence, competence, opting out, subsidarity and unanimity,* they added: "*in every nook and cranny*" which they defined as "a quaint English phrase to describe where Brussels bureaucrats would be if there were no subsidiarity" (December 14, 1991), p.54.

An industrious Frenchman, François Gondrand (1991), has complied a glossary of Euro-speak: *Parlez-vous Eurocrate?* with 1,000 entries!

13. From this perspective, the British allergy to the "F-word" which seems so ridiculous to a North American or German is well-founded. What they are objecting to is the possible emergence of a *stato*, i.e. any political form — however decentralized or deconcentrated — that accumulates sovereign powers within a single set of institutions at the European level. Cf. the discussion between Ian Davidson, "New era for Ec family" and Martin Wolf, "Federalism before a fall", *Financial Times*, December 3, 1991, p. 21. Samuel Brittan has attempted to clarify the terms of discussion for the British and concludes that "the true dividing lines are between different ideas on the role of the state rather than between countries or between federalists and nationalists". "Let fools contend about the forms", *Financial Times* (November 21, 1991).

14. A version of this scheme has appeared in Schmitter 1992a.

15. Admittedly, this leaves unexplained the relatively recent resurgence in interest in referendums and other devices of more direct democracy. They have, in fact, played a rather crucial role in the ratification of EC/EU agreements — often in countries that had little or no previous national experience with them.

16. For a brief account of the failure of Euro-corporatism, see Schmitter and Streeck, (1991).

17. I am endebted to Karl-Heinz Reif for allowing me to read several recent, but unpublished, essays of his analyzing the time-series data from *Eurobaromètre* on this variable.

18. For a succinct statement of this "transactionalist" approach to integration, see Deutsch et al. 1964. The *locus classicus* linking nationalism and social communication is Deutsch (1953). Donald Puchala has recently evaluated the contribution of this approach (1981).

19. Hence, the notion that the international system is becoming "neo-medieval" has gained some currency. See Bull (1977:264) for what seems to be the first appreciation of this. For more popular versions of this idea, see Eco (1986:73–86); Lapham (1988:8–9).

20. It should be stressed that in the diverse processes of nation-state-building, there has never been a pure case of peaceful, voluntary and negotiated integration of previously independent political units. The closest approximation consists in those cases that relied heavily on

marriage, dynastic alliances and family inheritance (the Hapsburgs being the most notoriously successful practitioners of this strategy — up to a point). Even those that did eventually arrive at some degree of national unity through alliances and treaties such as Switzerland, Germany and the USA experienced some significant episode of civil war or international conflict *en cours de route*. Canada and Australia might be considered exceptions, although the extent of previous independence of their constituent units is questionable.

21. For a particularly intelligent use of federalist theory to explore the emergent properties of the Euro-polity, see Sbragia (1992).

22. One thing, however, is abundantly clear: none of this experimentation beneath and beyond the SNS would be possible if it were not for the prior establishment of a "pluralistic security community" among the member-states themselves. Only in such a "Post-Hobbesian" context in which no participant can imagine any other participant using organized violence to impose its preferred outcome can one even contemplate a gradual and negotiated transition to such a novel polity of multi-levels and overlapping *compétences*. The prospect of a common *external* security threat, however, could very well enhance such a development — provided the *internal* members can agree on the nature of the threat and on the actions necessary to counter it.

23. This was first examined critically in Lindberg and Scheingold 1970. For a more recent re-appraisal of the spill-over hypothesis and its neo-functional foundations, see Schmitter 1992b.

24. See Schmitter and Streeck (1991); also Mazey and Richardson (1993).

25. William Wallace (1990:9) has recently suggested drawing a distinction between two parallel integration processes: "Informal integration consists of those intense patterns of interaction which develop without the impetus of deliberate political decisions, following the dynamics of markets, technology, communications networks, and social change. Formal integration consists of those changes in the framework of rules and regulations which encourage — or inhibit, or redirect — informal flows. Informal integration is a continuous process, a flow: it creeps unawares out of the myriad transactions of private individuals pursuing private interests. Formal integration is discontinuous: it proceeds decision by decision, bargain

by bargain, treaty by treaty." The book in which these remarks appeared, however, is devoted almost exclusively to bargaining among national states and the operations of international organizations.

26. One very salient example is the increased self-assertion of the German *Länder* with regard to the ratification of the Maastricht Treaty by the *Bundesrat*: "Ja, aber. Blockieren die Bundesländer Kohls Pläne einer Politischen Unions in Europa?", *Die Spiegel*, No. 13 (March 23, 1992), pp. 68–73. During the recent British elections, increased autonomy for Scotland became such a major issue that the Conservative foreign secretary, Douglas Hurd (1992), felt compelled to remind the Scots that it might not be so easy: "Scotland could not slide out of the United Kingdom on Monday and sidle into the Community as the thirteenth member on Tuesday. ... The lawyers would have a series of field days. There would be many months or years of disputes and uncertainty. ... Many European countries could put obstacles in Scotland's path as they would be reluctant to set a precedent for their own potential breakaway regions".

27. There is one, very important exception to this generalization. From very early on, the German *Länder* insisted that they be informed and participate at least indirectly in the deliberations of the Council of Ministers on issues assigned exclusively to them by the constitution of the Federal Republic. (Hrbek and Thaysen 1986).

28. This has long been a theme of Stanley Hoffmann. See, for example, the article cited in FN. 1. Also Puchala (1988) where it was found, even after the signing of the SEA, that "the weight of evidence tends to lie on the side of (European integration's having) strengthened states" (p. 461). Sharpe (1989) would also agree. For a more recent restatement, see Moravcsik (1994).

In my view, this conclusion is only plausible if one chooses to ignore (1) the extent to which a growing variety of domestic interests and passions are stimulated by the integration process to focus on a diverse set of state agencies — each of which develop independent relationships with EC/EU institutions, thereby, undermining the SNS's capability for unitary action; (2) the extent to which the proliferation of policy arenas at the supra-national level also encourages domestic interests and passions to circumvent national channels of decision-making, thereby, undermining the SNS's (putative) monopoly over political transactions with foreigners; (3) the extent to which domestic interests and passions in each SNS are capable of negotiating and contracting with each other, thereby, creating new forms of transnational "authoritative allocation" which cannot be easily "treatified" — much less controlled — by the SNS; (4) the extent to which national state actors — despite their best formal efforts at protecting their most exclusive property, i.e. sovereignty — often find themselves dealing with unintended consequences (backed by unexpectedly powerful sub-national actors) and are compelled to make significant concessions, if only to retain their credibility in the eyes of their fellow SNS; and, finally, (5) the extent to which within in the Council of Ministers (not to mention, its shadow organization, COREPER) the lines between "national" and "European" interests are blurred beyond recognition and the pressure to converge toward a regional norm become virtually irresistible.

It also helps if, as in Moravcsik's paper, one systematically confuses the role of the national government executive at any given moment with the longer term capacity of the national state. Not everything that strengthens the hand of the President or Prime Minister in a specific negotiation automatically enhances the long-run authority of the SNS.

In short, I find this conclusion to be very misleading. The only plausible grounds I can think of for accepting it are counter-factual, namely, that the role of the SNS would have declined even more in the absence of an EC/EU.

29. For an overview of this process of domestic regionalization, see Tarrow, Katzenstein and Graziano (1978); Mény (1982); Keating, (1988).

30. For an overview, see Marks in Sbragia (1992).

31. For an insightful analysis of how new bargaining arrangements are emerging between sub-national and national units, see Parri, (1989).

32. For some appropriately critical remarks on the likelihood of the emergence of a *"Europe des Régions"* rather than a *"Europe des Etats"*, see Marks in Spragia (1992:212–224) and Marks 1991. Also Alexander, (1991).

One of the most obvious impediments is the very asymmetric fashion in which regional governance is distributed across national polities in

Europe. Great Britain, for example, completely lacks this interme-
diate layer (although the issue of devolution of authority to Scotland
did emerge during the recent elections). Portugal and Greece have
only recently begun to experiment with regionalization in order to
attract more EC funds. Unfortunately for the issue of *economic and
social cohesion,* it is invariably the most developed internal regions that
are the best equipped and most eager to exploit the Bruxelles
connection.

For the enthusiastic endorsements of this idea, see Petrella (1978);
Pierret, (1984); Raffarin (1988); Ward (1991); Clement (1991).

33. With, of course, the notable exceptions of the British and, to a
lesser extent, the Danes — although I would concede that other de-
fenders of national sovereignty may be hiding behind these vociferous
opponents of supra-nationality.

34. Time and space preclude my delving into a related issue, namely,
whether it will be possible to reach a stable compromise on this
institutional question without tackling the prior issue of democracy
or, to resort to Euro-speak, without filling the EC/EU's "democracy
deficit". The fact that mass publics continue to remain national (or
sub-national), have little or no identification with Europe as such, and
tend to regard the politics of the EC/EU as excessively remote and
opaque casts a giant shadow over the entire process. It is one thing to
imagine an institutional arrangement that member governments,
national bureaucrats and Euro-associations could live with; it is quite
another to imagine one that individual citizens not granted the power
to hold the Commission accountable and sub-national groups and
movements not granted assured access would accept as legitimate in
the long run.

So far, the practice of modern democracy has been confined to nation-
states and their sub-units. Only polities with some minimal level of
shared identity seem to be able to generate sufficient trust among
politicians and solidarity across classes and regions to permit "con-
tingent consent" and "bounded uncertainty" — the two operative
principles of modern democracy.

In a recent unpublished essay, I have discussed this issue and concluded that the rules and practices of established liberal, representative and national democracy do not provide sufficient foundations for
the larger-scale, more remote and vicarious politics of the EC/EU. If

they decide to tackle this issue in 1996 or thereafter, the proponents of a democratic Euro-polity will have to come up with novel arrangements for accountability and new rights and obligations for citizens. "Democracy in the Euro-Polity: Temporary or Permanent Deficit?", paper presented at the European Dialogues Conference, Bruxelles, 24–25 February 1995.

References

Alexander, Jeffrey (1991), "Sceptical Reflections on a Europe of Regions: Britain, Germany and the ERDF", *Journal of Public Policy*, Vol. 10, No. 4, pp. 417–447.

Amsden, Alice H. (1985), "The State and Taiwan's Economic Development" in P. Evans, D. Rueschemeyer & T. Skocpol (eds.), *Bringing the State Back In*, Cambridge: Cambridge University Press, pp. 78–106

Moore, Barrington Jr. (1966), *Social Origins of Dictatorship and Democracy*, Boston: Beacon Press, p. xiii.

Brittan, Samuel (1991), "Let fools contend about the forms", *Financial Times* (November 21).

Brown, Seyom (1995), *New Forces, Old Forces and the Future of World Politics*, New York: HarperCollins, where this is referred to as "the problem of incongruence"(pp. 243–252).

Brzezinski, Zbigniew (1970), *Between Two Ages*, New York: Penguin Books, p.296.

Bull, Headley (1977), *The Anarchical Society: A Study of Order in World Politics*, London: Macmillan, p. 264.

Cavarrozi, Marcelo (1992), "Beyond Transitions to Democracy in Latin America", *Journal of Latin American Studies*, Vol. 24, No. 3 (October), pp. 665–684.

Clad, James (1994), "Disappearing States: Collapsing Governance in the Third World", in Armand Clesse *et al.* (eds.), *The International System After the Collapse of the East-West Order*, Dordrecht: Martinus Nijhoff.

Clement, Wolfgang (1991), "Auf dem Weg zum Europa der Regionen" in J.J. Hesse and W. Renzsch (eds.), *Föderalstaatliche Entwicklung in Europa*, Baden-Baden: Nomos Verlag, pp. 15–28.

Darnton, John (1994), "Stateless State: A New Specter Stalking Africa", *International Herald Tribune*, 25 May.

Deutsch, Karl (1953), *Nationalism and Social Communication: An Inquiry into the Foundations of Nationality*, Cambridge, MA: MIT Press.

Deutsch, Karl (1964), *et al., The Integration of Political Communities*, Philadelphia: Lippincott.

Eco, Umberto (1986), "Living in the New Middle Ages", *Travels in Hyperreality*, San Diego: Harcourt Brace Jovanovich, pp. 73–86.

Ernest, Gellner (1978), "Scale and Nation" in Fredrik Barth, *Scale and Social Organization* (Oslo: Universitetsforlaget).

Gondrand, François (1991), *Parlez-vous Eurocrate?*, Paris: Edition d'Organisation.

Hoffmann, Stanley (1982), "Reflections of the Nation-State in Western Europe Today", *Journal of Common Market Studies*, Vol. XXI, Nos. 1&2 (Sept.–Dec.), pp. 21–38.

Hrbek, Rudolf and Thaysen, Uwe (eds.), (1986), *Die Deutschen Länder und die Europäischen Gemeinschaften*, Baden-Baden: Nomos.

Hurd, Douglas (1992), *Financial Times* (March 21–22).

Davidson, Ian (1991), "New era for EC family" and *Financial Times*, (December 3), p. 21.

Johnson, Chalmers (1982), *MITI and the Japanese Miracle: The Growth of Industrial Policy*, Stanford: Stanford University Press.

Keating, Michael (1988), *State and Regional Nationalism: Territorial Politics and the European State*, London: Harvester-Wheatleaf.

Kohr, Leopold (1957), *The Breakdown of Nations*, London: Routledge & Kegan Paul.

Lapham, Lewis (1988), "Leviathan in Trouble", *Harper's* (September), pp 8–9.

Lindberg, Leon and Scheingold, Stuart, (1970), *Europe's Would-Be Polity*, Englewood Cliffs, NJ: Prentice-Hall.

Marks, Gary (1991), "Structural Policy, European Integration, and the State", unpublished paper, (March).

Mazey S. and Richardson J. (ed.), (1993), *Lobbying in the European Community*, Oxford: Oxford University Press.

Mény, Yves (1982), *Dix Ans de Régionalisation en Europe: Bilan et Perspectives (1970–1980)*, Paris: Editions Cujas.

Moravcsik, Andrew (1994), "Why the European Community Strengthens the State: Domestic Politics and International Cooperation", Working Paper #52, Harvard University, Center for European Studies.

Naisbitt, John (1994), *Global Paradox* (New York: Avon Books).

O'Donnell, Guillermo, (1993), "On the State: Democratization and Some Conceptual Problems: A Latin American View with Glances at Some Postcommunist Countries", *World Development*, Vol. 21, No. 8 (August), pp. 1355–1370.

Parri, Leonardo (1989), "Territorial Political Exchange in Federal and Unitary Countries", *West European Politics*, Vol. 12 (July), pp. 197–219.

Petrella, Riccardo (1978), *La Renaissance des cultures régionales en Europe*, Paris: Editions Entente.

Pierret, Georges (1984), *Vivre l'Europe ... Autrement. Les régions entrent en scène*, Paris: Jean Picollec.

Puchala, Donald (1981), "Integration Theory and International Relations", in R.L. Merritt and B.M. Russett (eds.), *From National Development to Global Community*, London: George Allen & Unwin, pp. 145–164.

Puchala, Donald J (1988), "The European Common Market and the Resilience of the National State", *Il Politico*, Vol. LIII, No. 3, pp. 447–466

Raffarin, Jean-Pierre (1988), *92 Europe: Nous sommes tous des régionaux*, Poitiers: Projets Editions.

Sale, Kirkpatrick (1980), *Human Scale*, New York: Coward, McCann & Geoghegan.

Sbragia, Alberta (1992), "Thinking about the European Future: The uses of Comparison", in A. Sbragia (ed.), *Euro-Politics*, Washington DC: The Brookings Institution, pp. 257–290.

Schumacher, E. F. (1973), *Small is Beautiful* (New York: Harper).

Schmitter, P.C. and Streeck W, (1991), "Organized Interests and the Europe of 1992", in N. J. Ornstein and M. Perlman (eds.), *Political Power and Social Change. The United States Faces the United Europe*, Washington, D.C.: The AEI Press, pp. 46–67.

Schmitter, P.C. (1992a), "Representation and the Future Euro-polity", *Staatswissenschaften und Staatspraxis*, III, 3, pp. 379–405, reprinted in *Jahrbuch für Staats- und Verwaltungswissenschaften*, Band 6 (1992–3), pp. 55–82;

Schmitter, P.C. (1992b), "Interests, Powers and Functions: Emergent Properties and Unintended Consequences in the European Polity", Second, Revised and Expanded Version, April 1992 – to be published in two separate chapters in Gary Marks, Philippe C. Schmitter and Wolfgang Streeck, *The Emerging Euro-Polity: Its Powers, Policies and Prospects*, Sage Publications.

Schmitter, P.C. (1995), "Democracy in the Euro-Polity: Temporary or Permanent Deficit?", paper presented at the European Dialogues Conference, Bruxelles, 24–25 February 1995.

Schmitter, P. C. (ed.), "Experimenting with the Scale of Production, Culture and Governance in Western Europe" to be published in *Experimenting with Scale in Western Europe*, forthcoming, Cambridge University Press.

Sharpe, L. J. (1989), "Fragmentation and Territoriality in the European State System", *International Political Science Review*, Vol. 10 (July), pp. 223–238.

Tarrow S., Katzenstein P. and Graziano L. (eds.) (1978), *Territorial Politics in Industrial Nations*, New York: Praeger.

The Financial Times (1989), "Where Large and Small Work Together in Perfect Harmony" (14 July).

Wade, Robert (1988), *Governing the Market: Economic Theory and Taiwan's Industrial Policies*, Princeton: Princeton University Press.

Wallace, William (1990), "Introduction: the dynamics of European integration" in W. Wallace (ed.), *The Dynamics of European Integration*, London: Pinter.

Ward, Colin (1991), "All Power to the Regions!", *New Statesman & Society* (December 6), pp. 30–32;

Wolf, Martin (1991), "Federalism before a fall", *Financial Times*, (December 3), p. 21.

by Johan P. Olsen,
University of Oslo,
Norway

Europeanization and Nation-State Dynamics

Search for a new political order

Asking whether a "Europeanization of the nation-state" is taking place, means calling attention to ongoing changes in the European political order. In particular, attention is directed towards the dominant institution of this order: the nation-state. Focus is on the interplay between changes in the relations *between* European states and changes *within* each state. How significant are processes of European integration and cooperation for the development of the nation-state as the loci of political power and legitimacy in Europe? How important is the nation-state for integration and cooperation at the European level? In the context of the *democratic* nation-state key questions are: What is the role of democratic governance and politics in European transformations? In turn, how is the relative importance of democratic institutions and processes affected by the search for European unity?[1]

For students of politics, the current situation presents both a challenge and an opportunity. On the one hand, the conditions under which the European integration process will persist, speed up, slow down, disintegrate or reverse itself, are not well understood. Neither is the impact of such changes on the nation-state.

No single approach or discipline is able to explain the complex dynamics of European integration (Dehousse and Majone, 1994). On the other hand, there is some evidence that periods of transition and transformation, generating debate and political struggle over the constituting principles and institutions of political life, also tend to stimulate theory building (Spragens, 1976).

In stable periods, studies of politics often focus on coalition-building and policy development. An often implicit assumption is that political processes reproduce, rather than change, existing actors and institutional and cultural frameworks. This assumption is problematic in periods of transition and transformation. Political discourses and struggles are then organized around questions like: How are political boundaries to be drawn and who is going to belong to a political community? What kind of political community is it possible and desirable to develop, and according to what principles and institutions are members going to live together? What principles and institutions will regulate interaction with outsiders (Kymlicka, 1993)?

In such periods we cannot take political structures and actors, boundaries and communities, collective identities and understandings, and distributions of resources and life chances, as given, i.e. as stable over the period studied. Instead, political processes have to be analyzed, not only in terms of their impact on policy content and coalitions, but also by their impact on political actors and structures. We need to understand what factors influence how political boundaries and communities are developed, constructed, institutionalized, maintained, modified and dissolved. Likewise, we need to understand on what basis various communities and associations are constituted — what ties members together and what holds them apart, what rights and duties membership gives, how tasks, authority, resources, and responsibility are distributed, and how tensions and conflicts are coped with.

The current European situation invites studies of how basic frameworks of political life might be changing, as Europeans cope with new challenges and opportunities. The primary aim of this paper is to suggest a few theoretical ideas that may throw some light over such possible transformations. First, the scholarly challenge of Europeanization processes is developed in more detail. Secondly, an institutional perspective on political change is sketched. This perspective is then illustrated in the three following parts. Some institutional characteristics of the modern, democratic nation-state, as a special type of political community, are analyzed. The perspective is used to discuss changes in the level of integration and cooperation at the European level, and, finally, some possible implications of changes at the European level for the nation-state are suggested.

Changing political boundaries and communities

In political life there are continuous processes of integration, disintegration and reintegration. People break out of old collectives, as they revolt against existing practices or ideas. Yet, they also develop new collectives and make new commitments. They draw and re-draw boundaries around large and small communities. They group and re-group themselves for a variety of reasons and purposes. They associate and disassociate in a multitude of ways on the basis of different principles, relationships and bonds (Dewey, 1927; Eisenstadt, 1987). Such processes create awareness of identity and distinctiveness. They produce relationships of group solidarity and trust, as well as perceptions of differences and conflict between groups (Coser, 1956; Schattschneider, 1960).

As political boundaries and communities develop, become institutionalized, and are modified or dissolved, a polity obtains or loses structure, and the nature of order changes. What, then, are the conditions under which polities gain or lose structure so that they become more or less coherent and coordinated? What are the processes through which changes, such as drawing boundaries, developing principles of inclusion and exclusion, and constructing the constituent rules of the community, take place? What are the conditions for the durable (long-run or equilibrium) impact of such changes — what traces does a history of (dis)integration leave, beyond the short-run (transition) effects of a specific period of (dis)integration (March og Olsen, 1995)?

247

The study of conditions for radical and swift change is linked to some of the major problems and controversies of social and political theory (Eisenstadt and Wittrock, 1995). Today, there is no strong theoretical or empirical basis for precise predictions of the likely magnitude and nature of change in the European political order. Change processes seem to be open-ended or beyond our comprehension. Yet, contemporary and historical processes of European integration and disintegration provide an opportunity for studying the conditions for political convergence and divergence at both the European and the national level, as well as the interplay between such processes. Specifically, historical transformations can be used to illuminate some old concerns in political theory, for example the conditions for radical and swift institutional change, and how such change might depend on shifting environments, the nature of a historically established order, and political purpose and conflict.

A Matter of choice? Inquiring into the processes through which European transformations are taking place, means facing an old puzzle in political theory: "To what extent forms of government are a matter of choice" (Mill, 1962). A theoretical interpretation of European integration and nation-state dynamics needs to reconcile three basic interpretations of the historical development of political systems. Explanatory factors are located in the objective characteristics of the contemporary context, in history, and in the purposes, reason and power of identifiable political agents (March and Olsen, 1989,1995; Olsen, 1992).

Functional efficiency. The first type of explanation assumes certain functional requirements or imperatives. A particular structure (institution, identity, moral or causal belief system, allocative principle, resource distribution) currently observed represents an efficient "match" with objective environmental conditions. Different environments dictate or provide incentives for different structures. Efficient matches are achieved through competitive selection or necessary adaptation to the changing opportunities and requirements arising from the environment. Inefficient structures are eliminated efficiently. Thus, in order to explain variation in structure, it is not necessary to consider the past, the generating processes behind a structure, or the characteristics of reformers trying to adapt the structure to its environment. Political actors are at the mercy of uncontrollable forces of, for instance, an economic, technological or divine nature. They may facilitate necessary adjustments and prevent the collapse of an order, but their primary role is that of bookkeepers of "the great necessities" (Seip, 1958). The best developed example of this type of interpretation is the static equilibrium theory of maximizing behavior under perfect competition (Basu, Jones and Schlicht, 1987).

Historical continuity and dynamics. The second type of explanation emphasizes the impact of history. Existing structures set boundaries for change. Transformations take the form of slow historical processes of sedimentation (Sait, 1938). Changes reflect a structure's "roots" and "routes" — the origins and the paths by which they have arrived where they are (Bendix,1968; Berman, 1983:v). Structures arise and change as a result of processes of contact, mutual learning, imitation and diffusion. Contact results in some kind of modification. Yet, whether the result is contradiction or copying depends on processes of interpretation which reflect an institution's identity, history and dynamics. For instance, the different routes leading to modern polities have distinctive consequences for how a system works and develops (Moore, 1966; Esping-Andersen, 1990; Greenfeld, 1992). Political cleavages and compromises are institutionalized and "frozen" and have implications long after the initial conditions producing them disappear (Lipset and Rokkan, 1967).

Political agency. The third type of explanation focusses on changes in the purposes, reasoning and power of identifiable political agents. A structure arises and changes as a result of problem solving and conflict resolution among purposeful actors. A structure represents a solution to a shared problem in a consensus system, or an imposed, coerced solution from a winning coalition or a conqueror. In all cases, a structure arises and is maintained or transformed as a function of the degree to which it serves the purposes of relevant actors. The task is to identify from where the political pressure for change comes and who is opposed. This is an interpretation which reflects democratic beliefs in human will, reason and control and a Demos with its future in its own hands (Dahl, 1989). It is also found (partly) in studies of the role of war and violence in political developments in Europe (Giddens, 1985; Tilly, 1992), and in studies of state- and nation-building (Rokkan, 1970; Eisenstadt and Rokkan, 1973; Tilly, 1975; Flora, 1983).

Reconciling the three interpretations raises questions about institutions' abilities to adapt spontaneously to major changes in their environments, the environment's ability to eliminate non-adaptive institutions, and the latitude of purposeful institutional reform (Olsen, 1992). From a democratic point of view the question is: What is politically possible in a modern democracy? That is, how different can political and social life be purposefully shaped (Dunn, 1990:161)? A challenge is to avoid political fatalism (nothing can be done) and political idealism (anything can be done). An institutional perspective on change is one way of approaching such questions.

An institutional perspective on change

An institutional perspective assumes that political life is patterned. There are organizing principles creating elements of regularity and stability, consistency, and coordination. A modern polity is neither a harmonious community unified by shared moral and causal beliefs, nor a collection of free floating, atomistic individuals continuously calculating what is in their best self-interest. Rather, the polity is constituted by its basic institutions — shared practices and rules embedded in structures of meaning (moral and causal ideas), and resources — which over extended timeperiods are taken as given by a large majority.

Institutions simultaneously create order and continuity and provide a dynamic element. The political order is temporary and imperfect. There is no complete integration and harmony, but fairly stable structures and patterns around enduring political discourses, tensions, and struggles. Different institutions embody and protect different principles and concerns, and change follows from the interaction and tensions between institutional practices, ordering principles and dynamics. A political order, as a config-uration of institutions, thereby comprises socially constructed boundaries for legitimate communities, actors, arguments and resources.

Institutions provide rules of exemplary or appropriate behavior. They create roles (citizen, prime minister, civil servant, judge) and define what it means to perform a role well in various situations. Even the "individual" is socially constructed and protected as society becomes willing to institutionalize individual rights. Prescribed and proscribed behaviors are embedded in codes of conduct and repertoires of standard operating procedures. The logic is rule-driven obligatory action, constraining behavior based on self-interest, emotions and instincts (March and Olsen, 1984,1989,1995).

Institutions give meaning to behavioral regularities. They provide purpose and legitimacy to rules and practices. They equip individuals with an identity and constitutive belonging, cultural affiliations and boundaries, and interpretations and accounts which help individuals make sense of life. Institutions are carriers of the basic codes of meaning, value commitments, symbols, and causal beliefs of a political community. They embody the central "themes for development" which guide institutional developments (Broderick, 1970:xvii).

Institutions create rights and resources and regulate their use. Institutions define public and private ownership of resources, and make us someone who owns or owes (Dworkin, 1986:vii). They construct and protect rights, powers and immunities. They also provide sanctions against violations of institutional rules (Rawls, 1971:55). Likewise, institutions regulate the use of public and private resources, rights and authorities. Thus they influence the ability of different actors to behave according to institutionalized rules and principles.

Institutions create, maintain and represent social groups. Social collectives, such as "the public", "the nation", social classes, strata and groups, are socially constructed, institutionalized and main-tained. Institutions, in turn, get their legitimacy and support from collectives of various sizes. Institutions represent social collectives and regulate their access to centers of decision-making and opinion formation (Rokkan, 1970). They thereby also affect who-gets-what in terms of well-being and life-chances.

Institutions do not adapt instantaneously or efficiently to minor changes in will, reason, power or circumstances; in particular not those integrated in encompassing political, cultural, economic and social configurations and orders. Equilibrium between environmental contingencies and organizational structures is not common (North, 1990; Orren and Skowronek, 1994). Comprehensive reform requires strong organizational capabilities to stabilize attention, mobilize resources and cope with resistance. Nevertheless, institutions are not static. Institutions develop, grow, or decay. They are transformed through the mundane processes of interpretation and adaptation, as well as the rare metamorphoses at breaking points in history (March and Olsen, 1989). They evolve routines for dealing with change, i.e. experience-based routinized responses to events and reform proposals (March, 1981). Still, sometimes they are overwhelmed by their environments, strong reformers, revolutionaries, or military conquerors.

There are periods when institutional inertia creates large gaps between existing structures and underlying realities. Conventions and organizational forms that have long gone untested from generation to generation become problems. Questions are raised as to why codes of conduct are different in one country, or in one context, from another (Elias, 1982:325). Key concepts, basic values, habitual routines, and distribution of resources and life chances are challenged. Concepts and theories are doomed or thrown into doubt by events because they fail to help people make sense of the world. Old categories change content as citizens reconsider, clarify or redefine what they want or believe, and as they renegotiate the terms of living together in a community (Herzog, 1989).

Trajectories depend on the type of change. Changes consistent with an institution's identity, traditions and dynamics are likely to be continuous and incremental. Change in opposition to an institution's identity, integrity and dynamics is likely to be episodic and problematic. Institutions will then defend their identity and integrity with the resources available. Radical and rapid transformations are likely only under special conditions. For instance:

- reform attempts, where considerable political energy and resources are mobilized over long periods of time by governments,
  political opposition, or social protest movements,
- collisions between major institutionalized rule sets, identities,
  inter-pretations and accounts of the world,
- deep performance crises according to the institution's own
  criteria of success,
- comprehensive external shocks, which in dramatic ways change
  the conditions under which the institution has functioned,
- shared expectations that either a performance crisis or an external shock is inevitable in the near future.

The type of order

Polities constituted on different institutional principles and social
relations are likely to have different dynamics. Likewise, we expect
dynamics to be affected by the degree to which polities are tightly
and loosely coupled systems.

Consider three alternative interpretations of how political communities are constituted (Yack, 1985). The *first* portrays a political
community as based on calculated self-interest. It is constituted on
the basis of continuous, individual calculations of the benefits and
costs of membership and is embedded in rational contracts. There
are few traces of earlier processes of integration and disintegration.
The *second* interpretation views the political community as a moral
community. The political organization is the expression and instrument of a pre-political cultural group. Individuals have internalized a commitment to a cultural heritage. Belonging to the
community is an integral part of individual identity, bringing about
loyalty, pride and emotional bonds. Consequently, history leaves
strong traces. The *third* interpretation understands the political
community as a democratic community based on informed and
reasoned acceptance of political agendas, institutions, and pro-

cesses. Individuals and groups agree on rules for peaceful, political co-existence. Public policy-making assumes that cultural norms and beliefs, as well as individual interests and instincts, are justified and critically assessed in public before collective decisions are made. Yet, there may be enduring conflicts of interest, and disagreements on moral and causal beliefs and what constitutes a good way of life. Here, history leaves moderate traces.

Change processes are also influenced by the degree to which polities are configurations of tightly or loosely coupled institutions (Cohen, March and Olsen, 1972). In a loosely coupled polity, institutional spheres are differentiated, separated, and partly autonomous. Different spheres have different dynamics and there may be considerable variations and lags in change processes. Events, decisions, and conflicts are kept apart, rather than attended to simultaneously. For instance, in a loosely coupled system political changes will not have immediate and direct effects on administrative, legal, economic, cultural and social affairs. Neither will changes in economic, cultural or social spheres have immediate and direct impacts on political, administrative or legal organization, behavior or thinking. In a tightly coupled polity, on the other hand, all spheres are likely to change in a synchronized way. The polity will move from one type of overall consistency and coordination to another type of order.

Loosely coupled systems are more likely to live with enduring differences and tensions than tightly coupled systems (Cyert and March, 1992). Yet, major societal transformations tend to replace sequential or differentiated attention with a felt need for joint decision making. Transformations, then, might affect citizens as a homogenous public. Political action takes the form of problem solving in the name of the common good and public interests. Tranformations might also affect the well-being and quality of life of various groups differently. For instance, modernization processes have both a creative and destructive potential (Black, 1966:27). Some groups are offered new opportunities. Others have their identity, beliefs and ways of life threatened. They may lose status, power and material benefits and security. As a consequence, change processes are likely to become conflicting and outcomes are likely to be dependent on the distribution of relevant resources.

Accumulation of crises is important for political developments (Rokkan, 1975), and the likelihood of episodic, radical and swift institutional transformations is linked to the inefficiency of ordinary processes of adaptation (March and Olsen, 1989:64,106). The more inefficient (or obstructed) ordinary processes of learning and adaptation are, the more likely a development characterized by big leaps rather than small steps. An institution or a regime may suddenly collapse or change fundamentally. "The intellingence of democracy" is to secure strong institutions for public debate and criticism, and thereby improve processes of experiential learning and incremental adaptation (Lindblom, 1965). Thus, in well-developed democracies, radical and swift changes are less likely than development based on incremental, autonomous, mutual adjustments.

In sum, an institutional perspective suggests that students of "Europeanization of the nation-state" need detailed historical-institutional knowledge in order to understand political dynamics. Here, we have to be content with a few illustrations, rather than a detailed analysis of the historical-institutional contexts of changes in the European political order.

The institutional complexity of he Nation-State

"The state" might refer to an abstract idea, or a historically concrete political form of organization (Skinner, 1989). It might signify a political community or an institutional arrangement. It is not obvious that "the state" refers to any coherent and consistent historical-concrete phenomenon, and scholars disagree over definitions and relevant analytical dimensions. Usually the list of defining criteria is long (Dunleavy, 1993: 611). Still, an attempt to understand current nation-state dynamics in Europe may benefit from avoiding detailed definitions at the outset. *If* the nation-state could be conceptualized as a unitary political organization, based on a coherent national culture, with one dominant and unambiguous trend of development, it would be comparatively easy to study possible impacts of Europeanization processes. A complication is that such assumptions are not very realistic in contemporary Europe.

The democratic nation-state is a special kind of historically developed political community and organization. It represents one possible answer to the questions of *external boundaries:* Who are to be included in the Demos as a self-governing political community? How are a territory and a population going to be divided, and according to what criteria will there be differentiated between insiders and outsiders, citizens and non-citizens? The nation-state also represents one possible answer to the question of *internal boundaries:* How are boundaries to be drawn between citizens, areas of activity, and institutional spheres within a specific polity and society?

The doctrine of national self-governance holds that political and cultural communities should coincide (Østerud, 1984, Gellner, 1993, Kedouri, 1993) and the doctrine of the sovereign nation-state emphasizes the significance of external borders and border control (Finer, 1974). The military and administrative power of a state can be measured by its ability to control the movement across borders of people, goods, and ideas (Rokkan, 1975, 1987:370). Political communities are defined by territorial borders, citizenship, nationality, and various rights which to a large extent determine the well-being and life-chances of individuals. It is legitimate to discriminate according to citizenship and nationality, and thereby to treat foreigners differently from compatriots. In addition, the doctrine of internal sovereignty ascertains the nation-state's final authority over all other collectives within its borders. History has made such claims and assumptions highly problematic.

National integration and differentiation

There has never been a nation-state with completely congruent political and cultural boundaries (Navari, 1981:13; Flora, 1992: 106). Still, some nation-states, like the Nordic ones, have come comparatively close. Within relatively stable territorial borders they developed congruence, not only between political and cultural boundaries, but economic and social boundaries as well. Nationalization of political, legal, cultural, linguistic, religious, economic and social boundaries and communities came, however, together with internal differentiation and specialization. The development of a centralized state capability and capacity was complimented by building institutions that could give direction to, and constrain, state power. Internal boundarydrawing may even be a condition for national integration.

State-building refers to processes of building or developing a national political center with considerable resources and thus capabilities and capacities to penetrate and control a territory and its population. In this context "the state" signifies a bureaucratically organized administrative and military apparatus (Eisenstadt and Rokkan, 1973; Tilly, 1975; Flora, 1983; Rokkan, 1987; Flora, Kuhnle and Urwin, 1995). The state, then, can be assessed as an instrument. Its value can be measured by its effectiveness and efficiency when it comes to defending the country, protecting law and order and contributing to economic prosperity or to social and cultural well-being.

Nation-building refers to a process of cultural standardization and homogenization within national borders, and differentiation from the rest of the world. A group of people come to consider themselves members of the same nationality. They develop a sense of national identity (Nationalgefühl) and act upon this belief, even if the concrete reasons for the belief vary greatly (Weber, 1978:395,398). In cases where the pre-political national basis, in terms of ethnicity, language, religion, common customs and memories, etc., was considered inadequate, political resources were mobilized to construct a national identity, and national interpretations and accounts. For example, mass education and socialization were used to develop "new citizens for a new society". That is, citizens with new national norms, loyalty, pride and a sense of belonging to a national community, in addition to citizens with new types of knowledge (Boli, 1989). Furthermore, the welfare state, with its national responsibility for the welfare of all citizens, represented a new, major step in nation-building and social inte-

257

gration. A growing public agenda also came with the integration of well-organized interests in public policy-making, a process which tended to strengthen the social basis of the state.

State- and nation-building processes were, however, balanced by the development of institutions intended to give direction to, or to constrain and control, the state's ability to mold society. Differentiation and separation of institutional spheres are significant aspects of the development of a liberal democratic polity (Walzer, 1983, 1984). A variety of institutional spheres achieved some degree of autonomy. They came to be (partly) shielded from government intervention and electoral politics, and also from each other. Drawing boundaries between institutional spheres meant constraining the legitimate use of resources (such as power, status, money, knowledge) from one sphere to another.

Institutional differentiation is reflected in both the political organization and in society at large. For instance, the *democratic* state assumes that state power is representative, responsible, and accountable, rather than personal and arbitrary. Informed citizens decide for what purposes, how, and when state power is to be used. The *constitutional* state and the *Rechtsstaat* define boundaries between the individual and the collectivity in terms of inalienable rights. Constraints on the legitimate use of state (coercive) power are defined in terms of separation of powers and the rule of law (Weber, 1978:909), giving bureaucracies and courts some autonomy from majority decisions. A *civil society* signifies the autonomy of a private sphere and a public space for free debate (Cohen and Arato, 1992). Voluntary associations, the family, organized religion, art, science, and the media are all assumed to have some autonomy. So are business enterprises competing in "free" markets.

A result of the dual process of national integration and differentiation is a political community embedded in nation-wide institutions and organizations, a national identity, and shared traditions of knowledge and interpretation. This is combined with strong internal boundaries between institutional spheres, identities, accounts, and resources. Governance in European democracies has come to refer to an institutional pattern of stabilized power and rule, principles and codes of conduct (Friedrich,

1963:182). At the same time, the state is an instrument of coercion, a community of calculated interest, a moral community, and a democratic community. The exact mix varies, yet institutions, identities, and worldviews usually have some value beyond their immediate instrumental effectiveness and efficiency. They have a direct impact on the legitimacy of political governance.

One implication is that the concept of the state as a unitary political organization with one center controlling the means of coercion, seems inadequate to grasp current structures and dynamics. Actual structures and dynamics involve complex combinations of institutional principles and rules organized into "archeological layers" reflecting the context and the time of birth and other critical experiences of various institutions (Stinchcombe, 1965; Østerud, 1979; Orren and Skowronek, 1994). They involve relatively stable, self-organizing networks of interdependent but partly autonomous actors with resources and rule structures of their own (Marin and Mayntz, 1991). Neither is the state embedded in a coherent cultural tradition which secures a shared identity and shared moral codes and meaning which facilitate social integration. Instead, there is a multitude of partly inconsistent cultural traditions and ideas, conglomerates of dis-parate and confused individuals (MacIntyre, 1984,1988 Eisenstadt, 1987).

The growth of the post war state, with its complex, mixed polity, inter-institutional networks, and hybrid organizations, has not been founded on, or followed by, any coherent reassessment of the legitimate constitutional principles of authority, power, and accountability. Legitimacy claims have been increasingly instrumental and are based on the ability of government to ensure continuing economic growth, to ward off economic crisis, and to guarantee citizens' well-being through the establishment of the welfare state (Graham and Prossner, 1988). This tendency was strengthened during the 1980s. At that time, most reforms in the public sector emphasized results more than legitimate structures and procedures, and competitive markets more than politics. Individuals were viewed as consumers and clients more than active and responsible citizens and members of a democratic community (Olsen and Peters, 1995).

If continued, this trend will turn the question of nation-state legitimacy and support into a calculation of the comparative effectiveness and efficiency of public and private institutions and organizations. The revival of nationalism and ethnic-based identities in Europe indicates, however, a more complex picture (Smith and Østerud, 1995). Institutions, identities, and beliefs have support beyond their instrumentality. Therefore, the Europeanization of the nation-state has to be understood against the background of varying mixes of calculated, moral, and democratic communities in different countries and institutional spheres.

In conclusion, some nation-states have come close to nationalizing a variety of communities and boundaries. At the same time, the polity became differentiated internally in institutional spheres. National communities and boundaries were, however, constructed in competition with both supra-national and sub-national boundaries and communities. They are also continuously challenged from "above" as well as from "below". Political parties, courts of law, cities, regions, minority groups, business enterprises, trade unions, professional associations, churches, and universities are all part of the institutional configuration on which a modern nation-state is constituted. All of them are also integrated in networks beyond the nation-state. Political, judicial, economic, cultural, linguistic, religious, scientific, and technological communities are dynamic rather than static. They are integrating and disintegrating in non-synchronized ways (March and Olsen, 1995).

An institutional perspective suggests that the "match" between, on the one hand, the institutional identity, traditions, and dynamics of a nation state, an institutional sphere, or a specific institution, and, on the other hand, characteristics of the evolving European polity, will have a significant impact on nation-state dynamics. Next, we look at some institutional developments at the European level and the degree to which they may present challenges or opportunities to nation-states.

Europeanization as institution building

European history shows continuous institutional development due to incremental shifts in identities, norms and their interpretation, causal beliefs, and resources. It also illustrates institutional breakdowns and radical change, where transformations have been coercive, hegemonic and a result of war, civil war, revolutions and revolts. Existing institutions and traditions have been seen as reservoirs of knowledge and norms based on the experience of generations. They have also been seen as outdated, based on prejudices and superstition, and in need of "Entzauberung" or rationalizing in order to improve performance and create progress. The modern idea of reform and willful design by applying reason and experience to all institutions and customs, and the possibility of designing institutions from "first principles", have co-existed with ideas about the constraints on political authority in terms of human rights, natural law and divine law (Berman, 1983:6,45,528).

Focus here is on processes of peaceful and non-coercive change. "Europeanization" refers to processes which make "Europe" a more significant political community and European boundaries thereby more relevant politically. Homogenization and standardization signify reduced variance in patterns of thinking, behavior, and organization. Integration means the construction of a political center with independent powers and jurisdiction over member-states — a "fourth level of governance" (Egeberg, 1980). The center is able to make, implement and control decisions and to interpret and assess reality with some authority. Political actors shift their attention, expectations, activities, loyalties or anger, toward the center. While there are many examples of European integration, the European Union, as the most developed example of such integration, is of special interest.

Cooperation and copying among states have a long history in Europe. Studying the development of administration, conscription, taxation, social services and education in Western Europe from 1660 to 1930, Barker concluded that all states are in debt to each other. Each has copied some institution or public service developed by others and each has been copied by others. All countries have studied, adopted, or tried to improve the methods of others, and thereby promoted the growth of a common European standard of administration and public service (Barker, 1966 (1944):93). Likewise, a multitude of institutions, associations, groups, and individuals have copied ideas and practices across national borders, contributing to some degree of political, cultural, social, and economic standardization, homogenization, and convergence.

Incremental, autonomous, and mutual adjustments might in the long run transform the viability of competing forms of political organization and culture. Therefore, homogenization and standardization might also reduce the importance of formal decisions to establish new institutional arrangements, or to eliminate old ones. Yet, political institution-building sometimes produces, rather than reflects, standardization and homogenization.

European integration and differentiation
What kind of political community is then developing in Europe (Galtung,1989; Wallace, 1990; Schmitter, 1992; Tassin, 1992)? What will be the mix of historical continuity and discontinuity? Who will be members and who will be excluded? Around what ideals, worldviews, principles, practices, and resources is a new order developed or constructed? Will there be cooperation and integration beyond a mere "partnership agreement" (Burke, 1968) or a calculated contract of organized interests wanting to rationalize economic production and exchange (Tassin, 1992:169)? How likely is the development of a political community based on shared cultures and values, a European identity and feeling of belonging, trust and loyalty, and shared interpetations and accounts? How likely is it that an old program of European unification will be implemented? That is, one which aims at "uniting the peoples of Europe in a single body politic while preserving for each their national independence" (Saint-Simon and Thierry, 1814). If it is likely, should the European political community be organized as some kind of a "welfare state" with a commitment to social

cohesion and collective responsibility for the well-being of all citizens?

The European Union is an emerging polity with an uncertain future. Expectations, hopes and perceptions vary enormously when it comes to how the EU will develop and function in the future. Some expect, hope for, or see, deep integration, removal of internal borders and barriers, and the development of "an ever closer union" and a strong federation. Some expect, hope for, or see, a more traditional type of inter-governmental cooperation. Others ask whether disintegration is likely in the West after the loss of the external foe in the East (Pohoryles, 1994).

Europe is currently trying to find a new balance between territorial and functional politics (Sbragia, 1993). Probably, the EU will develop into a unique form of political governance, something different from a superstate, an ordinary international organization, or a market. Conflicting influences seem to create indeterminate direction (Keohane and Hoffmann, 1991; Schmitter, 1992, 1995; Sbragia, 1992). Historically, the support for the idea of European unity has been rather uneven (Heater, 1992).

Usually, integration is justified instrumentally and functionally. A united Europe is supposed to make it easier to avoid war, to improve economic competitiveness, to reduce unemployment, to cope with environmental problems, to avoid excessive nationalism, or to defend a common culture. In reality, integration involves both joint problem-solving and conflict resolution. The quest for unity is taking place in the midst of a long history of antagonisms and wars. Like all modernization processes, Europeanization also affects different groups differently. It involves a tension between new technological and economic possibilities, historically developed institutions and traditions, identities and beliefs, and distribution of resources and privileges. Integration is an issue that evokes tensions around ethnicity and nationalism. It divides both governments and populations. In some countries, like Norway, European integration is perceived as an issue that challenges national unity and may have a potential to restructure the existing political cleavage system.

The traditional response to conflicts, stalemates, and reversals in the integration process has been to develop schemes of flexibility and differentiation. Existing differences have been recognized. It has been accepted that not all countries can or want to continue at the same speed, at least not in all policy areas. There have been exercises in boundary-drawing, as reflected in distinctions between a core and a periphery within the EU, and in expressions like "Europe a la carte", "variable geometry", "multi-speed integration", "differentiated integration", "concentric circles", and "opting out" (Laffan, 1992:13–14). Recent enlargements, including Austria, Finland and Sweden, and possible enlargements to the East and South, are likely to make differentiation an even more used technique. The impact of Europeanization on the nation-state, then, will depend on the future emphasis of political, economic, cultural, and social integration; that is, the relative priority given to building a European polity, a market, a welfare society, or a culture. Thus, we differentiate between a political agenda of developing institutions for regulation, reallocation, reinterpretation and reorganization (March and Olsen, 1995).

Regulation here means to take actors (and their interests, values, beliefs and resources) as given, and create rules of "fair competition". Governance is done by managing and facilitating voluntary exchange in order to discover or create Pareto-preferred solutions. The main European agenda has largely been consistent with such a view. The aspiration has been to remove barriers to trade among member-states, rather than strengthening the means of political intervention in economic affairs (Keohane and Hoffmann, 1991:23–4). The recent European development has been in line with a general convergence in the West around neo-liberal ideas of laissez-faire, deregulation and construction of competitive markets.

Redistribution means to take actors as given, yet influence the distribution of resources in order to ensure diversity and the ability to compete. For instance, in a welfare state, citizenship is defined in terms of universal social and economic rights. Reduced disparities in resources are supposed to make it easier for citizens to compete in politics and in the marketplace. Thus redistribution involves equalizing life chances and changes the social fabric of society. Diversity is promoted by subsidies and transfers to social and geographical groups, as well as to newspapers, political parties, language groups, and organizations. All this assumes considerable redistribution through the public sector. Reducing social and geographical disparities has been part of the European agenda. Funds for redistribution across national borders have been growing (Marks, 1992). Still, the issue of a "Social Europe" has tended to create conflict. Building a welfare society has been more a stepchild than a top priority (Liebfried, 1992; Streeck 1993). Limited ability to mobilize resources and budgetary problems have also reduced the role of the EC/EU as a redistributor and provider of social services, and therefore its ability to reduce economic and social differences, impinging on further integration.

Re-interpretation and re-education refer to governance by forming people and (re)constructing a culture. Citizens and officials are educated and socialized. Identitites are constructed and internalized. Norms of exemplary and appropriate behavior, acceptable accounts and interpretations, positive feelings and loyalties, are developed and spread. Culture-building can take place through general political discourse and information. It may be an aspect of educational, family, and media policies, as well as policies towards organized religion. The EC/EU has had some success in conceptualizing Europe as an economic unit, but less with the idea of political, cultural, and social unity in Europe based on a common heritage such as Christendom, Latin, and Roman Law, or common, future political projects. Culture-building has been part of cultural and media policies and of exchange programs for students and other youth groups. Yet, European policy-makers seem to have limited understanding of, and control over, the conditions under which a European identity and European accounts can be developed and mobilized (Schlesinger, 1995). While some elite groups have been socialized into strong believers in European integration, the "Europe of Maastrich" is an ideal which has been a modest mobilizing force among ordinary people. In a short time the success of political leaders in Maastricht was turned into one of the more severe crises in the history of European integration. Currently, the EC/EU seems to suffer from a crisis of ideals and values (Weiler, 1993). As argued by Delors, nobody falls in love with a large market (Delors, 1989).

Reorganization here implies governance by developing a political organization of society which makes it possible for individual Europeans to become, and to act as, democratic citizens. Governance as polity-building reflects a commitment to democratic structures and processes rather than to specific substantive outcomes. Governance involves affecting the frameworks within which citizens and officials act, and institutions, identities, accounts and resources are developed, maintained and changed. Governance establishes appropriate boundaries between institutions and groups, modifies or removes boundaries which are intolerable from a democratic point of view, and keeps institutions and groups within their appropriate boundaries.

The authors of the Treaty of European Union inserted a new part entitled "Citizenship of the Union" into the Treaty of Rome, and this has been interpreted as "one of the most significant steps on the road to European integration" (Commission, 1993). Clearly, the debate on European citizenship and the Political Union helped focus Europeanization as polity-building. This tendency may also be strengthened by the 1996 Inter-Governmental Conference. Still, citizens' rights and duties in the EU are modest compared to those of the nation-state. In addition, many architects of European unity, from Saint-Simon to post-war functionalists, have believed in integration legitimized by practical results rather than democratic structures and procedures. To a large extent, integration has involved a vision of the triumph of rational and technocratic governance over politics (Saint-Simon and Thierry, 1814; Laffan, 1992:9). Some of the same spirit is present in the functional, apolitical language of "subsidiarity", which may mean many different things (Blichner and Sangolt, 1994). Most often, however, the interpretation is instrumental: a problem should be solved at the lowest level, governmental or social, capable of doing so effectively. The underlying assumption is that it is possible to locate a "best" or "natural" locus of decision making and service provision. It is not assumed that the division of tasks, powers, and responsibility involves genuine political processes.

Democracies need the help of bodies not necessarily organized according to democratic principles. Thus it can be argued that the EU *should* be built on functional rather than direct democratic legitimacy (Gustavsson, 1994). It may also be argued that organization according to a functional logic is unavoidable in Europe. The spirit of a *necessary* development towards a stronger role for experts and non-majoritarian institutions is reflected in the prediction that there will be, in Europe like in the United States, a "fourth branch" of independent regulative agencies with far-reaching delegated powers. Their legitimacy will be functional, i.e. derived from their ability to cope with a complex and changing world. Efficiency will be the main normative criterion. Regulation will not (and should not) be used for redistributive and social policy goals (Majone, 1994).

Agreement on any description of the institutional configuration and dynamics of the EU is not to be expected soon. In an ambiguous and uncertain situation different groups read different things into existing structures and developments (Sbragia, 1994). Defining the situation is part of political discourse and struggle. Still, it can be argued that the European Union has developed an institutional configuration different from that of many nation-states. Compared to the Nordic countries, the European parliament plays a modest role. The Commission has only weak links back to a European electorate, and it depends on national administrations and military forces for the implementation of its decisions. The European Court of Justice is more activist. The role of the Committee of the Regions is uncertain. Expert agencies are shielded from the electoral process at the European level and the domestic politics of member states. An Economic and Monetary Union (EMU) will give a network of central banks sweeping statutory powers. Big business enterprises have come to dominate standardization processes and lobbying (Andersen and Eliassen 1991; Pedersen, 1994). Trade unions and other mass organizations are weakly represented. The level of public attention and the degree of politicization of European integration has, until recently, been low in most countries. Finally, popular attention to the democratic deficit has primarily been evoked by referendums.

The EU institutional configuration reflects a legacy of an "economic community" and a "common market". Its institutional centerpiece is the single internal market, and the logic of the market has spread to other institutional spheres. For instance, in opinion formation, the idea of public service broadcasting has lost ground to commercial media, thereby weakening a cultural logic and strengthening an industrial one (Schlesinger, 1995). Social and economic rights have often been discussed in a context of counteracting market failure, not as a constitutive principle in European society-building (Liebfried, 1992; Streeck,1993).

From an institutional perspective, a key question is how a European project focussed on eliminating national borders between member states, which act as barriers to the free movement of people, capital, goods and services, "matches" with a nation-state project emphasizing national borders, national self-governance, and national identity.

The future of the Nation-State

Bendix argued that "a historically delimited term like the 'state' implies not only a transition in the early modern period but sooner or later a transition to new and as yet unrealized or unrecognized institutional patterns in the future" (Bendix, 1968:9). Are we, then, in the midst of a new great transformation of the European political order, changing in fundamental ways the role of the nation-state as a distinct form of political community and organization? Is it likely that Europeanization processes, on par with the rising nation-state replacing feudal order, will eliminate, redefine or replace institutions and traditions, identities and belongings, norms and worldviews, as well as distributions of rights, privileges, and obligations (Black, 1966; Bendix, 1968:2; Tilly, 1975:39)? Or will the forces of historical continuity turn out to be stronger than the forces of discontinuity?

1989 has been described as "the year when the post-war order came crashing down" (Laffan, 1992:1). Since then, it has become obvious that some structures are not changed easily, even under extreme conditions. From an institutional perspective, the question is whether current processes of European integration constitute an external shock or a mobilization of political resources with the potential for radical and swift changes in the role of the nation state? Or has a continuous homogenization and harmonization reduced the drama of integration in Western Europe? Again, perceptions deviate strongly. There are competing interpretations of how different the polities of Europe are, how changes at the European level and nation-state dynamics are interrelated, and how the processes through which European change are eventually transmitted to the national level.

Consider a scenario of historical discontinuity in the political organization of Europe where the nation-state withers and most of its tasks, resources and support are transferred to institutions at the European, regional or local levels. This scenario is usually based on the assumption that the nation-state is no longer *functional*. It is "increasingly out of step with the necessities of the world in which we actually live" (Beetham, 1990:219). There is a growing disparity between its tasks and capabilities (Schmitter, 1991:16). It is at the same time too small and too big (Bell, 1987:14). A crisis is inevitable (Deutsch, 1981:340,341).

A functional interpretation assumes that the new political order in Europe depends on the comparative efficiency of structures at the global, European, national, regional and local levels. European institutions are to solve problems the nation-state or sub-national units cannot solve alone. Causal mechanisms are largely located in global competition and selection. Within this view, a perceived correlation between changes at the European and the national level is spurious. A testable implication is that membership in the EU will not have significant implications for nation-state developments. The fate of both member- and nonmember-states will be decided by global forces.

The functionalist story is an old one. Industrialization, modernization and progress are often assumed to reduce the range of viable institutions, identities and accounts, and by necessity to produce world-wide homogenization and a global civilization (Kerr, 1966). As we will soon see, it is not obvious that global economic and technological competition, or other functional "imperatives", dictate a polity of a particular size. Some of the best performing polities are small. Generally, it is doubtful whether it is possible to specify the optimal size of a polity, in particular in a situation with several competing criteria of success (Dahl and Tufte, 1973: 138,141).

An alternative scenario is one of historical continuity, with modest changes in the role of the nation-state as the dominant political form of organization in Europe. The challenge from international forces, which are difficult to control at the national level, is hardly new. Countries traditionally open to political, economic, cultural, and social impulses from the international community are unlikely to experience swift and fundamental changes in their political organization. More than in earlier periods, the nation-state has developed political shock absorbers (Østerud, 1994; Smith and Østerud, 1995).

Furthermore, predictions based on functionalism, which views all structures as instruments, underestimate the importance of cultural identities, belongings and feelings. Nationalism has proved to be a principle of extraordinary force as a justification and mobilization of political action (Tilly,1992). Economic globalization is, for example, unlikely to change the importance of nationalism. Assuming that it will is a mistaken belief in economic determinism in social life (Greenfeld, 1992:59). Instead, economic globalization and European integration seem to create national counterreactions, which may halt or reverse further integration. In a world of loosely coupled institutions, a combination of economic internationalization and cultural, ethnic, and national diversity is not a paradox.

In such a world there is also no reason to believe that levels of governance are involved in a zero-sum game. For instance, nation-states may lose policy instruments without any strengthening of European institutions (Scharpf, 1994; Kohler-Koch, 1996). Also, the two levels may become stronger simultaneously. In Spain, the construction of a European identity was one crucial mechanism in the process of the transition to democracy (Pérez-Díaz, 1993). As they are relieved of some problematic tasks, nation-states may be

270

strengthened (Milward, 1992,1996). Likewise, transfers of tasks to the European level may make it easier for minorities to claim self-governance and secession, and actually build new nation-states (Førland, 1993).

In addition, an increasing interaction and entanglement between national, supra-national and sub-national levels of governance, make it more likely that conflicts and coalitions may cross, as well as follow levels of governance (Moravcsik, 1994, Kohler-Koch, 1996). For instance, the symbiotic relationship developed between the European Court of Justice and national courts may become a role model for the European central bank and national banks (Sbragia, 1993:36–7), and other institutional spheres may follow. As a consequence, it becomes more difficult to say precisely what impact one level has on the others. It is not very likely that transformations of the European political order can be fruitfully conceptualized as a unitary process driven by a few causal factors. More probably, changes will be "driven by several engines operating according to different principles and sometimes out of sync" (Dehousse and Majone, 1994:92). European developments will be affected by a large number of events and decisions. There will be joint decisions and parallel decisions by non-coordinated actors, and there will be events and consequences not intended or foreseen by anyone.

Therefore, a theoretical discourse organized around the relative importance of (rational) European and nation-state actors is unlikely to capture what is going on (Matlary,1993; Dehousse and Majone, 1994). It is also doubtful whether major changes can be captured by the language of dependent and independent variables and the logic of regression analysis. It is more likely that transformations will take the form of a multitude of co-evolving, parallel and not necessarily tightly-coupled processes. "Europeanization" may signify a new constellation of change processes, not only a new type of polity.

Collision between institutional principles

In a world of intermeshed and co-evolving structures and processes, it is necessary to get beyond a discussion of the "Europeanization of the nation-state" as a question of dividing and transferring tasks, powers, attention, loyalty, and responsibility between levels of governance. A one-sided focus on Europeanization as the relation between two or more levels of governance, is most fruitful if each level can be conceptualized as unitary, separate actors. When both (all) levels are seen as configurations of loosely coupled institutions based on different principles, logics, and dynamics, we have to pay attention to how Europeanization might affect the relations and balance between major institutional spheres of the nation-state.[2]

In a differentiated, loosely-coupled polity, institutional spheres are affected differently and they are likely to attend to, interpret and respond to European developments differently and in non-synchronized ways. If there is a long-term tendency towards isomorphy between interacting and interdependent institutions, changes in terms of transfers of tasks, powers, and responsibility across major institutional spheres may turn out to be more significant than transfers between territorial levels of government. According to the principle of institutional "matches", an institution is unlikely to resist a development that is consistent with its own constituting principles and which gives higher priority, more power and status to the institution. Compared to, for instance, the traditional institutional configurations of the Nordic countries, central banks, courts of law, bureaucratic agencies, and business enterprises with international experience and expertise are least likely to fight European integration.

Given existing differences in institutional configurations in Europe, the implications for democratic politics is of special interest. This is the case not least in the Nordic countries, with their traditional emphasis on the primacy of political governance, well organized political parties, broad popular participation, consensus seeking, integration of organized interests into public policy making, and their claim that political democracy has to be supplemented by social and economic democracy (Allardt, 1981; Olsen 1983; Gidlund and Sörlin, 1991, 1993; Gidlund, 1993; Heidar and Svåsand, 1995).

Again, interpretations diverge. For some, European integration means democratic decay. Integration leads to a transfer of power to institutions and decision makers shielded from democratic politics and elections. This contributes to an increasing democratic deficit at both the European and the national level. National politicians have underestimated the impact of European developments on their own situation. Now they have to expect dramatic changes (Neunreither, 1994:303). The Nordic tradition of "anchoring" public policies in the population can not be upheld (Gidlund, 1993:201,202). The impact of democratic governance on society will decrease.

A competing interpretation is that European integration is a new step in the history of democratic development. European integration and cooperation is "the triumph of political reason over national passions and selfish interests" (Smith, 1991:151). High-ranking social democrats argue that social democracy in one country is now impossible. Strong European political institutions is the only way to secure democratic control over forces outside the reach of the nation-state (Färm, 1991:103, Brundtland, 1992). Democratic theory must free itself from the framework of the nation-state and stop ignoring the implications of international interdependencies and interactions (Held, 1991:143).[3]

Compared to the first half of the nineteenth century, when there was "almost universal agreement among the educated middle classes in Europe that the nation-state was the only viable political organization worthy an age of liberalism and enlightened politics" (Mommsen, 1990:211), things have changed. The idea that peace, prosperity and freedom would follow if Europe was reconstructed according to the principle of national self-government has lost some of its power. Excesses of nationalism, both in terms of aggression against other states and intolerance towards cultural minorities within its boundaries, have produced the feeling that the nation-state has lost its emancipatory character, has outlived its usefulness, and now spells disaster (Mommsen, 1990). Europe may be into a long-term political transformation. Yet, it is difficult to find strong documentation for sweeping statements, for example that the democratic nation-state will wither in the fore-seeable future.

In the present situation, there is a need for detailed historical-comparative studies of changes in all the major spheres constituting the institutional configuration of the democratic nation-state. This includes changes in the role of the political center and the administrative core of the state, as well as in the political, cultural, economic and social institutions and social groups supporting and constraining the use of state power. The lesson of referendums is that the task also includes studying variations and changes in public opinion (Listhaug, 1995). Attitudes and behaviors may be complex. The Norwegian case illustrates that organized groups against national membership in the EU still focus their attention, resources and behavior towards Brussels. Thy thereby make the EU a more relevant political unit and possibly contribute to European integration.

Small states

Studies of the smaller European nation-states may be of some interest as a supplement to current theories of interegration primarily based on the experiences of the larger European powers. Historically, a standard argument has been that small states, with limited material and cultural resources, will not alone be able to defend themselves or secure economic and cultural progress. They will, by necessity, be an appendix to the major powers (Moore, 1966:xiii; Rothschild, 1977; Höll, 1983). Lately, this interpretation has again become popular. It has been applied to the "quasi-states" of developing countries, that is, formally sovereign states without the ability to solve public problems and govern society (Jackson, 1990), as well as to the context of Europeanization.

Many smaller European states, however, have a good historical record when it comes to democratic development, peaceful co-existence, prosperity, welfare, equality between social classes, districts and gender, life expectancy, cultural development, and ecological consciousness. A democratic argument has been that the political community has to be small in order for citizens to have insight, participation, influence, and a feeling of belonging and trust. In terms of effectiveness, bigger states obviously have more

274

resources within their boundaries and it may be easier for them to impose their traditions, in terms of both policy style and substance, on the EU. Often, however, larger and more heterogeneous states also have more problems in coordinating a complex variety of interests, formulating a coherent policy, and acting decisively (Egeland, 1989). It is likely to be easier for smaller, homogenous states, than for larger, more heterogeneous states, to organize the public as a public and to develop a coherent political agenda and strong national institutions.

In addition, smaller and weaker states with open political, economic, cultural and social systems, have more experience than larger, dominant ones, in adapting to events and decisions over which they have little control. Therefore, the current situation, where it is emphasized that nation-states are not in control of their own fate, may be perceived as less new by smaller states than by the major ones with a legacy of world leadership. Because of their weakness, smaller states are more likely to construct institutional mechanisms for learning and adaptation (Deutsch, 1966).

Partly based on images of an uncontrollable environment and external threats, smaller states may develop internal solidarity and external flexibility (Katzenstein, 1984, 1985). Thus, they may have room for political maneuvering that larger and more hetero-genous countries do not have. For smaller states with well developed mechanisms for learning and adaptation, transformations are more likely to be stepwise than revolutionary, as long as no performance crisis is perceived or expected. Studies of how the Norwegian Ministry of Finance and the Ministry of Justice adjusted to Norwegian membership in the European Economic Area give some support to this conclusion (Farsund and Sverdrup, 1994).

To the degree that small, weaker and homogeneous countries and larger, dominant, and heteogeneous countries have different institutional configurations, policy profiles, and abilities to learn and adjust, "Europeanization" processes may mean different things to the two types of countries. Theoretical interpretations of European political transformations should pay attention to such differences.

Notes

1. I want to thank my ARENA colleagues and the participants in the Uppsala Symposium for interesting comments and conversations, Peggy Simcic Brønn for improving my English, and James G. March for more than twenty-five years of cooperation, through which most of the ideas in this paper have developed.

2. For instance, people may obey the law because they calculate the expected utility of following the law to be higher than the expected utility of breaking the law, because they agree with the moral content of the law, or because they agree with the processes and structures used in law-making (Tyler, 1990).

3. For a discussion of possible contributions from normative political theory to our understanding and assessment of Europeanization processes, see Eriksen, Føllesdal and Malnes 1995.

References

Allardt, E. (ed.) (1981), *Nordic Democracy*, København: Det Danske Selskab.

Andersen, S.S. and K.A. Eliassen (1991), European Community Lobbying. *European Journal of Political Research* 20:173–187.

Barker, E. 1966 (1944), *The Development of Public Services in Western Europe 1660–1930*. Hamden, Conn.: Archon Books.

Basu, K., E. Jones and E. Schlicht (1987), The Growth and Decay of Custom: The Role of the New Institutional Economics in Economic History. *Explorations in Economic History*, 24:1–21.

Beetham, D. (1990), The future of the nation-state. In G. McLennan, D. Held and S. Hall (eds.): *The Idea of the Modern State*, Milton Keynes: Open University Press.

Bell, D. (1987), The World and the United States in 2013, *Daedalus* 116 (3):1–31.

Bendix, R. (ed.) (1968), *State and Society,* Boston: Little, Brown and Co.

Berman, H.J. (1983), *Law and Revolution. The Formation of the Western Legal Tradition,* Cambridge, Mass.: Harvard University Press.

Black, C.E. (1966), *The Dynamics of Modernization. A Study in Comparative History,* New York: Harper & Row.

Blichner, L.C. and L. Sangolt (1994), The Concept of Subsidiarity and the Debate on European Cooperation: Pittfalls and Possibilities. *Governance* 7 (3):284–306.

Boli, J. (1989), *New Citizens for a New Society. The Institutional Origins of Mass Scholing in Sweden,* Oxford: Pergamon.

Broderick, A. (1970), *The French Institutionalists.* Cambridge Ma: Harvard University Press.

Brundtland, G.H. (1992), Norske utfordringer i en ny internasjonal virkelighet, Oslo: Innledning på Hordaland Arbeiderpartis årsmøte i Ullensvang, 4 April 1992.

Burke, E. (1968), *Reflections on the Revolution in France.* Harmondsworth: Penguin.

Cohen, J.L. and A. Arato (1992), *Civil Society and Political Theory.* Cambridge, Mass.: MIT Press.

Cohen, M.D., J.G. March and J.P. Olsen (1972), A Garbage Can Model of Organizational Choice, *Administrative Science Quarterly* 17:1–25.

Commission of the European Communities (1993), Report from the Commission on the Citizenship of the Union, Brussels: COM(93) 702.

Coser L.A. (1956), *The Functions of Social Conflict,* New York: Free Press.

Cyert R.M. and J.G. March (1992) (Second ed.), *A Behavioral Theory of the Firm,* Cambridge. Mass.: Blackwell.

Dahl, R.A. (1989), *Democracy and Its Critics,* New Haven: Yale University Press.

Dahl, R.A. and E.R. Tufte (1973), *Size and Democracy,* Stanford,CA: Stanford University Press.

Dehousse, R. and G. Majone (1994), The Institutional Dynamics of European Integration: From the Single Act to the Maastricht Treaty. In S. Martin (ed.): *The Construction of Europe. Essays in honor of Emile Noël* 91–112. Dordrecht: Kluwer.

Delors, J. (1989), Erklæring om retningslinjerne for Kommissionen for De Europæiske Fællesskaber, Strasbourg, 17/1/1989. Supplement to the Bulletin S.1/89: 5–26.

Deutsch, K.W. (1966), *The Nerves of Government*, New York: Free Press.

Deutsch, K.W. (1981), The Crisis of the State, *Government and Opposition*, 16 (3):331–343.

Dewey, J. (1927), *The Public and Its Problems*, Denver: Alan Swallow.

Dunleavy, P. (1993), The state. In R.E. Goodin and P. Pettit (eds.): *A Companion to Contemporary Philosophy.* 611–621. Oxford: Blackwell.

Dunn, J. (1990), *Interpreting Political Responsibility*, Princeton, N.J.: Princeton University Press.

Dworkin, R. (1986), *Law's Empire.* Cambridge, Mass.: The Belknap Press of Harvard University Press.

Egeberg, M. (1980), The fourth level of government: On the standardization of public policy within international regions, *Scandinavian Political Studies 3* (3): 235–248.

Egeland, J. (1989), *Impotent Superpower — Potent Small State*, Oslo: Universitetsforlaget.

Eisenstadt, S.N. (1987), *European Civilization in a Comparative Perspective*, Oslo: Norwegian University Press.

Eisenstadt, S. and S. Rokkan (eds.) (1973), *Building States and Nations (I,II)*, Beverly Hills: Sage.

Eisenstadt, S. and B. Wittrock (1995), Revolution and Social Theory, Jerusalem and Uppsala: Manuscript.

Elias, N. 1982 (1939), *The Civilizing Process. State Formation and Civilization*, Oxford: Basil Blackwell.

Eriksen, E.O., A. Føllesdal og R. Malnes (1995), *Europeanisation and Normative Political Theory*, Oslo: ARENA Working Paper 1995/1.

Esping-Andersen, G. (1990), *The Three Worlds of Welfare Capitalism*, Cambridge: Polity Press.

Farsund A.A. and U.I. Sverdrup (1994), Norsk forvaltning i EØS-prosessen — Noen empiriske resultat. *Nordisk Administrativt Tidskrift 75*, 1:48–67.

Finer, S.E. (1974), State building, state boundaries and boundary control, *Social Science Information*, 13 (4/5)79–126.

Flora, P. (1983), *State, Economy, and Society in Western Europe 1815–1975*, Frankfurt/London/Chicago: Campus/Macmillan/St. James.

Flora, P. (1992), Stein Rokkans makro-modell for politisk utvikling i Europa. In B. Hagtvedt (ed.): *Politikk mellom økonomi og kultur:* 81–134, Oslo: ad Notam.

Flora, P., S. Kuhnle and D. Urwin (eds.) (1995), *State Formation, Nation-Building and Mass Politics in Europe, The Theory of Stein Rokkan* (Forthcoming).

Friedrich, C.J. (1963), *Man and his Government*, New York: McGraw-Hill.

Färm, G. (1991), *Carlsson*, Stockholm: Tiden.

Førland, T.E. (1993), *Europeiske fellesskap?*, Oslo: ad Notam.

Galtung, J. (1989), *Europe in the Making*, New York: Crane Russak.

Gellner, E. 1993 (1983), *Nations and Nationalism*, Oxford: Blackwell.

Giddens, A. (1985), *The Nation-State and Violence*, Berkeley CA: University of California Press.

Gidlund, J. (ed.) (1993), *Den nya politiska konserten*, Malmö: Liber-Hermods.

Gidlund, J. and S. Sörlin (1991), *Ett nytt Europa*, Stockholm: SNS Förlag.

Gidlund, J. and S. Sörlin (1993), *Det europeiska kalejdoskopet*, Stockholm: SNS Förlag.

JOHAN P OLSEN

Graham, C. and T. Prossner (eds.) (1988), *Waiving the Rules: the Constitution under Thatcherism*, Milton Keynes: Open University Press.

Greenfeld, L. (1992), *Nationalism. Five Roads to Modernity*, Cambridge, Mass.: Harvard University Press.

Gustavsson, S. (1994), EG:s demokratiska legitimitet. SOU 1994:12 *Suveränität och demokrati, Bilagedel med expertuppsatser:* 117–174. Stockholm: Fritzes.

Heater, D. (1992), *The Idea of European Unity*, Leicester: Leichester University Press

Heidar, K. and L. Svåsand (1995), *Politiske partier og europeiserings-prosesser*, Oslo: ARENA Working Paper 8/95.

Held, D. (1991), Democracy, the nation-state and the global system. *Economy and Society* 20 (2): 138–172.

Herzog, D. (1989), *Happy Slaves. A Critique of Consent Theory*, Chicago: The University of Chicago Press.

Höll, O. (ed.) (1983): *Small States in Europe and Dependence*, Boulder/Wien: Westview/Wilhelm Braumnller.

Jackson, R.H. (1990), *Quasi-states: sovereignty, international relations and the third world*, Cambridge: Cambridge University Press.

Katzenstein, P.J. (1984), *Corporatism and Change*, Ithaca: Cornell University Press.

Katzenstein, P.J. (1985), *Small States in World Markets*, Ithaca: Cornell University Press.

Kedourie, E. (1993) (4. ed.), *Nationalism*, Oxford: Blackwell.

Keohane, R.O. and S. Hoffmann (1991), Institutional Change in Europe in the 1980s. In R.O. Keohane and S. Hoffmann (eds.), *The New European Community, Decisionmaking and Institutional Change:* 1–39. Boulder: Westview.

Kerr, C. et al. (1966), *Industrialization and Industrial Man*, Cambridge, Mass.: Harvard University Press.

Kohler-Koch, B. (1996), The Strength of Weakness: The transformation of Governance in the European Union (Chapter 7 in this book)

Kymlicka, W. (1993), Commmunity. I R.E. Goodin og P. Petit

(eds.): *A Companion to Contemporary Political Philosophy:* 379–393, Oxford: Blackwell.

Laffan, B. (1992), *Integration and Co-Operation in Europe,* London: Routledge.

Liebfried, S. (1992), Europe's Could-Be Social State: Social Policy in European Integration after 1992. In W.J. Adams (ed.): Singular Europe. *Economy and Polity of the European Community after 1992:* 97–118. Ann Arbor MI: The University of Michigan Press.

Lindblom, C. E. (1965), *The Intelligence of Democracy,* New York: Free Press.

Lipset, S.M. and S. Rokkan (1967), Cleavage Structures, Party Systems and Voter Alignments: An Introduction. In S.M. Lipset and S. Rokkan (eds.): *Party Systems and Voter Alignments. Cross-national Perspectives,* New York: Free Press.

Listhaug, O. (1995), Komparativ offentlig opinion, nasjonale forskjeller og europeisering: En oversikt over nyere forskning. Oslo: ARENA Working paper 1995/2.

MacIntyre, A. (1984) (2nd. ed.), *After Virtue,* Notre Dame, Ind.: University of Notre Dame Press.

MacIntyre, A. (1988), *Whose Justice? Which Rationality?,* Notre Dame, Ind.: University of Notre Dame Press.

Majone, G. (1994), The European Community as a Regulatory State. Florence: European University Institute: Manuscript.

Marin, B. and R. Mayntz (eds.) (1991), *Policy Networks,* Frankfurt am Main: Campus.

March, J.G. (1981), Footnotes to Organizational Change, *Administrative Science Quarterly,* 26:563–577.

March, J.G. and J.P. Olsen (1984), The New Institutionalism: Organizational Factors in Political Life, *American Political Science Review,* 78:734–749.

March, J.G. and J.P. Olsen (1989), *Rediscovering Institutions,* New York: Free Press.

March, J.G. and J.P. Olsen (1995), *Democratic Governance,* New York: Free Press.

Marks, G. (1992), Structural Policy in the European Community, In A. Sbragia (ed.): *Euro-politics. Institutions and Policymaking in the "New" European Community:* 191–224. Washington DC.: Brookings.

Matlary, J.H. (1993), Towards Understanding Integration: The Role of the State in EC Energy Policy, 1985–1992, Oslo: University of Oslo. Unpublished Doctoral Thesis.

Mill, J.S. 1962 (1861), *Considerations on Representative Government,* South Bend, IN.: Gateway Editions.

Milward, A.S. (1992), *The European Rescue of the Nation-State,* London: Routledge.

Milward, A.S. (1996), The frontier of national sovereignty, Chapter 6 in this book.

Mommsen, W.J. (1990), The Varieties of the Nation State in Modern History: Liberal, Imperialist, Facist and Contemporary Notions of Nation and Nationality, In M. Mann (ed.): *The Rise and Decline of the Nation State:* 210–226. Oxford: Blackwell.

Moore, B., Jr. (1966), *Social Origins of Dictatorship and Democracy,* Boston, Mass.: Beacon Press.

Moravcsik, A. (1994), *Why the European Community Strengthens the State: Domestic politics and International Cooperation,* Working paper # 52, Harvard University, Center for European Studies, .

Navari, C. (1981), The Origins of the Nation-State, In L. Tivey (ed.): *The Nation-State. The Formation of Modern Politics:* 13–38. Oxford: Martin Robertson.

Neunreither, K. (1994), The Democratic Deficit of the European Union: Towards Closer Cooperation between the European Parliament and the National Parliaments, *Government and Opposition* 29 (3): 299–314.

North, D.C. (1990), *Institutions, Institutional Change and Economic Performance,* Cambridge: Cambridge University Press.

Olsen, J.P. (1983), *Organized Democracy,* Oslo: Universitetsfor-laget.

Olsen, J.P. (1992), Analyzing Institutional Dynamics, *Statswissenschaften und Staatspraxis* 2: 247–271.

Olsen, J.P. and B.G. Peters (1995), *Lessons from Experience. Expe-*

riential Learning in Administrative Reforms in Eight Democracies, Pittsburgh: Pittsburgh University Press (forthcoming).

Orren, K. and S. Skowronek (1994), Beyond the Iconography of Order: Notes for a "New Institutionalism", In L.C. Dodd and C. Jillson (eds.): *The Dynamics of American Politics. Boulder:* Westview Press.

Pedersen, O.K. et al. (1994), *Demokratiets lette tilstand,* København: Spektrum.

Pérez-Diaz, V.M. (1993), *The Return of Civil Society,* Cambridge, Mass.: Harvard University Press.

Pohoryles, R.J. (ed.) (1994), *European Transformations: Five Decisive Years at the Turn of the Century,* Aldershot: Avebury.

Rawls, J. (1971), *A Theory of Justice,* Cambridge, MA: Harvard University Press.

Rokkan, S. (1970), Nation-Building, Cleavage Formation and the Structuring of Mass Politics. In S. Rokkan et al.: *Citizens, Elections and Parties: Approaches to the Comparative Study of the Processes of Development:* 72–144. Bergen: Universitetsforlaget.

Rokkan, S. (1975), Dimensions of state formation and nation-building: A possible paradigm for research on variations within Europe. In C. Tilly (ed.): *The Formation of National States in Europe:* 562–600. Princeton: Princeton University Press.

Rokkan, S. (1987), *Stat, nasjon, klasse,* Oslo: Universitets-forlaget.

Rokkan, S. og D.W. Urwin, (1983), *Economy. Territory. Identity. Politics of West European Peripheries,* London: Sage.

Rothschild, Joseph (1977), Observations on Political Legitimacy in Contemporary Europe. *Political Science Quarterly 92* (3):487–502.

Saint-Simon, H. de og A. Thierry 1814, The Reorganization of the European Community. Or the necessities and the means of uniting the peoples of Europe in a single body politic while preserving for each their national independence. In H. de Saint-Simon (1964), *Social Organization, The science of man and other writings,* New York: Harper.

Sait, E.M. (1938), *Political Institutions — A Preface.* New York: Appelton-Century Crofts.

Sbragia, A.M. (ed.) (1992), *Euro-Politics. Institutions and Policymaking in the "New" European Community*, Washington D.C.: Brookings.

Sbragia, A.M. (1993), The European Community: A Balancing Act, Publius: *The Journal of Federalism* 23 (Summer): 23–38.

Sbragia, A.M. (1994), From "Nation-State" to "Member-State": The Evolution of the European Community. In P.M. Lützeler (ed.): *Europe After Maastricht: American and European Perspectives:* 69–87, Providence RI: Berghahn Books.

Scharpf, F. (1994), Community and autonomy: multi-level policy-making in the European Union, *Journal of European Public Policy* 1 (2): 219–242.

Schattschneider E.E. (1960), *The Semi-Sovereign People*, New York: Holt, Rinehard and Winston.

Schlesinger, P.R. (1995), Europeanization and the media: National Identity and the Public Sphere. Oslo: ARENA, Working Paper 1995/7.

Schmitter, P. (1991), The European Community as an Emergent and Novel Form of Political Domination, Madrid: Estudio/working paper 1991/26.

Schmitter, P. (1992), Representation and the Future Euro-Polity, *Staatswissenschaft und Staatspraxis* 3:379–405.

Schmitter, P. (1996), If the nation-state were to wither away in Europe, what might replace it (Chapter 8 in this book)

Seip, J.A. (1958), *Teorien om det opinionsstyrte eneveldet*, Oslo: Universitetsforlaget.

Skinner, Q. (1989), The State. In T. Ball, J. Farr and R.L. Hanson (eds.): *Political innovation and conceptual change:* 90–131, Cambridge: Cambridge University Press.

Smith, A.D. (1991), *National Identity.* London: Penguin.

Smith, D. and Ø. Østerud (1995), *Nation-State, Nationalism and Political Identity.* Oslo: ARENA Working Paper 1995/3.

Spragens, T.A. jr. (1976), *Understanding Political Theory*, New York: St. Martin's Press.

Stinchcombe, A.L. (1965), "Social Structure and Organizations", In

J.G. March (ed): *Handbook of Organizations:* 142–193, Chicago: Rand McNally.

Streeck, Wolfgang (1993), From market-making to state-building? Reflections on the political economy of European social policy. Madison, Wisconsin: Paper presented at the 89th Annual Meeting of the American Sociological Association, Miami, Florida, August 13–17, 1993.

Tassin, E. (1992), Europe: A Political Community? In C. Mouffe (ed.): *Dimensions of Radical Democracy:* 169–192. London: Verso.

Tilly, C. (ed.) (1975), *The Formation of National States in Western Europe*, Princeton N.J.: Princeton University Press.

Tilly, C. (1992) (paper back ed.), *Coercion, Capital, and European States, AD 990–1992*. Cambridge: Blackwell.

Tyler, T. (1990), *Why people obey the law*, New Haven: Yale University Press.

Wallace, W. (1990), *The Transformation of Western Europe*, London: Pinter.

Walzer, M. (1983), *Spheres of Justice*, New York: Basic Books.

Walzer, M. (1984), The Resources of American Liberalism. Liberalism and the Art of Separation, *Political Theory* 12 (3):315–330.

Weber, Max (1924) 1978, *Economy and Society.* Edited by G. Roth and C. Wittich, and translated by E. Fischoff et al. from Wirtschaft und Gesellschaft. Berkeley: University of California Press.

Weiler, J.H.H. (1993), Europe after Maastricht — Do the New Clothes have an Emperor? In *Democratic and Legal Problems in the European Community:* 113–148. Oslo, Senter for Europa-rett, IUSEF no. 12: Universitetsforlaget.

Yack, B. (1985), Concept of Political Community in Artistotle's Political Philosophy, *The Review of Politics*, 47 (1):92–112.

Østerud, Ø. (1979), *Det planlagte samfunn*, Oslo: Gyldendal.

Østerud, Ø. (1984), *Nasjonenes selvbestemmelsesrett*, Oslo: Universitetsforlaget.

Østerud, Ø. (1994), *Antinomies of supra-national state-building*, Oslo: Universitetet i Oslo, Institutt for statsvitenskap: Forskningsnotat 7/94.

Biographical Notes

Sverker Gustavsson is associate professor at the Department of Government at Uppsala University. His publications are on research policy, welfare state theory and European integration. Currently he is working on a book dealing with the democratic deficit issue of the European Union.

Geert Hofstede was the founder and first director of the Institute for research on Intercultural Cooperation (IRIC), an independent foundation cooperation with other universities in the Netherlands. He is also emeritus professor of Organizational Anthropology and International Management at the University of Limburg and a member of many other research associations. His academic and professional experiences are in both Social Psychology and international management. He is the author of *Cultures and Organizations: Software of the Mind* (1991), and several other books articles.

Beate Kohler-Koch is Professor of Political Science and International Relations at the University of Mannheim and director of the department of European Integration at the Centre of European Social Sciences of this university since 1990, after having been Professor in Darmstadt (1972–1990) and Visiting Professor in Bologna and Maastricht. She has published widely on different aspects of European integration and international relations. Her present projects concern the transformation of European systems of public and private interests, the role of regions as political actors in the EU, the perspectives of European Governance as well as the future of the nation-state under the conditions of growing globalization.

Leif Lewin is Johan Skytte Professor of Eloquence and Government at Uppsala University and Dean of the Faculty of Social Science. He has done research on modern Swedish history of ideas, democratic theory, electoral behaviour, rational choice, corporatism and European parliamentarianism. His books include *The Swedish Electorate* (1972), *Governing Trade Unions in Sweden* (1980), *Ideology and Strategy* (1988) and *Self-Interest and Public Interest in Western Politics* (1991).

Alan S. Milward is Professor of Economic History at the London School of Economics & Political Science and Cabinet Office Official Historian for the UK government. He is the author of several works on the modern economic history of western Europe and also on the European Communities. In 1992 he published *The European Rescue of the Nation State* and in 1993, with other authors, *The Frontiers of National Sovereignty.*

Anne Murcott has an M.A. in Social Anthropology and a Ph.D. in Sociology. She is author of numerous articles on various aspects of health as well as diet and culture, and was editor of the international journal *Sociology of Health & Illness* from 1982–1987. Her most recent book is *The sociology of Food* (with Stephen Mennell and Anneke Van Otterloo). Currently she is Director of the Economic and Social Research Council (U.K.) Research Programme "The Nation's Diet: the Social Science of Food Choice" and holds a research post as Professor of the Sociology of Health at South Bank University London.

Johan P. Olsen is director of the Programme "Advanced Research on the Europeanization of the Nation-State" (ARENA), financed by the Norwegian Research Council, and professor in Political Science at the University of Oslo. He received his PhD from the University of Bergen and is a member of the Norwegian Academy of Science and Letters. Together with James G. March he has co-authored *Ambiguity and Choice in Organizations* (1976), *Rediscovering Institutions* (1989) and *Democratic Governance* (1995). He is also the author of *Organized Democracy* and several books in Norwegian and Swedish.

Richard Pipes is Baird Professor of History at Harvard where he has taught since 1950. His speciality is Russia during the Imperial period and the Revolution. He has also written on contemporary events and in 1981–82 served as Director of East European and Soviet Affairs in the National Security Council. His books include *Formation of the Soviet Union* (1953), *Russia under the Old Regime* (1974), *The Russian Revolution* (1990) and *Russia Under the Bolshevik Regime* (1994). He is currently working on the history of private property and its effects on political freedom in England, Russia and several other countries.

Sandra Scarr is Commonwealth Professor of Psychology at the University of Virginia. Her publications includes work on intelligence, child care and family issues. She is also editor, or co-editor, of several journals in psychology, and has been elected a Fellow of the American Academy of Arts and Sciences. Among her publications are *Mother Care/Other Care* (1985).

Philippe C. Schmitter is professor of political science at Stanford University. He has done research on European integration, corporatism and transition to democracy in different parts of the world. Among his publications are *Still the Century of Corporatism* (1975), *Transitions from Authoritarian Rule* (1986, with Guillermo O'Donnell), *Experimenting with Scale* (forthcoming) and *The Emerging Euro-Polity* (forthcoming with Gary Marks and Wolfgang Streeck).

Alexandra Ålund is an associate professor at the department of Sociology at Umeå University. She has, since 1970, continuously worked on studies of international migration and ethnic relations. She is the author of *Paradoxes of Multiculturalism; Essays on Swedish Society* (Avebury 1991) and many other books. Her present project concerns the significance of transethnic social relations and appearance of bridge-building cultural systems of meaning in modern multiethnic societies in western Europe.

Index of names

Index of subjects

nation-state, 268–275; and
networks, 193, 196, 228; policy-
making process of, 181, 227; and
research policy, 183, 192;
and regional policy, 179,
193f., 197, 230; and
security,149f.; and social
policy, 179; and sovereignty,
170–197; and Sweden, 149,
272; and welfare, 262, 264f.;
see also Governance, Interest
and Sovereignty
EURATOM, 229
Eurocentrism, 91
European Central bank, 271
European Court of Justice, 175f.,
199, 267, 271
European Parliament, 164, 176,
267
European Single Act, 155, 176,
179
European Steel and Coal
Community, 158, 161, 165,
228
EVSS (European Values System
Study), 28
Family-friendly policies, 112, 124;
and careers, 113; and
economic effects, 109f., 112f.;
and EU, 115; and welfare,
122f.; see also Gender and Labor
force participation
Fatalism, 142, 250
Femininity, 27, 36ff.
Food: as communication, 53, 68;
and national identity, 50f.,
56, 60f., 64, 69
Free-rider, 150f.
Functionalist theory, 153f.; see
also neo-functionalist theory
Fundamentalism, 31, 42

Geimeinschaft, 87f.
Gender, 91; and careers, 116–118,
122; equality, 108–126; and
discrimantion, 116; and family
policy, 109, 112, 114, 124; and
motherhood, 112, 118, 125; see
also Affirmative action and
Family-friendly policies
Genetic explanations, 22
Governance: and bargaining, 171;
changes of, 171; concept of,
186–195, 197, 261, 263,
266; levels of, 272; and
networks, 187f., 189
Heimat, ideal of, 87–88
Historical explanations, 249
History, two concepts of, 63
Human rights, see rights
Idealism, 250
Identity, 60f.; collective, 92, 97f.;
contructions of, 95–99; crises
of, 95; European, 262, 270;
levels of in Europe, 230ff.; and
institutions, 138, 251; national,
26, 43, 135, 217, 257, 268;
modern, 89; quest for, 95; and
social order, 97f.; and symbols,
96; and tourism, 67;
transetchnic, 97; see also Civil
society, Commuity, Food,
Mental programming
Ideology, 111, 134, 211, "blut and
boden", 82, 95; imperial,
137; see also Culture
Immigration, see Emigration
Imperialism, 147f., 217
Individualism, 36ff.
Industry strategies, 159, 187
Institutional change, 187, 250ff.,
261f.
Integration, 44, 152, 158, 270; and

For Product Safety Concerns and Information please contact our EU
representative GPSR@taylorandfrancis.com
Taylor & Francis Verlag GmbH, Kaufingerstraße 24, 80331 München, Germany

www.ingramcontent.com/pod-product-compliance
Ingram Content Group UK Ltd.
Pitfield, Milton Keynes, MK11 3LW, UK
UKHW021833240425
457818UK00006B/178